CATERING The Art, Science & Mystery

CATERING The Art, Science & Mystery

MICHAEL ROMAN

*"Catering is the art of selling, producing, and performing
outstanding food and beverage, while practicing
the science of earning a profit."*

CaterSource®

w w w . c a t e r s o u r c e . c o m

CaterSource®, Inc. P.O. Box 14776, Chicago, IL 60614

Cover & Book Design: Eric Craig
Editorial Assistance: Bernice Phillips

Copyright © 2001
Published by CaterSource®, Inc.
PO Box 14776
Chicago, IL 60614
e-mail: info@catersource.com

To Order: 800-932-3632 or www.catersource.com

Printed in the United States of America

10 9 8 7 6 5 4 3 2 1

ISBN 0-9702342-2-8

Table of Contents

PREFACE

CHAPTER 1: INSIDE LOOKS

CHAPTER 2: MARKETING

Table of Contents

CHAPTER 3: BROCHURES

CHAPTER 4: KITCHEN

CHAPTER 5: SALES

Table of Contents

CHAPTER 6: PRICING

CHAPTER 7: PROPOSALS

Table of Contents

Table of Contents

Preface / Acknowledgements

Preface

The business of catering is growing at an amazing rate. The combined annual revenue for off-premise catering and banquet facilities is in excess of six billion dollars per year. Catering businesses range from startups doing under $50,000 per year to those doing in excess of $10,000,000! Caterers are quality people who have dedicated themselves to selling, producing, and serving outstanding food and beverage hospitality to a public that unfortunately usually shops for the lowest price when selecting a caterer.

Most caterers know how to cook wonderful food. However, many of these same caterers don't understand how to market themselves, price their catering, and manage their growing business. This book is dedicated to this end, to help catering professionals achieve their goals for personal and business success.

I've had the privilege of meeting hundreds of caterers over the last twenty-five years who have provided me with countless ideas to share with other caterers. In this book, you will find a combination of my own observations, plus many of the ideas and examples given to me by caterers.

Today's caterer works sixty to ninety hours each week. They make huge sacrifices in trying to balance their business and personal lives. Today's caterer realizes the importance of marketing and selling. After all, these days a buyer can get food from so many sources. Today's caterer understands the need to also sell themselves to the shopper in addition to their menus. Today's caterer realizes the importance of being more selective on the types and number of clients they choose to work with. Today's caterer understands that the two most important words to remember while making business decisions are "it depends".

Caterers need to constantly change. They need to move to higher levels of professional standards and success. This book provides caterers with an opportunity to learn about alternative ways to approach the business of catering. Students of catering will be able to accelerate their learning curve in this intriguing profession. Why should they make the same mistakes that others have already made. Instructors of catering may use this book to present real world catering solutions to their students.

Catering is the art of selling, preparing, and performing outstanding foodservice, while practicing the science of making a profit. It is an unforgiving business. So many caterers work for many years and never get their just rewards. Being artistic is only part of the equation for catering success. Understanding the science of catering is just as important. This book is filled with information that will provide both the artistic and scientific sides of the amazing business of catering.

What about the mystery of catering? Most caterers will verify that there are very few constants in catering. It seems that each customer wants things done differently than what others do. They all have unique wishes and wants for their catering. Each party or event a caterer does is brand new and original. Each catered event is like opening night in a new restaurant. It's a mystery because no one really knows what might happen. Will circuit breakers blow due to the excess need for electricity in a home setting; will the air conditioning in a banquet center go out! This is the strength as well as the weakness of selling catering. This book will examine these mysteries and offer varied solutions that will prepare caterers for overcoming the unkown.

Most caterers thrive on the excitement that crisis brings. Sometimes the crisis is caused by last minute changes from the customer. However, most crisis is brought on by the caterers themselves due to lack of planning and not paying proper attention to detail. Successful catering comes from managing the small things. This book presents a variety of ideas that will help control crisis and provide action plans to help owners and managers organize their energies to create win-win scenarios between the customers and the caterers.

For those who have taken time to read this preface, I have a pledge, ... if you ever need to ask a question or clarify any of the education in this book, I will be happy to assist you... simply email to questions@catersource.com and I will respond. Your success is my goal. The resources of CaterSource stand ready to help.

Finally, whether you are a student of catering thinking about becoming a caterer or a tried and true experienced caterer, let's not forget that catering is an extremely exciting and gratifying profession. Caterers help people. Caterers make a lot of friends. Being a caterer is a wonderful opportunity to participate in foodservice hospitality at its highest. Caterers, in their own way, make a difference in our world.

Acknowledgements

CaterSource wishes to thank all of the caterers who have contributed to the educational materials in this book.

INSIDE LOOKS

CHAPTER

1

TABLE OF CONTENTS

CHAPTER

1

"Doing off-premise catering is like a sports team that always plays away games!"

CaterSource Journals

Take a L👁OK Inside...
The Pages of the CaterSource Journals!

Off-Premise - *Fine Catering by Russell Morin • Attleboro, MA*

CaterSource spent 14 happy hours watching the catering team at, Fine Catering By Russell Morin, set-up, serve, and breakdown this event for 1100 guests. The event was really two events in one, with two different menus.

The event was for the Rhode Island State Bi-Centennial Committee and was held both in the RI capital building, and in a tent attached to the historic site. Over 120 catering staff worked diligently to make this multi-floor special event happen successfully.

Fine Catering by Russell Morin has been catering since 1911 and this year will have an annual sales volume of 5.5 million. This event, which took four days of preparation, was only part of the total catering effort. President, Russell Morin told us, "As proud as I am of our catering team at the state capital event, I'm just as proud of our staff that catered four other events, feeding over 700 guests on the same day!"

As CaterSource watched this event take place, it was quickly apparent that these catering professionals knew what they were doing. Everything was organized and everyone knew what their job was. We saw boundless energy and hospitality from this fast moving catering team.

The hosts and guests presented some last minute changes that were quickly and efficiently handled. Also, it was obvious that a special spirit existed within the great looking staff. They knew who they were, what they were supposed to do, and what was important to the hosts.

All in all, this well executed catered event ranks in the top ten that we've seen over the last five years! Congratulations from CaterSource!

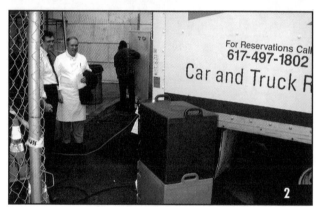

1. Creative Director, Stephanie Straight, (left), President, Russell Morin and Banquet Chef, Sharon Champagne (right) sixteen hours into their 20 hour day! **2.** The load in was slowed due to security. **3.** A view of the tent that was attached to the state capital of Rhode Island.

Off-Premise - *Fine Catering by Russell Morin • Attleboro, MA*

1. The view under the attached tent. The grass floor caused the usual problems. 2. Individual menu cards on each table made it easier for the guests to know what was ahead for them. 3. The block of wood was a simple, yet effective, solution to the lawn problem. 4. The chefs used a charcoal grill in the cook tent outside the attached tent. 5. These large blue containers are purchased from the fishing industry. They are used to hold fresh fish during processing. Here they're used to keep large amounts of ice from melting.

MENU

THE COCKTAIL RECEPTION IN THE CENTURY PAVILION

Passed hors d'oeuvre Selection
•
Gorgonzola Basil Purses
•
Caribbean Crabcakes with a Balsamic Molasses Glaze
•
Maple Glazed Salmon on Crisp Sweet Potato Rounds
•
Coconut Shrimp with Tamarind Vinaigrette
•
Fire and Spice Tenderloin Morsels
•
Ginger Chive Crepes with Asian Pork
•
Marinated Veal Asparagus Roulade
•
Baked Vegetarian Spring Roll with Sweet and Pungent Fruit Sauce
9.50 per person

CENTENNIAL BALL STATEHOUSE ROTUNDA DINNER

Sole Lobster Roulade
Medallions of Lobster Tail with a Lemon Sabayon and Tamale Sauce

Mache Salad
Delicate Lambs Tongue Greens served over Grilled Bruschetta with Artichokes,
Roasted Baby Fennel and Red and Yellow Tomatoes splashed with an infused Orange Balsamic Reduction

Roast Tenderloin Jus Lie
Herb Roast Tenderloin of Beef with a Velvety Red Wine Au Jus over an Asparagus Wild Mushroom Timbale served with a Trio of Vegetable Bundles

53.95 per person

Chocolate Royal Treasure
A Delicate Cappuccino Mousse encased in a Chocolate Pouch brushed with Gold Leaf
tied with a White Chocolate Tassel

add 2.00 per person

Off-Premise - *Fine Catering by Russell Morin • Attleboro, MA*

Procedures
Given to the staff

THE GRAND PAVILION BUFFET DINNER

• As guests enter the tent, all managers should have a table layout and seating assignments to assist guests as needed.

• Floor Managers are there to assist guests in any way necessary and assist staff if need be. Staff should be well versed on the menu.

• The room will be divided into 4 sections with a floor manager and lead waitstaff for each section.

• There will be special vegetarian requests and those guests will be pointed out. A special procedure will be set up in advance for these guests.

• The salad and roll baskets will be pre-set.

• Staff will advise guests to start at the buffet when they are ready and will direct them to their recommended buffet location.

• Wine will be served at the table as guests begin their salad course.

• It is important that wine, water and bread is constantly replenished throughout the meal.

• Clearing of dirty plates will also be an issue since people may return to the buffet for seconds.

• 2 double Dessert Buffets will be ready with 4 coffee stations ready as well.

• Coffee will not be offered at the table.

• There will be a handicapped table assignment, (please refer to layout).

• Porta Johns should be noted.

• Some guests from the Rotunda will be joining the festivities under the tent after dinner.

• There are cocktail tables located along the dance floor and stage area where these guests can be directed for seating.

• There will be 4 bars in this area with 6 bartenders.

• These bars will remain open throughout the evening.

• Bars will officially close at 11:30 pm for all alcoholic beverages only.

• A 5 minute warning will go off to alert guests to the start of the fireworks display at approximately 11:25 p.m.

• Guests are expected to move out from under the tent onto the lawn or up to the Century Pavilion.

• Fireworks will last until about 11:50-11:55 which will then mark the close of the Centennial Ball.

• As people return to their seats or begin to leave, this could become chaotic.

• All staff will have to be attentive to whatever may arise.

• At this point, most of the staff will be out of the Rotunda ready to assist if needed.

Off-Premise - *Fine Catering by Russell Morin • Attleboro, MA*

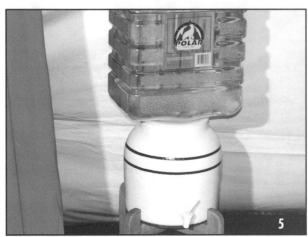

Off-Premise - *Fine Catering by Russell Morin • Attleboro, MA*

1. One of the buffets in the outside tent. **2.** As usual, young energetic staff added to the event's success. **3.** The cook tent that was attached to the outside tent. **4.** The dessert buffet under construction. **5.** Water coolers were placed around the exterior of the tent so quests could see the quality of the water supply. **6.** The salads for the outside tent buffet were assembled under the cook tent. **7.** The salads were then stored in a refrigerated truck to insure proper serving temperature. **8.** & **9.** Views of the elaborate sweet table. **10.** This was very interesting. Plates were heated with sterno and foil right on the buffet! A unique idea! **11.** A second cook tent, outside the front of the building, was used just for the hors d'oeuvre that were served to the inside guests.

Off-Premise - *Fine Catering by Russell Morin • Attleboro, MA*

MENU

CENTENNIAL BALL
GRAND PAVILION BUFFET

Pre-Set Asparagus Salad
with Roasted Herbs, Chevre and Gremolata Croutons on a
bed of Romaine and Bibb Lettuces lightly tossed with a
Lemon Herb Vinaigrette

....

Carved Lemongrass Tenderloin
Roast Tenderloin of Beef Seasoned with Lemongrass served
with a Teriyaki Wild Mushroom Sauce or a Thai Red
Onion Marmalade

....

Lemon Saffron Brochettes
Grilled Breast of Chicken with a
Lemon Saffron Sauce

....

Lime Tequila Seafood Brochettes
Shrimp and Scallop Skewers in a
Lime Tequila and Garlic Marinade

....

Spring Vegetable Farfalle
Bow Tie Pasta with Asparagus, Artichoke and Sugar Snap
Peas in a Lemon Basil Mint Pesto Cream Sauce

....

Grand Dessert Buffet
A Lavish Display of Assorted Tortes, Cakes,
Tarts, Miniatures, Fresh Fruit, Chocolates,
Nuts and More

45.50 per person

All above Buffet Menus will be served with
Seasonal Baby Spring Vegetables, Potato and
Hearth Baked European Style Breads

Off-Premise - *Fine Catering by Russell Morin • Attleboro, MA*

1 - 3. Views of the hors d'oeuvre tent in action. 4. Now we're upstairs in the capital building viewing the plating of the different salad course for the inside guests. 5. The finished salad. 6. Care was taken to rack the salads, and cello wrap the entire rack for sanitation purposes.

Procedures

Given to the staff

THE BREAKDOWN

- We will proceed for breakdown as per usual.

- Centerpieces will be removed by florists in both locations.

- We will strip linen and turn over to Chris at Drapery House.

- We will determine where the linen will be left.

- Bars will be broken down that night and alcohol removed from premise.

- All leftover wines from Wayne Dist. will be secured in a designated room of the Statehouse.

- Quality Rental will be arriving for table and chair breakdown.

- We will remove all other equipment, etc. on Sunday beginning at 9:00 am.

- A coffee cambro and soft drinks will be set-up for breakdown crews for the night, along with left over pastries.

Off-Premise - *Fine Catering by Russell Morin • Attleboro, MA*

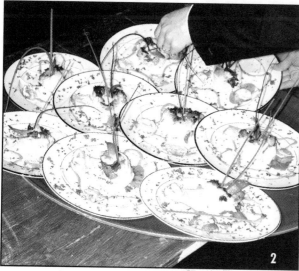

1 - 3. The Plated Sole Lobster Roulade in action!
4. The sorbet palate refresher being prepped.
5. One of the bars was placed at the building's front entrance immediately in front of an historic cannon. We wonder if the bartenders wish it was a working cannon!

Off-Premise - *Fine Catering by Russell Morin • Attleboro, MA*

Off-Premise - *Fine Catering by Russell Morin • Attleboro, MA*

MENU

BAR & BEVERAGE SERVICE

We will provide a total of (**10**) bars
throughout the evening, (**6**) bars open
during the cocktail reception:

(**4**) bars in the Pavilion and
(**1**) double in the Statehouse

(**4**) bars will open in the Grand Pavilion as guests
move in for the Grand Buffet and will stay open
throughout the remainder of the evening.
We will reopen at least (**2**) bars as needed in the
Century Pavilion as guests move into this area
for dancing after dinner.

(Complete Top Shelf Premium Bars 10.00 per person)

Linen

100	120" Ivory @ 10.00 ea = 1,000.00
20	90" Ivory @ 8.00 ea = 160.00
1000	Damask Ivory Napkins @ .65 ea = 650.00

1. A view of the tables that were set in the hallways of the Rhode Island State Capital building. **2.** The bundled veggies being heated for the entree plate. **3.** The dishup station worked extremely well. **4.** That's Russell along the wall, with his son Michael, who is a fourth generation caterer! **5.** The finished entree plate. **6 - 7.** Dessert being prepped and served!

Off-Premise - *Fine Catering by Russell Morin • Attleboro, MA*

Procedures
Given to the staff

THE SET-UP / TABLE SETTINGS

• All rentals arrive Thursday.

• Our linen will be placed on Friday afternoon in both locations along with toppers inside the Statehouse.

• Toppers for the Grand Pavilion will be placed early Saturday morning.

• Centerpieces should arrive by 11:00am Saturday.

• Florists need about 1-1/2 to 2 hours for their set-up.

• We need to be completely set-up and ready by 4:00 in both locations.

THE GRAND PAVILION

• 55 tables of 10, 6 tables of 12, 20 cocktail tables as additional seating for dancing after dinner.

• These tables will be set as usual for a Buffet with only 1 wine glass and with double knife.

• Dessert flatware will be taken at Dessert Buffet.

• Coffee cups will be at Coffee Stations only.

• There is a special 3 pointed fold for the napkins.

• Committee will be placing table #'s. Favors and programs will be placed on the seats.

THE ROTUNDA

• 18 tables of 10 on the 2nd floor Rotunda with 10 tables of 10 in the Stateroom.

• 20 tables of 10 on the 3rd floor Rotunda. (this # will be confirmed Monday)

• This is a full formal place setting with ind S&P.

• Champagne glasses will be set and offered with dessert.

• Special 3 pointed napkin fold.

• Ind Menu Cards will be placed at each setting.

• Table #'s will be placed by Committee.

On-Premise - *Mintahoe Hospitality Group • St. Paul, MN*

The Mintahoe Hospitality Group is one of the largest independent caterers in the twin cities of St. Paul and Minneapolis. The company, which started in 1993 from the back of a bowling alley, is a wonderful success story. Today, the company, under the leadership of Kelvin and Annette Lee, sells over five million dollars in annual catering sales... this is quite a remarkable fact in just six short years!

Mintahoe employs over 140 staff. One interesting observation is that even though the company has grown, Kelvin Lee still personally signs each vendor and payroll check. According to Kelvin, "I just feel it keeps me in touch with our business".

The company has three divisions ... on-premise, off-premise, and commercial contract catering. Our story is about their on-premise banquet and event business.

Mintahoe owns three banquet facilities with over 66,000 square feet of event space. They have exclusive contracts that give them an additional 20,000 square feet. In each of these facilities they offer Perfect Host Catering with traditional menu offerings and Apples Catering offering up-scale and creative alternatives.

Apples is resident caterer at Blaisdell Manor, a graceful Georgian Mansion in the historic Whittier Neighborhood, conveniently located blocks from Downtown Minneapolis. Blaisdell Manor has the largest single room seating capacity of any similarly styled mansion, as well as complimentary parking for the guests.

In addition to Blaisdell Manor, Mintahoe Hospitality Group also owns and manages two other unique sites to host an event at . . . St. Anthony Main Event Centre, nestled on the banks of the Mississippi River with a view of Downtown Minneapolis . . . and Bandana Banquet & Conference Centre, with spacious rustic elegance in historic Bandana Square in Saint Paul.

During our one day December visit, we visited three different venus and observed three different events. Needless to say, things were really happening on this December Saturday!

Vice-President Jolene Ihle, told us "Even though our business seems to be constantly growing, our wonderful team of professionals seem to also be increasing their intensity to stay on top of each and every event."

What we witnessed during our visit was top-notch hospitality and catering success. The events sere on time and provided beautiful food presentations. We were impressed with the energy for success exhibited by the Mintahoe catering team!

On-Premise - *Mintahoe Hospitality Group • St. Paul, MN*

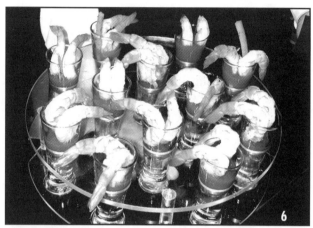

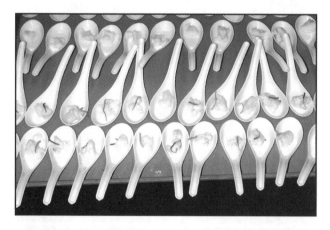

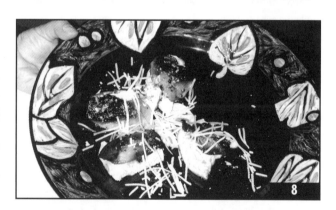

1. The Bandana location. **2.** The Blaisdell Manor. **3.** St. Anthony's Event Center. **4.** Table setting at Blaisdell. **5.** Passed hors d'oeuvre ready to leave the kitchen. **6.** We loved these passed Shrimp Shooters! This was worth our whole trip! **7.** Buffet stations featured display cooking. **8.** Beautiful and creative serving pieces seemed to be everywhere. **9.** This photo shows the special painted ceiling at Blaisdell Manor. Guests love the feeling of the clouds.

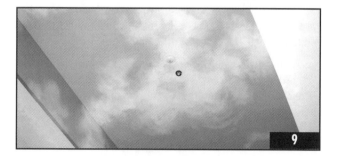

On-Premise - *Mintahoe Hospitality Group • St. Paul, MN*

As You Wish Desserts

Priced per serving. Minimum 3 dozen servings per item.

Millennium Celebration Cakes . . . 4.95
individual pyramid dark chocolate decadence cake
layered with hidden gem of coulís, truffle, or ganache,
and garnished with ginger cream and sculpted
gold fleck chocolate

•

Rhonda's 'Out of this World!' Assortment . . . 3.95
Three petit pieces per serving. Assorted hand crafted truffles,
chocolates and confections

•

*Available individually boxed, a perfect take home
treasure, or gift for someone special . . . 5.25*

•

*Poached Pear and Raspberry Trifle with
Orange Custard . . . 75.00*
Served per trifle, approximately 35 servings each.

•

Warm Mocha Spoon Cake . . . 3.75
Served self-service buffet style, attendant required.
Made with butterscotch bits and served over
vanilla ice cream

•

Faery Cakes . . . 1.95
an assortment of citrus cakes with coconut topping, and blossom
topped chocolate cupcakes with
fluffy icing

•

Mint Pavé . . . 3.95
mint bavarian chocolate sponge cake garnished with red currants
and mint leaves

•

Apples' Signature Pear Walnut Muffin . . . 3.95
topped with a trio of apples sautéed in apple jack butter, garnished
with cinnamon sticks, whipped crème, and dried berries

10. Stations were highly designed. 11. Desserts ready
for guests. 12. A Paella Station using huge saute pans.
13. A Presentation Cooking Station. 14. An entree plate
for the sit-down event we observed. 15. An Asian Station.
16. A Coffee Station.

On-Premise - *Mintahoe Hospitality Group • St. Paul, MN*

On-Premise - *Mintahoe Hospitality Group • St. Paul, MN*

Embellishments

(50 servings per platter unless otherwise noted.)

Pistachio Crusted Salmon Platter . . . 125.00
surrounded by a sage and cranberry wreath,
served with herbed crostini and artichoke tartar sauce

•

Baked Goat Cheese . . . 65.00
with roasted garlic and caramelized onion, served
with rosemary focaccia

•

Spicy Barbecue Shrimp and Jack Lasagna . . .95.00
served with bell pepper and onion salsa, 25 servings

•

Slow Roasted Vegetable Platter . . . 85.00
brussels sprouts, carrots, squash, red skin on potatoes,
yams, bell peppers, and fresh rosemary served with
gorgonzola walnut dip and raspberry honey mustard

•

Vegetable Cobbler . . . 95.00
eggplant, mushrooms, zucchini, artichokes, garlic,
roasted red peppers, fresh spinach and parmesan served
with white cheddar and sage buttermilk biscuits

•

Winter Fruit Platter . . .85.00
sliced kiwi and star fruit, kumquats, pineapple, man-
darin oranges, and gingered pear cranberry compote

•

Peppered Beef Tenderloin . . . 135.00
garnished with roasted green topped carrots and served
with roasted garlic slather and a caramelized onion
marmalade and sourdough rolls

Faeries
Are tiny supernatural beings
in human form
depicted as clever, mischievous
and capable of
assisting and harassing humans.

They live in an imaginary land
called Faeryland.
A very charming and
enchanting place.

19

17. One of the interesting themed stations we viewed was the Faery Dessert Station which featured an actor portraying a Faery. The desserts were placed on tables around the faery. **18.** The event space at Bandana. **19.** Guests are given this wonderful and poetic printed sheet when they approach the Faery Dessert Station.

Drop-Off - *Russo's Gourmet Express • St. Louis, MO*

Russo's Gourmet Catering is a family business! This St. Louis catering company started as a restaurant in 1961. In 1987 all five Russo children joined the company. Today, the business sells over 4 million dollars of full and self-service catering a year.

This story deals with Russo's newest division, Russo's Gourmet Express, which offers self-service corporate and social catering to the St. Louis marketplace.

With more than ninety employees the company, under the leadership of John Russo, caterers to thousands of customers each month. Their goal in the Express division is to make a catered lunch more like dining in a fine restaurant.

The company's overall success and longevity is due to the remarkable team of family members who have successfully worked together making a contribution to the business while maintaining the art of family living!

Frances Russo, the matriarch of the family, who was on hand when the first catered meal went out, is still the driving force behind both the company's success and the family's endurance.

According to John, "Our company's success is the result of hard work, quality products, learning from failure, loyalty to our customers and overall persistence".

During our visit, on a busy December day, we watched as the catering team prepared, packed, and delivered fifty-six different catering orders. We marveled at their systems and especially the way they package their food.

The catering team at Russo's really understands the meaning of quality!

Drop-Off - *Russo's Gourmet Express • St. Louis, MO*

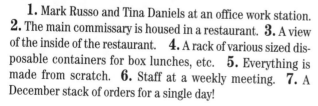

1. Mark Russo and Tina Daniels at an office work station. **2.** The main commissary is housed in a restaurant. **3.** A view of the inside of the restaurant. **4.** A rack of various sized disposable containers for box lunches, etc. **5.** Everything is made from scratch. **6.** Staff at a weekly meeting. **7.** A December stack of orders for a single day!

Drop-Off - *Russo's Gourmet Express • St. Louis, MO*

THE NEW RUSSO'S GOURMET EXPRESS MULTI-PAGE MENU BOOKLET.

HOMESTYLE COMFORT FOODS -

OLD-FASHIONED YANKEE POT ROAST
Fork-tender beef medallions oven-braised with roasted vegetables, and garnished with lots of peas, carrots and pearl onions.

GRANDMA RUSSO'S HOMESTYLE MEATLOAF
Fresh ground beef with lots of fresh herbs and vegetables, baked with honey tomato glaze and served with thyme gravy.

ITALIAN SPEDINI
Beef medallions pounded thin and rolled with fresh basil, Roma tomatoes, imported Italian cheeses, onions, Italian breadcrumbs and marinara sauce.

DUMPLINGS & CHICKEN
Guests may fight over these dumplings. White meat chicken slow-simmered with chunky vegetables and three-herbed homemade dumplings.

PRICE PER PERSON
12 to 29 . . . . . $10.95   30 to 49 . . . . $9.95   50 to 74 . . . . . $8.95

MEATLESS ENTREES -

SPINACH & BABY SWISS QUICHE
Lots of fresh spinach, cheese, whipped eggs and herbs in a flaky crust.

ROASTED VEGETABLE LASAGNA
Fire-roasted zucchini, onions, red peppers, carrots, spinach and broccoli with imported Italian cheese and Alfredo sauce.

STUFFED EGGPLANT ASIAGO
Fresh basil, Asiago cheese and sundried tomatoes sandwiched between sliced eggplant. Rolled with Italian breadcrumbs and baked in a zesty pommodoro sauce.

SMOTHERED PORTABELLA MUSHROOM STEAKS
Wait till you cut into this steak! Giant Portabella mushrooms lightly marinated in aged balsamic vinaigrette. Char-broiled and topped with julienne vegetables, toasted leeks and mozzarella cheese. Served with a smoky chasseur sauce.

SOUTHWEST GRILLED POLENTA
Light polenta cakes grilled and served with mixed julienne vegetables, roasted corn, and black bean relish.

PRICE PER PERSON   12 to 29 . . . . $11.45   30 to 49 . . . . $10.45   50 to 74 . . . . $9.45

SIDE DISH SELECTIONS
Roasted garlic potatoes • Capellini Primavera in butter garlic • Bahamian peas & rice
Seven grain rice pilaf • Glazed carrots • Seasonal fresh vegetable medley • Broiled parmesan potatoes
Snap pea & carrots • Herbed rosemary potatoes • Green bean & tomato sauté • Confetti Couscous
Balsamic grilled vegetables

Our hot entreés are delivered in thermal insulated containers and accompanied by all necessary
serving utensils and paper products.

Hot Entrees

In House Bakery/Handcrafted Desserts

Cold Appetizers

Box Lunches/Salads/Soup of the Day

Additional Lunch Selections/Hot Appetizers

Food Bars/Join Us For Lunch

Beyond The Call

Call 427-4955   Fax 427-5911   www.russosgourmet.com

Drop-Off - *Russo's Gourmet Express • St. Louis, MO*

8. John Russo and a view of one section of the kitchen. **9.** Everything is made in-house, including cakes and desserts. **10.** A traditional box lunch. **11.** All lunches are packed in larger boxes for appearance and easy handling. **12.** Larger trays go into larger custom boxes that allow them to be stacked.

Drop-Off - *Russo's Gourmet Express • St. Louis, MO*

13

15

```
              RUSSO CATERING COMPANY          12-07-99
                   Sales Order #:80949

         Name: WASH U SCHOOL OF LAW*        Event Date: TUE 12-07-99
      Contact: Sharon Strathman            Event Type: GOURMET EXPRES
      Address: 1 Brookings Dr,Campus Bx 1120 Deliver: 11:15A   Serve: 12:00P
               St Louis MO 63130                  Phone: 935-6420

    Customer No.: 4614              PO#/REF:

    Location: MX-WASH U SCH                  Guests: 25
    Packaging: ROOM 593                  Entry Date: 12-02-99
        Setup: HOT/PLT   KITCHEN OUT TIME: 10:30A   Entered By: TMD

    ┌─────┐                                    ┌──────────┐
    │FOOD │                                    │ SERVINGS │
    └─────┘                                    └──────────┘
      DCL-GRILLED ROSEMARY CHICKEN               25
      EPS-PASTA PRIMAVERA                        25
      BB-CAESAR SALAD                            25
      BBD-ASSORTED SALAD DRESSING                 1
      KBP-FRESH FRUIT SALAD                      25
      G-FRENCH BAGUETTES                          2
      G-WHEAT BAGUETTES                           2
      K-1+DZ COOKIES (DOZ)                        2
         KDP-CHUNKY CHOCOLATE CHIP COOKIE PLATT   9
         KDP-SUGAR COOKIE PLATTER                 6
         KDP-HONEY WALNUT OATMEAL RAISIN COOKIE   6
         KDP-CHUNKY WHITE CHOCOLATE MACADAMIA     4
      KV-BUCKET & ICE                             2
      KZ-DISPOSABLE DINNERWARE                   25
      KZ4-LIQUID CHAFER FUEL                      4
      KZ-PAPER TABLECOVER 54X108                  2

    ┌──────────────┐
    │FOOD REMARKS  │
    └──────────────┘
      ROSEMARY GRILLED CHICKEN - 3OZ SIZE**
      CAESAR SALAD WITH EVERYTHING ON THE SIDE INCLUDING ASSORTED DRESSING
      FRUIT SALAD
      BAGUETTES INSTEAD OF ROLLS
      REST AS SHOWN
      .

    ┌──────────────────────┐
    │SPECIAL INSTRUCTIONS  │
    └──────────────────────┘
      DELIVERY AND SETUP BY 11:30A
      WASH U SCH OF LAW
      5TH FLR - FACILITY COMMONS - 593

    ┌──────────────────┐
    │BEVERAGE REMARKS  │
    └──────────────────┘
      2 BUCKETS OF ICE ONLY

    ┌────────────────────────────┐
    │EQUIPMENT/SUPPLIES REMARKS  │
    └────────────────────────────┘

      DISPOSABLE
      2 PAPER TABLECOVERINGS
      4 STERNO
```

14

16

Drop-Off - *Russo's Gourmet Express • St. Louis, MO*

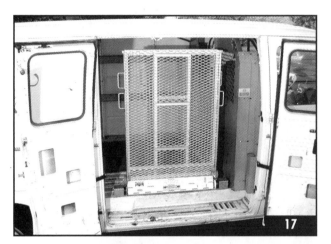

13. We loved the fact that the tape dispenser was chained to the rack! This way it won't disappear. **14.** An example of an order as it comes from the computer. **15.** Again, everything leaves in boxes. **16.** Even the cookies are 95% made in-house. **17.** The vans are equipped with handicapped ramps, which allow for easy loading and unloading. **18.** Operations Manager Jeff Robinson in action. **19.** Chef Kevin Jacobs taking a break from the action!

CaterSource Journal Subscriptions

These are CaterSource's incredible bi-monthly CaterSource Journals! The stories you just reviewed in chapter one are taken from these Journals. To get a sample, and subscription information, please call 800-932-3632 or go online www.catersource.com

CHAPTER 1  QUESTIONS

1. What did you find interesting while reviewing the photos of these caterers in action?

2. Did you see concern for sanitation?

3. What unique equipment did you see?

4. What did you notice about the staff?

5. What catering tips did you learn?

6. What did you see that didn't seem right?

7. Which of the caterers seems to be the one that is most like what you do or want to do?

8. How did these caterers work ahead?

9. What are the apparent differences between on and off-premise catering?

10. Which style of service do you like best... buffet or plate service?

MARKETING

CHAPTER

2

M · A · R · K · E · T · I · N · G

TABLE OF CONTENTS

CHAPTER

2

"Caterers never have enough working space at a party location!"

Demonstration Marketing is the Best

What can we do to make cold calling "warmer"? How can cold calling bring in more dollars? How can we give a salesperson a reason to do cold calling?

A super way to achieve success, and create a positive answer to the questions above, is to offer group tasting to your marketplace.

Here's how to go about it:

1. Decide on a geographical area that you wish to canvas. It could be a suburb, a building, a city, an industrial park etc.

2. Next, find a location in that area that will happily let you use their facility to hold a sampling open house for people in the area. You probably need a location that will hold 100 people including your buffet set-ups.

Carpet stores, automobile dealers, theater lobbies etc. all work well. Most of these places will let you use their place free since you are helping them become acquainted with the area's buyers also.

"Hi, my name is Bob Smith and I'm the owner of ABC Catering. We're looking for a place to set-up some catering buffets and serve about 100 people some samples of our food. Would you consider letting us use your showroom to invite these business people to come on our invitation. It won't cost you a cent and you'll get the same list of attendee's names that I will."

3. Now, pick a date for your sampling open house. Wednesday just might be the best day for it, but other days can work just as well. Your invitation will invite them to come between the hours of 11:30 AM and 2:00 PM.

4. Now it's time to go out and canvas the area selected! Carry with you some sort of food give away such as a brownie, chocolate dipped strawberry or a special cookie.

It is also best to work in teams of two. You actually look less dangerous to those who you approach. Walk through the door; go right up to the first person you see or the receptionist, smile and say:

"Hello, my name is Bob Smith and this is Mary Jones and we're from ABC Catering. (give away your food treat) Here's a little something special for you! We're looking to introduce our catering to those who haven't used us so we can build our business. We want to invite some people from your company to come to our free food tasting next Wednesday at the USA Carpet Showroom. Here's an invitation. Who do you think would like to come? Do you think you might have more than five people wanting to come?"

5. Try to ascertain the "temperature" of the idea in the mind of the person you're talking with. If possible ask if you can speak with the person who does the ordering from caterers.

6. Now is the time to put an invitation down on their desk. It actually works better if you set it down instead of wait for them to take it from your hand. As they look down at it you might say:

"Here's an invitation that we're passing out in the area. We expect about 200 people to come. As you can see, this invitation is for a group of five people from your company. If you have any questions please call the number on the invitation. By the way, you don't have to R.S.V.P. to attend. Do you have any questions? Thanks, hope to see you there!"

7. At the open house offer samples of your entire product line from simple box lunches to whatever. In some cases you should have some buffets just for show.

This system of marketing cold calling has helped many caterers increase their business dramatically. It is also good because it gets everyone in the company involved in an exciting promotion

SAMPLE INVITATION

ABC Catering
Invites You To Our 3rd Annual
"Tasting For New Customers"

at

USA Carpet Showroom
222 S. Jefferson

from

11:30 AM until 2:00 PM

This Invitation Will Admit FIVE
For other information call 555-5555.

Marketing Plan Template

Here is a marketing plan template that you might find useful when looking for investors or investment money.

1. The executive summary

    A. Explain who you are.

2. Introduction

    A. Tell them what you are going to be telling them.

3. Situational analysis

    A. Outline the demand for your catering.

    B. Discuss the trends in catering.

    C. Give the demographics of your marketplace.

    D. Explain how the industry has been doing.

    E. Provide the facts on any new political or legal situations pertaining to catering.

4. Overview of the marketplace

5. The competition

    A. Name them and explain your U.S.P's.

6. Your company

    A. Explain what you believe in.

    B. Make them taste and see your catering.

    C. Tell about your customers...list them by name.

    D. Include some of your menus and recipes.

Marketing Plan Template

7. The target market

A. Explain who you are going after.

8. Problems and opportunities

A. Give an honest appraisal of how you see it.

9. Goal of the marketing energy

A. This is where you tell them how much you are going to return.

B. Build sales forecasts.

10. Marketing strategy & Tactics

A. Give them actual marketing materials i.e. ads, brochures, bluelines etc.

B. Take them step by step through your time line.

11. Implementation & control

A. Discuss at what level you will attain your break-even point.

B. Give the names of anyone else who will be monitoring your progress.

C. Mention your start-up costs and other budget matters.

D. Give a detailed answer as to how you will be able to change direction... if necessary.

E. Be sure to tell them who they call for answers.

12. Summary

A. Tell them what you just told them!

B. Bring in testimonials.

13. Appendices

A. Put in everything... including the kitchen sink! The longer it is the better!

Evaluating Your Marketing Strategy

What is consulting? To me, consulting is evaluation and comparison. First you evaluate what conditions exist, then you compare these conditions with those that exist elsewhere.

This is why the world has consultants. Not for their expertise, but for their exposure to diverse conditions. Most caterers have never been to many other catering operations to see what is happening. I've been fortunate to have personally visited more than 900 catering companies over the last 20 years.

That's what this new series of articles is about. I hope to give our readers some guidelines for "self-consulting".

It is important that catering businesses receive ongoing evaluation in order to continually reach for higher levels of success.

Definition of Marketing

Marketing is what a company does to locate new buyers; confirm for past buyers that they are already with the best caterer; and finally, to prepare the shopper for the sales program!

The Goals of Marketing

Marketing has only two goals. First, it needs to make your phone ring or get prospective buyers to come into your place of business. Second, it needs to create a sales opportunity by preparing the shopper to better understand your differences from other caterers.

The "Heart"of Marketing

1. Separate your company's actions and policies from what is perceived to be industry standards.

2. Take the risk out of buying for the client.

3. Market differently to different groups and individuals. This is not easy, but it's important.

4. For social catering stress entertaining and status.

5. For corporate catering stress sales results and employee happiness.

6. Teach the business of catering to your marketplace.

7. Always answer the question of WIIFM in everything that you do... what's in it for me!

8. Use testimonials... they are powerful in catering.

9. Try to deliver more then you promised!

10. Remember that in most cases caterers are not taken too seriously by those wanting to buy catering.

Ways To Measure Your Marketing Temperature

1. Talk with your present buyers. Ask them what they like best about your service. Ask them what they like least.

2. Ask your present buyers what they would do if they owned your company for a day and could change anything that they wanted.

3. Talk with your own staff. Ask them what they would do to make the company better and then listen to their answers.

4. Figure out how you can get a detailed demonstration of what and how your closest competitors do with their catering. Why not purchase some catering from them without them knowing it is for a competitor!

5. Take an honest inventory of where your company stands in the "mind of the buyer" in these categories as a guide:

> **A.** Overall image
>
> **B.** Knowledge of your product/service
>
> **C.** Sensitivity to buyer wishes
>
> **D.** Enthusiasm for catering
>
> **E.** Professionalism

How To Be A Market Leader

1. Master the ability to recognize the opportunity for new service and products quicker than others.

2. Have total concentration for success and to win over your competition.

3. Have a clearly written mission statement.

> ... THINK OF THESE TIPS, TACTICS AND IDEAS AS A STARTING POINT FOR DOING SELF-CONSULTING FOR YOUR OWN BUSINESS.

Evaluating Your Marketing Strategy

4. Educate your entire team and potential clients to the advantages of your service.

5. Have valid cost control efficiency.

6. Constantly take the pulse of the marketplace.

7. Like to win!

8. Know what will be needed five years from now.

Develop Value-Added Marketing

Below are the cornerstones in establishing value-added catering. This is where a catering sales force can't be afraid of pointing out why they are better and different than the competition!

1. Food

2. Serving Staff

3. Knowledge

4. Experience

5. Equipment

6. Sanitation

7. Delivery Methods

8. Price Advantages

9. Technology

10. Guarantees

11. Professionalism

12. Style

13. Testimonials

14. Themes

You need to nurture these concepts to take full advantage of them when marketing your catering to a competitive marketplace!

A successful marketing program needs a commitment to keeping the mind of the buyer constantly thinking only of us when they think of catering!

Rules, or Goals of Your Marketing Program

1. You sell more catering when your marketing energy demonstrates to the buyer what the catering will do for them and their situation.

2. The marketing must overcome the false and true beliefs that they have about catering.

3. Catering marketing must take the risk out of decision making for the buyer!

4. Remember: Most people buy the most familiar brand.

5. Most people buy by simply choosing ... catering marketing needs to permit buyers to decide to buy from you rather than from the most familiar.

6. To keep a client loyal, your marketing must continually remind them that they are with the best already!

7. To take buyers from another caterer you need to give them a chance to use you just once... not forever!!

8. Effective catering marketing demonstrates the downside of the alternatives to catering.

9. Higher prices are not defended in catering marketing. They are explained by showing how they provide less disaster (or more success) over the competition's lower prices.

10. Catering marketing needs to show that in catering you get what you pay for!

A caterer can never spend too much time or money on marketing. It's really quite simple, you can't grow a company faster without quality marketing to new and past clients. The CaterSource Journal is full of examples of successful marketing techniques and ideas!

Important Concepts in Marketing

What are the catering markets?

1. Social
2. Corporate
3. Budget
4. Contract
5. Wholesale
6. Retail

Sales ratios in change

1. 80% Corporate/20% Social
2. 60% Corporate/40% Social
3. 60% Corporate/20% Social/20% Other
4. 25% Corporate/65% Social/10% Other

Some Catering Marketing Niches

1. Private labeling of foods.
2. Executive jet feeding.
3. Catering for under 10 guests.
4. Movie and production shoot feeding.
5. Kosher catering.
6. Corporate gifts.
7. Upscale or fashion catering.
8. Budget or fast food catering.
9. Corporate catering.
10. Social catering.
11. Picnics.
12. Selling foods to other caterers.
13. Disaster catering.
14. On-Premise Banquet Halls.
15. Sub-contracting out to help hotels.
16. Food styling.
17. Coffee and meeting breaks.
18. Last minute catering.
19. Award programs.
20. Charity fundraisers.

Information That Starts Your Marketing

1. What types of people purchase from my company already?

2. How do these buyers feel about our catering?

3. What are the steps buyers take to purchase from us?

4. How many different groups buy from us?

5. I need to understand what to look and listen for when selling a buyer.

6. I should maintain a data base of my buyers and update it continually.

7. I need to understand what foods, styles of service and trends are really in.

8. What parts of my business are expensive in the mind of the buyer?

9. What parts of my business are looked upon as "added value"?

10. Do I know what other buyers say about our catering?

11. Do I know the strengths and weaknesses of our kitchen?

12. Am I aware of past and present advertising and marketing statements?

13. Do I know the story behind the start of my company?

14. I need to really taste my company's foods.

15. Have I spent time talking to others about our product & service?

16. Do I really understand and know about my company's product lines?

17. Do I understand what my company's guarantee policy is?

18. Am I aware of my competitor's marketing?

Foundations for Catering Marketing

1. Separate your company's actions and policies from what is perceived to be industry standards.

2. Take the risk out of buying for the client.

3. Market differently to different groups and individuals.

4. For social catering stress entertaining and status.

5. For corporate catering stress sales results and employee happiness.

6. Teach the business of catering to your marketplace.

7. Always answer the question of WIIFM in everything that you do... what's in it for me.

8. Use testimonials... they are powerful in catering.

9. Try to deliver more then you promised!

10. Remember that in most cases caterers are not taken too seriously by those wanting to buy catering.

11. Talk with your present buyers. Ask them what they like best about your service. Ask them what they like least.

12. Ask your present buyers what they would do if they owned your company for a day and could change anything that they wanted.

13. Talk with your own staff. Ask them what they would do to make the company better and then listen to their answers.

14. Figure out how you can get a detailed demonstration of what and how your closest competitors do with their catering. Why not purchase some catering from them without them knowing it is for a competitor!

15. Take an honest inventory of where your company stands in the "mind of the buyer" in these categories:

    A. Overall image

    B. Knowledge of your product/service

    C. Sensitivity to buyer wishes

    D. Enthusiasm for catering

    E. Professionalism

16. Decide on what area of your business you need to market first.

17. Develop some small marketing programs first. Wait till later for the mega dollar promotions. Remember what George Patton said, "A good plan today is better than a great plan tomorrow."

18. Think of your business from the buyers point of view.

19. Decide what part of your business is ripe for a change.

20. Live by the motto that every product/service can be improved!

Planning for a Marketing Program

1. Decide what promotion fits in with your overall marketing goals.

2. Concentrate on increasing the most profitable parts of your business.

3. Write down what you expect this promotion to bring you.

4. (a) Make sure you know what Unique Selling Propositions you will be marketing to.

4. (b) Determine what you are going to offer and to whom.

5. Create your theme, point of interest, gimmick, attention getter or whatever you wish to call it!

6. Figure how you can get your entire staff involved in the promotion.

7. Test your ideas with your various mentors.

8. Put a budget together to look at the numbers. Remember, if a catering business is earning 20% profit on every dollar sold, then you get back $2.00 for every $100.00 of stuff you sell. So, if a promotion is figured to cost you $1,000.00 of your hard earned money, then you will need $5,000.00 in sales from the promotion just to break even!

9. Create a realistic timetable and assign tasks to create the promotion for yourself and the staff.

10. Put the promotion aside for a few days. Let it roll around in your head. If it still makes good sense and nobody is able to critique it... put it in motion.

Getting Money From Your Vendors

It may not seem correct to solicit dollars from purveyors to help pay for our marketing energy, but many are doing just this! In fact, most other industries use the concept of "one company takes care of the other". If you still aren't sure about this concept, just review your accounts payable to several of your purveyors. Here's a letter that might help:

Date:

MEMO

From: Jim Smith

To: Bob Jones

I really need your help... but first let me tell you once again what a super job you and your crew are doing for us! I receive nothing but raves from my clients and their guests about your products.

Bob, I've arranged to do some marketing during the months of November and December targeted at getting more business during our slower season of January through March. The total budget is $4,800 for some ads in the City Light magazine and a direct mail letter to 3,000 people in the Plum Grove area.

Since we both will gain from the success of this marketing, I'm asking my suppliers for their financial support in this marketing program. Please consider investing 10%, or $480, in our marketing efforts.

You may send us a check directly, or if it's better for you, you can make the check out to one of the companies that I need to pay for the marketing i.e. postage, printing ad design etc.

In either case, please call us before September 25 with your decision. You may ask for me or Margaret. Thanks for your consideration!

P.S. Why don't we meet for lunch!

Starting a Social Self-Serve Division

Below is an advertising template to capture a new niche in your marketplace. This new division which could be named "Social Self-Serve", is for your social customer. It is usually geared for both week night and weekend sales. Some caterers will be wise to place higher minimums on Saturday orders.

One of the questions that some caterers might ask is "Will this self-service division take away from my full service business?" CaterSource can assure you that, with very few exceptions, this new division will increase your full service business! Most of your clients will use your self serve division only for less critical entertaining situations i.e family and friend gatherings. All of the guests who come to this self serve event will learn of your company, self and full serve divisions from their hosts... therefore... referrals.

You will find that the average order will be about 32 guests. Remember, this is designed to be a one-way delivery. The customer will transfer your foods to their stuff after you deliver. You should be able to charge for delivery and any special services that the client wishes. However, the most important rule for a self service division is Food only... No serving staff supplied... no exceptions.

You may wish to run your advertisement in various local newspapers or in a postcard format to mail to targeted areas of your marketplace. This type of marketing and selling program should benefit your company with its larger market base who really doesn't want to "waste" money on staff and equipment rentals.

Ways to Outlive the Catering Cycle

1. Catering is like most businesses. The life cycle starts with a dream... which moves into the launch... followed by growth... reaching a plateau... which is the beginning of the decline.

2. This is how many of our customers see us... in one of these stages of life. Everyone wants to buy from the "new kid on the block". Because of this, we lose some business no matter what marketing we do.

3. What's interesting is that caterers, unlike many other types of business people, tend to look upon their work as a life... not just a livelihood.

4. One of the best ways to cheat this process is to begin again! Create a new division, a new concept, a new company, a new logo, a new department, a new service motto or anything else that will bring you face to face with what you need... challenge and "non-life-threatening" crisis!

5. Another way to help yourself is to secure bank, or "angel" financing for your marketing programs.

Template for a PR Release

ABC Catering Company To Teach "Kitchen" Classes To Young Children

On June 25, 1990 ABC Catering will be announcing the sponsorship of special "free" kitchen classes for children between the ages of seven and nine years of age.

The children will learn how to decorate cup cakes, make chocolate dipped strawberries and a variety of other skills that will permit them to be exposed to the fun of working in a kitchen.

These are the first classes to teach children about how kitchens work!

For more information contact:

Bob Smith at 555-555-5555.

Proven & Experimental Marketing Ideas

1. Make speeches to clubs, etc.

2. Place news releases with local and city newspapers.

3. Get on a radio talk show.

4. Tie in marketing with various charities.

5. Find an important person to feature in your advertisements.

6. Create a newsletter.

7. Write a column for the newspaper.

8. Let your regular buyers rent some equipment from you even when they are not buying the food from you company.

9. Send congratulatory letters to key business figures that win awards or are written about in the business sections.

10. Create a traveling information booth to take to shopping malls and community trade shows.

11. Rally around a common problem of the community.

12. Provide your prospective callers with hard-hitting testimonials from happy clients.

13. Provide food for the Chamber of Commerce meetings.

14. Create marketing value with all sorts of checklists for buyers.

15. Make a percentage contribution to a charity based on each sale.

16. Send birthday cards or cakes to important people.

17. Look in Thomas's Register of Manufacturers to learn about 5, 10, 15, 20 and 25 year corporate anniversaries. Then send them a pleasant letter!

18. Put catering displays in other business's windows.

19. Invite your best buyers to a party.

20. Send a picture postcard of your staff.

21. Put best buyers names up on a billboard.

22. Use sealing wax for a finishing touch on your letters.

23. Put a scent into your letters.

24. Offer to buy back one of the host's pictures to add to your collection!

25. "Win Our Chef" For One Night Promotion

26. Give part-timers business cards with their name & yours on them.

Proven & Experimental Marketing Ideas

27. Invite people into your kitchen and sales office for an open house.

28. Give an educational seminar for corporate clients on "What's Hot & Not in Corporate Catering In The 1990's"

29. Offer gift certificates in denominations of $1,000 and $5,000!

30. Handle RSVP's for your buyers.

31. Sell two for the price of one weddings.

32. Create a newsletter carrying your name but containing articles, notices and information given by the community.

33. Develop a scratch & sniff ad

34. Buy three events and get the fourth one at 1/2 price.

35. Get specially printed messages placed in fortune cookies.

36. Hold a "Fall" and or "Spring" fashion show of your foods and entertaining styles.

37. Send Thanksgiving cards instead of Holiday cards.

38. Create hot lines for special types of orders or information.

39. Offer 100% money-back guarantee.

40. Sell a limited number of party permits.

41. Give commissions to clients who recommend people who buy.

42. Offer evening business hours for clients to call.

43. Create a division to handle catering for second marriages.

44. Use at least one of the client's recipes at the event.

45. Provide souvenir menus for the guests to take with them.

46. Hold a cooking contest for corporate Presidents only.

5TH CALLER GETS 50% OFF THEIR NEXT SELF-SERVICE ORDER.

Catering Business Builders

#1. Newspaper Column - In most areas of the nation, and Canada, smaller to mid-size community newspapers are always searching for materials to print. Start by creating some 200 to 400 words articles on catering and entertaining. Then send these articles to various newspapers in care of the "features editor". They just might print them.

#2. Handle RSVP's For Clients - An interesting concept is to tell certain corporate and social clients that if they wish, you will be happy to have their guests write, or call your office to confirm that they are coming to the event. In this way you give your buyer added value and you also get a chance to touch a whole bunch of potentially new customers.

#3. Business Card For Part - Timers - Provide your part-time event staff with their own personalized business card. For many of them it will be the first business card they've ever had. They will pass them out everywhere! Also, they will now have something to give a guest when they're asked "Who did the catering?" It might be wise to print onto the front of the card "For information please call (your name) at (your phone).

#4. Special Message In Fortune Cookie - A great business builder is to give your regular corporate buyers a tray of fortune cookies with a customized message inside i.e. "ABC Catering wishes to thank you for your continued support" or " ABC Catering knows that good fortune is on the way for you!" Give us a call if you wish to know how to order these custom cookies.

#5. Evening Office Hours - Both on and off-premise caterers should consider marketing the fact that they are always available to talk on the phone, or in person, during specified evening hours. Monday and Thursday evenings are probably the best. This will make it easier for those people who find it difficult to call, or visit, during daytime hours.

#6. Dedicated Tasting Sessions - As both a marketing and cost cutting activity, dedicate two times per month when a potential buyer may come into your company for a group tasting. One weekend day and one weekday evening seem to work best. "Mrs. Smith, we really don't hold private tasting simply because it's very difficult to capture what we do for just two or three people. But, we've set aside two days a month when customers may come in for a tasting of a wide variety of our menu items. Usually there are about twenty customers like yourself who attend, so we can really go all out to present our food. Would you like to come on either..."

#7. Special Cooking Contest For Corporate Presidents - This is a fun marketing idea. Place an ad in your city's business journal, or where companies will see it. Announce the 1st. Annual President's Chili Cookoff Contest. The prize is a contribution to a charity of their choice. You will be amazed at how this marketing idea excites people! Choose your judges wisely.

#8. Food Critic For A Day - Invite about 100 potential, or regular, buyers to come in an critique your foods. Tell them that you need to to try out some new menu items before you offer them to the public. When they arrive, give them a souvenir apron that says "Food Critic For A Day", and a list of the new foods with space for them to write their comments (a clipboard helps). Be sure to label your menu items on the buffets so they can correctly tell you what they think!

#9. Generic Birthday Cake - Offer your best corporate buyers a free birthday cake once a month that says "Happy Birthday To Our (place month) Birthdays". In this manner the company can celebrate all of the birthdays for a particular month at the same time.

#10. Cater To Other Caterers - Yes... this is really a great business builder. Send letters to other caterers letting them know that you would be happy to create some food for them to use at their events. Give them a wholesale price for everything from chicken breast to tossed salad. You're probably thinking that this won't work... but it does. Call me and I'll be happy to explain this in greater detail with you.

#11. Scratch & Sniff Ads - Call your printer and ask them how much it costs to create a scratch & sniff promotional piece. You will be amazed at how reasonable it is to do this. Also, it's dynamite marketing because your marketplace has never received a promotion of this type from a caterer.

#12. $5,000 Gift Certificates - Why not? It will cause mayhem in buyer's minds when they see a promo offering them ... and you might even sell one!

Why Catering is so Tough to Market

1. When you market catering you are marketing something that can not be taken off a shelf and examined by the buyer.

2. When marketing catering to a buyer it is difficult to demonstrate your product/service like you can a camera or a new car. Many buyers have never really understood what catering really is!

3. The marketer usually is marketing a product that they have never really purchased themselves. So, they really don't have a clear understanding of what goes through the mind of a buyer.

4. When you sell catering the buyer doesn't take the party home with them. They have to trust you... and that is very scary!

5. Some of the most expensive cameras sell for under $2,000.00. But a wedding may cost $15,000.00. Because of this buyer tend to get very cautious, simply because of the total amount of money they are spending.

6. Buyers know that they cannot return the catering after the party for a refund or an exchange. This makes the salesperson's task even harder.

7. In most catering sales situations, the buyer gets an entire proposal and contract to take with them before they say yes to the caterer. Because of this, the buyer is able to put things "under a microscope" and compare your bid with others. But the bids being compared are very seldom at the same quality level as yours.

Open Houses Really Work

Open houses are one of the strongest marketing moves you can make! The total energy, which is focused on the common goal of getting new business from both old and new clients, increases the total morale of a catering company.

These four pages give you a little insight into the successful open house given by **Carlyn Berghoff Catering** (Chicago, IL) They mailed out 1,500 invitations to both old and new clients and had over 450 people r.s.v.p's who attended this gala evening.

CaterSource spent the evening watching as the guests sampled the foods and felt the warm hospitality of the CBC team. "Crowd" control was a factor, especially when it came time to refill the buffets. It's amazing what people will do for free food and beverages!

If you've ever done an open house, you know that it is a lot of work and worry. This is a time when everything must be proper and correct.

CBC's open house was to let everyone see their new 10,500 square foot facility and to renew friendships. CBC asked for, and received, great support from their vendors with respect to economic breaks on the ingredients that went into this marketing event.

The CBC Team (L to R) Carlyn Berghoff, Dina Vivada, Michelle Willey, John Tutaj, Jennifer Perna, Margaret Ortiz, Kate Flynn, and Robert Hollenbeck.

Carlyn Berghoff greeted everyone at the door as they entered. This is a vital part of an open house!

You are invited to see how a west-loop bicycle factory has been converted into state-of-the-art catering studios and fabulous kitchens!

Carlyn Berghoff

C A T E R I N G INC.

1001 West Van Buren Street
Chicago

THURSDAY, FEBRUARY 23, 1995
5:00 - 8:00 p.m.

**PLEASE JOIN US FOR A FESTIVE TOUR
AND OPEN HOUSE**

✿ ✿ ✿

COCKTAILS AND HORS D'OEUVRE

✿ ✿ ✿

CULINARY DEMONSTRATIONS
by Chef Robert Hollenbeck and Chef John Tutaj

Music throughout the evening
Special Night-of-Event Drawing
Grand Prize - Dinner Party for Ten Guests

This invitation admits you and one guest
Please respond to our party hot line on or before Friday, February 17th
(312) 432-0200

Complimentary parking in West Van Buren lot at corner, west of entrance
Complimentary Shuttle Bus Return to Northwestern and Union Stations

This is the front and back of the invitation that was mailed to 1,500 regular and potential clients.

Open Houses Really Work

Braised Duck Gratin
with black beans and sweet potatoes

California Crudite
A wild variety of fresh crisp vegetables
cool, creamy herb dip

Chips, Chips, Chips,
Lightly seasoned crispy vegetable chips
cumin sour cream
green onion dip

An Assortment of Cocktail Sandwiches
Grilled flank steak on corn muffins
chipotle sour cream

Thinly sliced vegetables and a variety of
sprouts on multigrain rolls
lemon avocado coulis

Mint-marinated breast of chicken on pita bread
hummus bi tahini

House smoked salmon on black rye rolls
lemon scented cream cheese

Shaved ham with on poppy rolls
apricot dijon mustard

Open Houses Really Work

Guests at the open house could choose from three bar locations and five food stations spread around the CBC offices and kitchens.

This is the postcard that started it all. Clients were informed of the new CBC home from this cheerful photo.

Open Houses Really Work

Win One Great Cooking Lesson

Dinner for Ten...

In our Kitchen!

Consult with the chef ahead of time to shape a menu to your tastes as you learn how professionals plan menus. Then work with him (and your friends) to create your own delicious three course dinner from start to finish. Learn the chef's secrets as you go. Finally, relax and enjoy what you've made!

* * *

A selection of Passed Hors d'Oeuvre

First Course
A combination first course pairing vinaigretted greens and warm cheese
Served with bread and herb butter

Entree
A mixed grill of beef tenderloin and fresh salmon with complementing sauces
Served with carefully selected vegetable and grain accompaniments

Dessert
The chef's nationally recognized signature dessert,
Two Chocolates
Served with coffee, decaffeinated coffee, and tea

* * *

Carlyn Berghoff Catering will supply service, tables, linen, place settings, flowers, everything! And we'll set it all up in the newest, most advanced catering kitchen in the city.

A drawing will be made from all business cards received by 7:45. Winner need not be present to win. Your participation (and that of your guests) is, of course, optional- but we don't think you'll want to miss it! Not valid Sundays, holidays, some Saturdays, or during the months of May, June, October, or December. Other restrictions may apply.

Above: One of the ways to get better participation by the guests was the above contest announced on giant posters around the offices during the open house. Below: Another giant poster thanked all the vendors that helped CBC.

This evening has been made possible in part by generous contributions from:

Ivan Carlson & Associates
Hall's Rental Service, Inc.
BBJ Boutique \ Mr. Bill Pry
Kloeckner Preferred Flowers
Carmel Music & Entertainment
A New Dairy, Inc.
The Seafood Merchants, Ltd.
Buedel Food Products, Inc.
Highland Baking Company
Testa Produce Company
Casper Food Service
Mr. Sol Heifetz

All photos on this page by Phil Farber-Photo Images, Inc.

Image: Is it Everything

Is image everything? Yes. The important educational concept to understand is that you have several images. One is your actual image. Next is the perceived image. Third is what you think about your image.

Let's say that you serve egg salad on one buffet, while at another event you are serving French Rack of Lamb. Your actual image is that of a catering company that handles a full range of culinary foods.

However, your perceived image is in the eyes, minds, and gossip of those attending your two events. The guests who saw the Lamb are perceiving you as a high end caterer. Those who only tasted your egg salad are perceiving you as a much simpler caterer.

Of course, if you are serving egg salad canapes with a dollop of caviar on them, you still have a differently perceived image.

If you are only viewed as a box lunch caterer, many clients won't perceive you as one who can do a large corporate event. Is this fair? No. But that's the way it is in business. What some caterers find even more disturbing is the simple fact that what some people believe to be true just isn't!

The first conclusion for our "Image" concept is that perceived image is the most deadly! It's unfair, but your simple actions, or inactions, can cause a set of buyers to incorrectly judge you for life!

Here's some examples of the kinds of things that can cause you to have an incorrect public perceived image:

1. When you deliver an order your delivery person is not clean looking or in uniform. This results in a perceived image that the rest your kitchen must be not up to par either.

2. When calling your company, the person handling the call doesn't show courtesy or provide a feeling of caring. This leads to the perceived image that you will not be there to support them when they need you.

3. You send too much food. Therefore people begin to talk about the fact that they can under order for certain parties and still have enough food.

4. A valet parker is curt with a guest. This leads to the perceived image that the rest of your company has rude people.

5. You tell your potential buyers before they decide that they are going to use you that if they cancel you are going to keep some of the deposit. This leads to the perceived image that you are only concerned about dollars and that for some reason a lot of your clients cancel.

Here's some examples of some positive perceived image situations:

1. A client makes an appointment for you to come and see them, or to come into your banquet facility. You write them a handwritten note confirming the appointment and thanking them in advance for the opportunity. This results in the perceived image that you are intensely professional and organized.

2. When delivering an order the delivery person tells the client that the chef has given them some free samples of some new dishes. This creates a perceived image that you are investing in your customers.

3. Call a customer moments before your delivery van leaves for their event. Tell them that the food looks great! This relieves the client and gives you a perceived image of caring. By the way, your last minute call will almost always will have incredible impact on your client.

4. Ask a client who is calling for information if they wish you to take the lead, or do they know what they want. This gives a perceived image of cooperation.

Does this make any sense to you? Some caterers work their whole life without understanding the importance of perceived image.

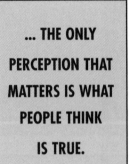

... THE ONLY PERCEPTION THAT MATTERS IS WHAT PEOPLE THINK IS TRUE.

The third type of image perception is the one that you believe to be true. This is the most dangerous perception of all! We all think that things are better than they really are. Also, it takes a special person to really tell us what they really think about us. In other words, no one likes too much confrontation. In this form of "self-perception" we often lull ourselves into a false sense of safety.

Image: Photos Help or Hurt

Linda West, the owner of Melange, told us that they saved $3,000 by doing their own food styling for the photographer. Linda convinced the food photographer to do the work on a straight trade where she got the professionally done photos, and the photographer got beautiful samples to show his new clients!

Linda also cautions anyone doing this type of work to, "Get a real food photographer!"

The back of each piece carries a high quality sticker with company information and phone numbers.

Linda told CaterSource, "Since we've developed this photo concept, we don't need to use our cumbersome portfolio of pictures when visiting potential clients. In fact, it seems that this new promotion gives us instant credibility and demonstrates our style and quality. It was one of the best moves we made!"

From The Front Cover

How does an up-scale caterer offer simple self-service catering without losing their up-scale image? This is how Melange Catering (Houston, TX) solved the problem.

They created beautiful four-color photos and printed them with great care onto 8.5 x 11 glossy high quality card stock. In addition, they also created a custom folder that has a four-color photo on the front cover to hold the set of four image photographs. It cost them a lot of money, but it helped them accomplish their goal of letting both their new and old customers know that self-service can be done with high style ... even with plastic ware.

When the buyer looks at both the "office lunch" photo above and the "events" photo to the right, also on the front cover of this Journal, they can see that they will be getting high style by using Melange!

Whether it's using plastic or silver, the marketing message is focused on style and quality!

The total amount printed was 5,000 sets of four photos and a folder. It cost $5,000 plus an additional $3,000 in trade for the printing. Also, they used the services of a design house that charged $10,000 in trade to set-up the design concept in the photos and do the four-color separations for the printer.

Image: Can We Have Both Sides of the Coin

Can a caterer successfully sell both up-scale and down-scale menus to the same marketplace... under the same trade name? Engroff Catering (Topeka, KS) has done just that for the last fifteen years!

The photo to the right is an event for 750 graduating lawyers from a state college. The photo at the bottom is a 200# pig for a pig pick'n event of 300 for the President of a different university.

The tablecloth reception, using china, was a brunch hors d'oeuvres event for 11/2 hours costing $6.50 per guest. The pig pick'n cost $10.00 per guest.

Jay Engroff started as a caterer with the pig roasts and moved into the more formal style of catering as more, and more, clients requested it.

In 1994 Engroff Catering will sell $600,000 of catering with a 14% profit.

Jay told us that he orders his pigs from a meat purveyor that has the ability to smoke the pig for him. They charge $35 extra for this service.

Theme menus offered by Engroff Catering include Mexican, German, Italian and Chinese. These menus are sold for $8.50 (10-30 guests) $8.25 (31-70) $8.15 (71-199) $7.95 (+200).

It is usually easier for a caterer to move from up-scale to down than it is to go from down to up... we congratulate Engroff Catering!

Image: Company Name Changes

Why would a caterer ever change their company's name? Let's look at some situations and strategies for changing your brand in the marketplace.

Suppose your company name is "Roman's Catering" or "Catering By Roman". The case can be made that no matter how successful your company is, when you try to sell it you will have some problems.

The buyers will know that long after you leave, customers will be asking to speak with Roman when they call. Most people want to talk with the owner when they know who it might be.

Many reading this article already know, even when they have no intention of selling their business, that all callers want to speak with the person whose name is on the company.

Here's one way of solving this situation. Start by adding a tag line to your original name. "Catering by Roman" now becomes "Catering By Roman's Grand Events". You start answering the phones that way and you change your letterhead.

In a year, or two, you start dropping the size of the logo print on your letterhead and business cards. "Catering By Roman" becomes smaller and "Grand Events" becomes larger.

The same concept is used when answering the phones. "Catering By Roman's Grand Events" becomes "Grand Events Catering". This really works if you wish to take the time to do it. In most cases, owners who have done this are extremely happy with the results.

The next scenario is different. Suppose you have a brand name that is a little tired, or has suffered some embarrassment in the marketplace. What should you do?

Many caterers have simply started another company under the same roof as their primary one. So, "Catering By Roman" could form a new business called "Applause Catering".

After talking with your attorney, you would simply acquire separate phones, accounting systems, etc. and start to sell the new brand to the public.

You would place a separate yellow page ad, do separate advertising for the new entity. While you would not deny that you owned the new business, you won't be telling people at first.

By the way, have you ever considered doing what many restaurants and retail businesses do... "under new management". The reason this is done is because of a real, or false, perception by the public, that a particular catering business is no longer viable.

Often, the move is done internally simply as a bold marketing move. Recently, a caterer who had suffered a serious food borne illness case, used "under new management" to save their business from disaster. While this is a tragic situation, the owners of the catering business used sound marketing techniques to overcome a difficult business dilemma.

Many caterers choose to move to a different level of price when they open a new sister company. Sometimes a lower priced caterer will use the new company to get away from the typecasting that the public feels about the primary company name. In other words, if you are know as a "sandwich" caterer and you wish to do formal weddings, the move to a new company makes a lot of sense.

Others will opt for moving down in price when forming a sister company. Sometimes, a high end social caterer will move towards a picnic, or bbq, business with the new company.

Think of it as Marriott Hotels, Residence Inns, Courtyard by Marriott, and Fairfield Inns. All of these brands are owned by Marriott, but they all have a different meaning in the marketplace. They all have different price points..

It is interesting to note that often Marriott builds a Courtyard By Marriott, a lower priced product, right on the same property as a higher cost Marriott Hotel.

This means that you probably don't have to build a secret second company if you wish. Your customers can understand your need for diversity and growth.

But sometimes it's best to keep it a secret for a little while. Did you know that Campbell's Soup owns Godiva Chocolate? This is a secret to most people, because marketers understand that, while it's not necessary to be top-secret, this type of confused branding might cause some people to react differently to the products.

Many caterers have learned that when they have two brands out in the marketplace, they often compete with each other. Buyers call both companies and compare pricing. Before you consider this, remember that Pontiac and Oldsmobile are all made by the same company. Also, a Mercury Sable and a Ford Taurus are virtually the same car! Interesting... isn't it?

The concept of changing a catering company's name, or the addition of a new company is a valid choice for many caterers. How you accomplish the task is the only concern.

What's in a Name?

A brand name is merely one that is distinctive in the mind of the buyer. Can it put your company at an advantage over others? Can it put your company at a disadvantage?

These are valid questions for any caterer. The important point is that any caterer reading this page has already named their company. So, what's the point?

Well, this information may be of assistance in understanding the marketing implications of the type of name you selected. Also, quite a few caterers make the marketing move to change, or adjust, their company's name. More on that in the next issue of the CaterSource Journal (#24).

First, let's review the marketing concepts behind a name. Brand names or "branding" are most important when you consider the impact that a particular name might have on someone encountering it for the first time in the yellow pages or on a brochure.

1. Personal names... Mike's Catering, Catering by James, George's, Roman's Catering & Special Events are examples of these types of names.

By far, these types lead the pack when you look through the yellow pages for caterers. It's only natural for someone starting a catering business to use their own name for the company.

While there is nothing wrong with this concept, many caterers have learned that as they grow their business using this form of a name, most first time callers want to speak with the person whose name is on the business. How many calls can one person handle?

2. Place names... Highland Park Caterers, Washington Square Catering, New York Caterers, West End Catering are examples of these types of names.

This type of name can be excellent because it gives the caller a quick understanding of the type of people you might already do business with. But, that can be the downfall also. Suppose your "place" has had a change in its popularity?

In addition, this type of "place" name can give the shopper a wrong idea of how far you will travel to do catering. Can you get to them on time? Will bad weather cause you to be delayed because you're so far away. All of these feelings are called "buyer's prejudice" and they can have a good, or bad, result on your growth.

3. Status names... Upper Crust Caterers, Gold Label Caterers, Gourmet Classics are examples of these types of names.

With respect to "buyer prejudice" these are the most dangerous types of names to use. If you are called Upper Crust... then you must be expensive... and maybe they don't want to buy expensive. Or, their boss has told them to buy down on the next catering order.

Can you see how this type of name can work against you? It's unfair, but this marketing truth has great impact on your future.

Remember, a shopper will never call you and tell you "I saw your name in the yellow pages, but I decided not to use you because your name sounds too expensive... I just wanted to take time to call you to tell you this".

4. Descriptive names... Festivities Catering, Picnics R' Us, The Corporate Caterers, Box Lunches ToGo, Applause Catering, and Ovations Caterers, are examples of these types of names.

We've saved the best for last. These types of names are the most ideal. They have less "buyer prejudice" and are based usually on what your catering company does or what the results of your catering will be.

These types of names also give the reader a quick understanding of what you probably do as a caterer. A good goal for marketing your brand is to help the buyers associate your name with your company instead of another. It should make them aware of exactly who you are and what you sell and stand for.

A brand needs to provide a point of difference for the buyer! The name Applause Catering puts a positive difference into the mind of the buyer, while the use of the word "Gourmet" in your name might have a positive, or negative, influence on the decision of the shopper to pursue the sale further.

Don't take this education too seriously. However, there may be some truth as it applies to your own business. Feel free to call and speak with Mike Roman about this concept further, Next month we'll tell you how some caterers changed their names.

Frequent Buyer Program

This is a CaterSource, Inc. template which you can use as a subscriber. It may be used in several ways. First, it may be a "stand alone" promotion. Second, it may be printed right into your menu. Some caterers might find it best to use it only for a group of special buyers, to provide them with perks, and the feeling of being special.

1. This promotion is often successful even when the buyers don't take advantage of the awards. This type of promo offering "bonus points" is being used by many other types of businesses and services.

2. Pretty simple! Spend a dollar and get a point towards the award redemptions. You can also offer "bonus points" for certain circumstances that will help you build your business, such as breakfast.

3. The awards are also simple. They can range from a simple birthday cake to a trip to NYC. The important concept is that the awards be the kind that will be appreciated in your area.

4. Yes, let your buyers keep the records for redemption by saving their invoices from your catering. This also allows the buyer to determine what award they are going after and provides less work for you!

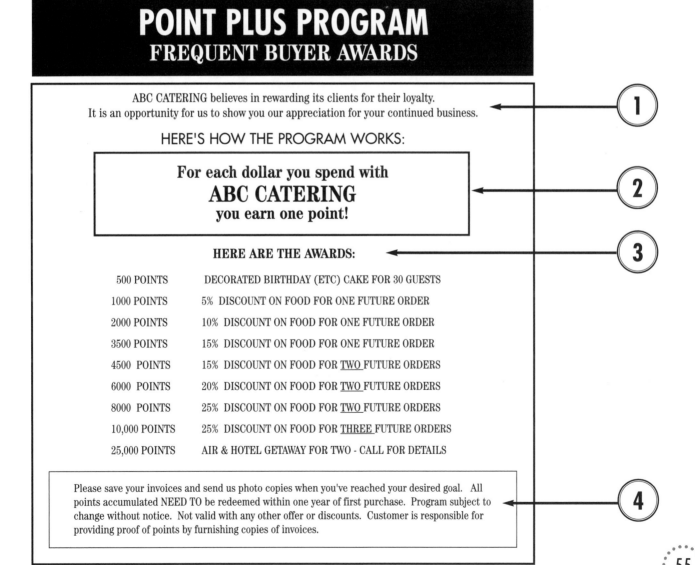

POINT PLUS PROGRAM
FREQUENT BUYER AWARDS

ABC CATERING believes in rewarding its clients for their loyalty.
It is an opportunity for us to show you our appreciation for your continued business. ← **1**

HERE'S HOW THE PROGRAM WORKS:

For each dollar you spend with
ABC CATERING
you earn one point! ← **2**

HERE ARE THE AWARDS: ← **3**

500 POINTS	DECORATED BIRTHDAY (ETC) CAKE FOR 30 GUESTS
1000 POINTS	5% DISCOUNT ON FOOD FOR ONE FUTURE ORDER
2000 POINTS	10% DISCOUNT ON FOOD FOR ONE FUTURE ORDER
3500 POINTS	15% DISCOUNT ON FOOD FOR ONE FUTURE ORDER
4500 POINTS	15% DISCOUNT ON FOOD FOR TWO FUTURE ORDERS
6000 POINTS	20% DISCOUNT ON FOOD FOR TWO FUTURE ORDERS
8000 POINTS	25% DISCOUNT ON FOOD FOR TWO FUTURE ORDERS
10,000 POINTS	25% DISCOUNT ON FOOD FOR THREE FUTURE ORDERS
25,000 POINTS	AIR & HOTEL GETAWAY FOR TWO - CALL FOR DETAILS

Please save your invoices and send us photo copies when you've reached your desired goal. All points accumulated NEED TO be redeemed within one year of first purchase. Program subject to change without notice. Not valid with any other offer or discounts. Customer is responsible for providing proof of points by furnishing copies of invoices. ← **4**

Branding is Not Just for the Big Guys

1. A brand name is merely one that is distinctive in the mind of the buyer.

2. Brand names or "branding" are developed from these types of names:

> **A.** Personal names... Mike's Catering
>
> **B.** Places... Highland Park Caterers
>
> **C.** Status names... Upper Crust Catering
>
> **D.** Good association names... Gold Label Catering
>
> **E.** Descriptive names... Festivities Catering

3. A good goal for marketing your brand is to help the buyers associate your name with your company instead of another. It should make them aware of exactly who you are and what you sell and stand for.

4. A brand needs to provide a point of difference for the buyer! The name Applause Catering puts a positive difference into the mind of the buyer.

Focus Points for Marketing

1. Working spouses.

2. Cocooning.

3. Supermarkets.

4. Maturing markets.

5. Baby boomers.

6. New tax law.

7. Not enough staff.

8. Second marriages.

9. Less lead time.

10. People want to buy more but shop less.

11. Credit cards.

12. Buying perks.

13. Adult education.

14. Sanitation.

15. Value.

About Corporate Catering

1. At least four general categories.

A. Self-Serve   **B.** Full-Serve   **C.** Special Services   **D.** Permanent Operation

2. The types of events & situations that corporations need caterers for:

A. Open houses or product announcements.

B. Grand openings.

C. Galas or special celebrations.

D. Office parties including holiday events.

E. Picnics

F. Ground breakings.

G. Retirement parities and welcomings.

H. Inventories sessions.

I. Plant tours & other off premise situations.

J. Strikes & emergencies.

K. After hours activities.

L. Board Meetings & other management sessions.

M. Gifts.

N. Training sessions.

    …and much more!

EXAMPLES OF THE LATEST THINKING ON CORPORATE CATERING:

1. Corporations are selecting caterers as they would any supplier or vendor.

2. The corporate client wants convenience and "on time" performance from all vendors.

3. Cost is looked upon as an expenditure in the pursuit of an end.

4. Corporations are fully aware that entertaining will increase their sales.

5. Corporations understand staff turnover, therefore they are more interested in buying from a company and relying on an ordering system rather than salespersons only.

6. Corporations want perks from caterers.

7. Corporations don't like surprises!

8. On the same day a corporate client may need 56 box lunches @ $4.75, a self-serve cold buffet for 32 @ $9.75, a served board luncheon for 22 @$41.00, an afternoon tea for 9 @ $10.00, an evening cocktail event for 350 @ $27.00 and a continental breakfast the next morning for 50 @ $5.25.

Promotions for Corporate Catering

Caterers are always searching for new things to do with, and for their present, and new, corporate catering clients. Most of a caterer's corporate catering clients market their own goods and services in an aggressive manner. It is only natural that these same clients don't understand why a caterer, as a business person, doesn't do the same.

In other words, the corporate buyer is either marketing their own stuff, or they are being marketed by those who wish to sell them stuff! Yes, it's true that a caterer's food is a great marketing tool, but it might be better to create and launch some marketing concepts for different types of corporate buyers.

Here's some examples:

1. For 1st time buyers... After the corporate buyer purchases two cold buffets luncheons for 30, or more, guests, they get their next order, from thirty to fifty guests, for one-half the price.

2. For regular buyers... market the RAD... Referral Appreciation Discount! Each time your buyer gives you a lead for a new client, they receive a 10% discount on their next order and the new buyer gets the same.

3. For all buyers... Give Bonus Points... just like the airlines. One dollar equals one point. Don't worry about bookkeeping. Have the buyer keep their own totals by redeeming photo copies of their past invoices.

4. For all buyers... Market a Retainer Program where the company prepays $2,000, for example, and you continually deduct their purchases from this amount. One check... one invoice cuts down on their cost of bookkeeping.

5. For all buyers... Form a Customer Advisory Board. This makes them feel loved and gives you a testimonial!

6. For regular buyers... Start a Catering Newsletter that brings "food news" to your buyers.

7. For new buyers... Start cold calling & warm calling. The business is out there... go after it!

8. For new buyers... Hold Educational Seminars i.e. "What's Hot & Not in Corporate Catering."

9. For all buyers... Announce Open Houses and Tours of your own business & kitchen. Be sure to schedule these sessions on both weekdays and weekends.

Six New Divisions

L et's look into some interesting new ideas for marketing your business to sell more corporate catering. Each of these ideas have some unique twists. After reading the information below, feel free to call Mike Roman at CaterSource to ask additional questions.

1. Corporate-Social Division

This is selling social catering to corporate clients in a corporate manner. Corporate executives are used to buying catering in a quick and concise manner.

Unlike buyers of social catering who wish to be involved with everything that happens, corporate buyers wish to get it done! They wish to rely on the talents of a professional salesperson.

So, in the case of buying a wedding, the corporate person doesn't want to dedicate unlimited amounts of time to decide on menus, decor, etc. When they learn about your Corporate-Social Division, they get the message that the buying process need not involve a lot of time and conversation.

2. Customized Foodservice Division

This is selling employee cafeterias and corporate executive dining rooms. The message that you wish to send to your existing buyers is that your company, besides being a great caterer, can organize and establish an on-going foodservice relationship.

Your main focus is on your food quality, especially your food taste, and that you are a member of their immediate community. This means that you will be able to give them quick response to any situations that might arise.

3. Corporate Event Planning Division

Take the team approach with this one. Your marketing needs to stress that at your company, there is a team of three, or four, professionals that specialize in planning large corporate events... with, or without, your company doing the catering.

You charge by the hour or project. You'll find the venue, develop a proper theme, create the menus and coordinate the total event from beginning to end.

4. Employee Incentive Division

Because of the on-going corporate layoffs, companies are searching for ways to increase employee morale. Such events as award luncheons, safety dinners, employee of the month breakfasts, and nutrition breaks are being instituted.

It is best to approach this new division with total dedication to the task. You need to offer corporations the excuse to buy your ideas that will include the food, motivational speakers, awards and plaques, posters, pamphlets, contests, etc.... all geared to creating better morale between the employees and management.

5. Food As Marketing Division

This is getting one corporation to purchase food for another corporation. This is a hot idea! Why shouldn't an insurance company want to give a continental breakfast to the 300 employees of a company it insures?

This division lends itself to direct mail marketing. It's important to provide a list of menus that range from very low to very high. An example of a low cost would be $1.75 per person for a fruit kabob display.

6. Indoor Picnic Division

The caterer who finds locations to offer for winter, or inclement weather, picnics will make a lot of money! Corporations are moving towards picnic and BBQ (see article on Ranch Hands® on page 4) concepts because they carry less liquor and sexual harassment liability... and cost a lot less than more formal events. Picnics are families and beer, while the annual holiday event is scotch and trouble.

Ideas to Market to Corporations

1. Become a consultant
2. Surprise Package
3. Establish FAX link
4. Establish computer link
5. Become a partner
6. Sell event planners
7. Sell Volume Discounts
8. Write Request for Bid Letters
9. Give ID Numbers
10. Use Plastic Cards
11. Charge Account Program
12. COD Discounts
13. Give equipment
14. Build Catering Pantry
15. Run-Out Buffets
16. Time-Released Marketing
17. Free Small Orders... when you get big ones!

Caterers are always searching for new things to do with, and for their present, and new, corporate catering clients. Most of a caterer's corporate catering clients market their own goods and services in an aggressive manner. It is only natural that these same clients don't understand why a caterer, as a business person, doesn't do the same.

In other words, the corporate buyer is either marketing their own stuff, or they are being marketed by those who wish to sell them stuff! Yes, it's true that a caterer's food is a great marketing tool, but it might be better to create and launch some marketing concepts for different types of corporate buyers.

Here's some examples:

1. For 1st time buyers... After the corporate buyer purchases two cold buffets luncheons for 30, or more, guests, they get their next order, from thirty to fifty guests, for one-half the price.

2. For regular buyers... Market the RAD... Referral Appreciation Discount! Each time your buyer gives you a lead for a new client, they receive a 10% discount on their next order and the new buyer gets the same.

3. For all buyers... Give Bonus Points... just like the airlines. One dollar equals one point. Don't worry about bookkeeping. Have the buyer keep their own totals by redeeming photo copies of their past invoices.

4. For all buyers... Market a Retainer Program where the company prepays $2,000, for example, and you continually deduct their purchases from this amount. One check... one invoice cuts down on their cost of bookkeeping.

5. For all buyers... Form a Customer Advisory Board. This makes them feel loved and gives you a testimonial!

6. For regular buyers... Start a Catering Newsletter that brings "food news" to your buyers.

7. For new buyers... Start cold calling & warm calling. The business is out there... go after it!

8. For new buyers... Hold Educational Seminars i.e. "What's Hot & Not in Corporate Catering."

9. For all buyers... Announce Open Houses and Tours of your own business & kitchen. Be sure to schedule these sessions on both weekdays and weekends.

Ideas for Corporate Sales

The following ideas are provided for subscribers to utilize, to get or "firm-up" corporate catering accounts. We're confident that once you read them, you will be able to make them better!

1. R.A.D.

"Referral Appreciation Discount"

This is a simple program that will might turn your corporate clients on! It is best to use with clients who buy from you on a regular basis.

You introduce it in the following manner:

> *"Mary, you've been ordering from us for over a year now, and it appears that you really enjoy our food and service. Here's some information on our newly developed Referral Appreciation Discount program which is geared to give a "buying advantage" to new, first time clients and to the company that refers them to us.*

> *It's really quite simple. You can give us a name of someone, or a company you think would also enjoy our fine food and service, or you can have them call us directly. On their first order they receive a 20% 'welcome' R.A.D. and as a thank you for your effort your company receives a 20% discount on your next order. Does anyone come to mind that I might contact?"*

2. Equipment Loans

Coffee is sold to offices because the vendor lets the office have a "free" coffee maker. The office may keep the "free" coffee maker as long as they keep buying their coffee supplies from this vendor.

CaterSource believes that this is a natural extension for most caterers. A caterer could give a corporate client a stove, refrigerator, microwave, chafers, trays, electric oven, etc. that could be used to heat, hold or present the caterer's menu items.

Yes, they could keep this as long as they continued to give that caterer the level of buying loyalty required. The numbers add up... a $500 stove for a continued purchase commitment of $3,000 per month.

3. Retainer

CaterSource has talked about this in their seminars for the past three years. It's a great idea that makes it easier for regular clients to order more.

The catering retainer is no different than a lawyers retainer. The client gives the caterer a sum of money in advance of their purchases which are then deducted from the amount given.

So, a client may pay $2,000 per month with one check and the caterer keeps track of what's spent. As the amount gets down to $150 the caterer requests additional money.

From the client's point of view, it is easier to deal with one check and only one invoice a month. The caterer's joy comes from the increased buyer loyalty. CaterSource has been told by some caterers that each check a client sends costs that client a processing fee. The retainer concept is considered to be very favorable by many large corporations.

4. Educational Seminars

Caterers are experts at feeding large groups. Why not use this expertise to generate new business by telling people more about what caterers do.

Hold informal seminars at your location, school, or hotel to provide "marketing education" on catering.

Here's some of the topics that will bring new and old buyers in for education:

A. "What's Hot & Not in Corporate Catering"

B. "What's Hot & Not in Picnics"

C. "What's Hot & Not in Social Catering"

D. "Ten Ways To Get Better Prices From Caterers"

E. "The Liability of Hosting Catered Events"

F. "New Catering Themes For 2002"

Some caterers charge $25 for each company attending (which includes lunch), while others give them free. You will get more attendees if you hold your seminar at a local hotel, rather than in your own facility.

CaterSource participated in a seminar on picnics, where those attending heard from Mike Roman, a local lawyer, a local insurance agent and the caterer's chef.

Over 90 companies attended and over $100,000 worth of catering was sold as a result of the meeting. To get your message, or the invitation, out use normal direct mail concepts as explained in past CaterSource Journals.

The important thing about marketing and selling to corporations is to keep coming at them with new ideas that keep demonstrating to them that your company is still one of the market leaders in your area! Corporate buyers enjoy buying from companies that remind them of themselves!

Simple Business Builders

The fax machine is a friend to a caterer when it comes to self-service orders coming in from corporate clients. Example 1 is based on Truffles & Tarts Caterers (Carmichael, CA) "faxable" menu. CaterSource likes this format because it is direct, simple and easy to use by both the clients and the kitchen. It also is a low cost business builder.

We suggest that you create your own faxable menu in an 11 x 14 inch format. We also suggest that you have the copy store print them and then make them into gummed, peel off pads of 100. When your clients receive them, they will understand what they are for, and having them in pads, ready to be pulled off and used, will give your clients a sense of your professionalism. Be careful of the color paper you select (white might be the best) because of the effect it might have when coming back

EXAMPLE 1 (ACTUAL SIZE 11 X 14 INCHES)

Company logo

FAXABLE FEAST
GOURMET BOX LUNCHES BY FAX
FILL OUT AND FAX US AT
(555) 555-3333
Order preferred by 5pm on day before delivery

CONTACT	
COMPANY	
DELIVERY ADDRESS	
ROOM/FLOOR	PHONE
DELIVERY DATE & DAY	DELIVERY TIME

Payment by: ❑ Cash ❑ Check ❑ MC/Visa/AMEX

► ENTREES ◄
Served with fresh baked bread & butter

BREAST OF CHICKEN BALLANTINE
Marinated chicken breast stuffed with spinach, feta & ricotta cheeses, almonds & herbs. Served over pasta salad of the day.
7.25 each   No. of orders

BEEF SATAY
Beef medallions over Thai peanut pasta, tossed with seasonal veggies creamy peanut dressing.
7.45 each   No. of orders

►SANDWICHES◄
All sandwiches served on housemade bread with tomato & lettuce + chef's salad of the day.

SAGE ROASTED TURKEY
Beef medallions over Thai peanut pasta, tossed with seasonal veggies creamy peanut dressing.
6.45 each   No. of orders

BLACK FOREST HAM & CHEESE
A big seller! This traditional favorite will keep your guests happy.
6.95 each   No. of orders

SANTE FE BEEF
Roast beef, hot pepper jack cheese & the power zest of pepperoncini peppers.
6.75 each   No. of orders

CAJUN MEATLOAF
Our chef's secret recipe!. A traditional meatloaf with the unique taste of New Orleans!
5.95 each   No. of orders

VEGETARIAN
A top seller! Combination of cream cheese, cucumbers, avocado & sprouts.
6.35 each   No. of orders

CLUB SUB
Black forest ham, sage roasted turkey, smoked bacon & cheddar cheese make this a winner!
6.95 each   No. of orders

►ENTREE SALADS◄
All salads served with freshly baked, housemade bread and butter.

MEDITERRANEAN SALAD
Marinated feta with roasted vegetables & pepperoncini peppers on mixed greens with vinaigrette.
6.25 each   No. of orders

CURRIED CHICKEN SALAD
Fresh roasted chicken with toasted almonds & coconut in our mild curry dressing over greens.
6.55 each   No. of orders

CAFFE SALAD
Avocado, kidney & garbanzo beans, cheddar cheese, new potatoes with ranch dressing.
6.75 each   No. of orders

CHINESE CHICKEN SALAD
Chinese flavored chicken tossed with seasonal veggies & almonds with soy-lime dressing.
7.95 each   No. of orders

CHEF SALAD
Julienned turkey, ham, cheddar & jack cheese, egg, tomato & olives on greens with ranch.
6.50 each   No. of orders

ROASTED CHICKEN SALAD
Marinated chicken, mushrooms, carmalized walnuts on greens with honey-mustard dressing.
6.95 each   No. of orders

► DESSERTS ◄
For each box lunch you may also wish one, or more, of our tantalizing sweets

CHOCOLATE CHIP COOKIES
1.10 each   No. of orders

FUDGE BROWNIES
1.45 each   No. of orders

FRESH FRUIT TARTS
2.25 each   No. of orders

LEMON BARS
1.25 each   No. of orders

CHOC. DIPPED SHORTBREAD
1.00 each   No. of orders

BLOND BROWNIE
1.45 each   No. of orders

.85 each   No. of orders

►BEVERAGES◄
SPRITE	1.00	No.
COKE	1.00	No.
DIET-COKE	1.00	No.
ICED TEA	1.00	No.
MINERAL WATER	1.25	No.
ROOT BEER	1.00	No.

FAX to us at 555-3333!   Talk to us at 555-5521.

Here's a quick, inexpensive promotion idea to build business from The French Gourmet (San Diego, CA).

Example 2 is a printed sheet that has a rotary file index card to punch out.

They stuff these in all mailings, including billings, as a marketing tool.

They purchased them from Jilcraft at 800-545-2723 for $170 per thousand. This price includes type setting. Why not give it a try?

EXAMPLE 2 (ACTUAL SIZE 8.5 X 4 INCHES)

CATERING
(619) 488-1725

FRENCH GOURMET.
Party Trays to Elegant Events
CORPORATE • WEDDINGS • SOCIAL
COCKTAIL PARTIES • OPEN HOUSES
THEME PARTIES • BOX LUNCHES
DINNERS • OFFICE PARTIES
(619) 488-1725 ❑ FAX: 619-488-1799
960 Turquoise Street, San Diego, California 92109

Punch Out of Performance

YOU'VE GOT
OUR NUMBER!!!

**Please add our card
to your rotary file
... we're only a phone call away!**

How Corporations View Caterers

Corporate catering is what most caterers want. It is usually easier to sell and deliver than social catering like weddings. Let's look at corporate catering from the buyers point of view.

First, to be a successful corporate caterer you need to be looked upon by corporate buyers as a source for solutions. In addition, you need to be different from the other caterers who are also looking to sell their catering to corporations.

Here's a few reminders on how many corporate buyers view caterers:

1. They can get food from dozens of other places. Why shouldn't they keep a lot of caterers on call? After all, why would I order Mexican catering from a German caterer?

This has always been a problem for many caterers. Corporate buyers wouldn't think of eating in the same restaurant each and every day. So, why would they want to buy from the same caterer every time they need catering.

Obviously, caterers need to provide a wide variety of menu items demonstrating their ability to cater all ethnic styles a buyer may want.

In addition, caterers would be wise to offer a seasonal change of menus. For example, offer a spring and a summer menu. The important concept here is that the corporate shopper gets the feeling that your business is constantly changing to offer the latest and best in different cuisines.

Your battle is to let your corporate client understand that while there are other caterers, you are the only and best choice since you offer a source of solutions to whatever they might need.

2. They can get cheaper food from dozens of other places. After all... isn't a chicken salad sandwich the same whether you pay $5.50 or $4.75?

To understand the impact of this ask yourself this question. When you buy Driscoll strawberries for you business, don't you shop for the lowest price? Isn't your assumption that a Driscoll brand strawberry is the same no matter where you buy it?

That's just the point. To your buyers the brand is the product line, or chicken salad sandwich, not the caterer who is making it for them. So, the obvious solution is to stress the benefits of your brand name over others.

You would do this by stressing that your price contains much more than just the words "chicken salad sandwich". Your price includes the highest quality purveyors, 6 ounces of salad, temperature control, on-time delivery, sanitation and overall quality service. This is hard to do in a society where most people are looking for price advantages.

3. They don't believe that caterers will give them the value they wish! After all... my other corporate vendors give me "free" stuff for being a loyal customer... so thinks the corporate buyer of catering.

To counter these unique thoughts you first need to make your buyers feel loved. The best way is to stop by and shake their hand. By doing this you will get to know them better and build your relationship with them.

Next you should send in some exciting extra food samples from time to time. Everyone likes to get something free. Remember, we're not suggesting that you give a "kick-back" or free food to them to take home for a party they're giving to friends or family. This could get you in trouble with their, or your, company policy manual.

Some caterers are using some sort of a "bonus point" system for their corporate buyers to offer the entire company a benefit for purchasing from one catering vendor. See CaterSource Journal #7 page 2 for an example of such a bonus point program.

Approach the buyer of corporate catering from a "Hospitality" point of view... you sell, or can arrange for, everything they need to make their needs, wants, dreams and situations become o.k! Be their problem solver! In short, you need to be all things to a corporate buyer.

This is usually easier thought, or said, than done. Often, corporate buyers are on a power trip and look upon the caterer as a "necessary evil". This usually stems from the fact that one, or more, caterers have let this buyer down in the past.

To overcome, or neutralize, this you need to have some sort of a 100% satisfaction guarantee to offer your corporate buyers. At first this might seem too dangerous, but we can assure you that it will increase your overall sales.

Finally, never before has it become so important to resell and sell more to our buyers! As the younger generation might say... you "need to be in their face" at all times. What we mean is that being in their "ear" is not good enough in the 90's. There are too many other caterers who are willing to give the time it takes to grow a corporate business in a tough competitive marketplace!

Use Emotional Words

- Tell instead of inform
- Tough instead of difficult
- Let instead of allow
- Help instead of assist
- Answer instead of reply
- Better than instead of superior to
- Take care of instead of service
- Get instead of receive

- Buy instead of purchase
- Pick instead of select
- Hold instead of reserve
- End instead of terminate
- Right now instead of immediately
- Good for instead of beneficial
- Asked for instead of requested

EMOTIONAL INSTINCTS THAT "TURN-ON" BUYERS OF CATERING

1. Saving Money
2. Saving Time
3. Avoiding Criticism of Others
4. Increasing One's Reputation
5. Avoiding Hard Work
6. Fun
7. Showing Off / Scoring Points With Friends
8. Learning About Catering

A One Minute Radio Ad

Here's a template for a one minute radio commercial. Radio is working for many caterers to build new business. Try to trade with the radio stations when possible to keep your costs down. The normal trade ratio is two radio dollars for every catering dollar.

The last time you put together a party it probably took weeks of planning. What would you do if you suddenly had to do some entertaining with only a few hours notice? Wise hostesses know the answer to that one. They call ABC Catering. ABC Catering has literally created stunning arrangements for large parties on as little as four hours advance notice. You may not be able to do that with your kitchen, but ABC Catering can, thanks to a talented staff of experts and the most modern cooking equipment. ABC is a family run business. They supervise each and every order. They will consult with you to create a menu for your special occasion, even if there's just a few days or hours notice. So, the next time you find out in the middle of the day that you need to entertain guests for dinner, don't panic... just call ABC Catering...555-5555... jot down the number and keep it handy... 555-5555... ABC Catering.

Tips for Selling Over the Phone

Here's some tips for getting better results while selling over the phone:

1. You need to be a good listener.
2. Take notes as you talk with your contact.
3. Stay on track.
4. Concentrate on what you say, how you say it and the tone of your voice.
5. Turn a negative response into a sales advantage.
6. Never apologize for calling.\
7. Explain your offer in clear terms with "WIIFM" (what's in it for me) to the buyer in the forefront.
8. Write a script or checklist to follow during the call.
9. Smile while you are speaking to the potential client... it really works!
10. Tape record your side of the conversation so you can review it later.

Places to Find Sales Leads

Here's some obvious, and not so obvious, places to search for leads to sell your catering:

1. Visiting office to office.
2. Yellow Pages.
3. Reverse telephone directory.
4. Business newspapers.
5. Customer lists from your suppliers.
6. Customer lists from realtors.
7. Lists from party rental companies.
8. Anyone that you spend money with.
9. List of your past clients.
10. Lists of people who didn't buy from you.

Know Your Competition

Sometimes caterers work so hard at what they do that they don't take the time to check-out and analyze their competition. Most caterers, who are determined to win big in their marketplace, try to learn as much as they can about those caterers that they seem to be competing with.

For sure, a caterer needs to know about those caterers who they lose bids to. To get you in the mood for doing this detective work, CaterSource, Inc. has created a list of actions and some ideas for you:

1. Know who your competitors are. Drive by their location and observe.

2. Talk to others who have seen your competitors up close i.e. rental dealers, bartenders, waitstaff, etc.

3. Know the names of the leaders and key players at your competitors. Learn what they did before.

4. Be aware of the competition's quality, styles and prices. Talk with clients. Get copies of their proposals.

5. Get copies of any advertisements or brochures that your competitors have used.

6. Attempt to discover the strengths and weaknesses of the competition.

7. Check with your city to see if the competitors are legally licensed to do catering.

8. Purchase tickets, and attend, any function that your competitors do for charities.

9. Determine in what marketing direction you think your competitors are moving.

Taking a Telephone Survey

The purpose of the script below is to permit anyone in your company to take the "hospitality temperature" of your product/service system. It may be used with your old time buyers or with clients who have just purchased. It will work with both full-service and self-service clients.

Your Caller: "Hello, Mrs. Smith, this is Mary Fisher and I've been retained by ABC Catering to call some of their clients to find out if all of your expectations with their catering were met. Do you have about three minutes to listen to some brief questions now, or should I call back at a different time?"

1. Was your catering delivered to you as you requested?

2. Was the driver pleasant and helpful?

3. Were the event staff on time and helpful? (full-service)

4. Did any of the food spill while being delivered? (self-service)

5. How were the portions? Was there a lot left over?

6. Do you feel that the price you paid was too low, too high or just right?

7. Have you used other caterers during the last three months? If so, how do they compare with ABC Catering?

8. What would you like ABC Catering to know when I write my report about our talk together?

Checking Out the Competition

1. The easiest way for a caterer to check out the competition is through the purchase of catering from the competitors! Order what you wish to check out... a simple box lunch, a cocktail event, picnic or holiday party.

2. Of course, you don't want them to know it is you until after the food arrives. Can't you just see it... all of your chefs, sale people, etc. getting a chance to see, eat and digest the competition. Only two things can happen. You are either thrilled at how many mistakes the competitor makes, or you're destroyed by their greatness! In either case, this reverse engineering, as it's called, will help you find out what you need to know.

3. Here are some reasons for checking out the competition:

    A. To insure your survival.

    B. To discover their strengths and weaknesses.

    C. To take advantage of any, and all, opportunities that you become aware of.

    D. To fulfill your curiosity.

    E. To stay competitive in the marketplace.

The Basics of Yellow Page Ads

Yellow page advertising is a major cost to most caterers. Let's examine the hypothetical ad below. Notice that in the ad our imaginary caterer has placed the greatest emphasis on their company name by making it almost 50% of the ad. If you review your own city's yellow page directory, you will notice ads similar to our example below.

Catering for all occasions!

ABC CATERING

Since 1974

- Anniversaries
- Weddings
- Picnics
- Box Lunches
- Cocktail Events
- Reunions
- Open Houses
- Buffet Dinners

1122 N. Spring Street
Anytown, IL 55555

555-1111

Many caterers have concluded that shoppers, when searching the yellow pages, are looking for what caterers sell instead of what, or who, caterers think they are! In other words, placing more emphasis in your ads on the type of catering you do, or the types of themes you have, will probably bring better sales results than boasting about how long you've been in business or that you have the best food in town.

What does a buyer, or shopper , go into the yellow pages to find... a particular name of a caterer... or a type of catering they need?

For example, when a secretary looks in the yellow pages, after being told to find a caterer for a cocktail reception does she:

A. Search for the name of a company that sounds good?

or

B. Look for an ad that mentions cocktail receptions or hors d'oeuvres?

The conclusion is not that your company's name is unimportant. It is simply that the first goal of this shopper is to locate some companies to call about a cocktail reception. It seems logical that she would call those companies that mentioned "cocktail receptions", or hors d'oeuvres, in their ad copy.

CaterSource Rule #17. Never make your company's name the primary focus for a yellow page ad.

CaterSource Rule #9. Advertise what your company makes... not who you are.

Another concept that is often overlooked by caterers planning a yellow page ad is "buying prejudice". Most buyers are influenced by what they read and see in your advertisement. Buyers react in either a positive, negative or impartial manner to everything in your ad.

When you advertise "Since 1954", or anything like this, some buyer's reactions are that you must know what you are doing. Others will think that your company is old and couldn't know anything about newer foods and styles.

The same is true when placing your address into the ad. Some buyers will look favorably on your address because you're close to them, while others will not call you because of their worry that you are too far away and might have problems with weather conditions or traffic.

CaterSource Rule #33. Limit the number of items in your ad that can be judged in a prejudicial manner causing confusion, suspicion or doubt by shoppers.

With respect to #33, it is also silly for a caterer to think that shoppers are not concerned with getting the best chance at a good price when calling a caterer. If you have a "silver tray" or "tuxedoed" drawing or feeling in your ad, you probably won't be getting as many calls as you should. Be careful of words like "culinary" or "gourmet", since these often are prejudged to mean expensive to a shopper.

CaterSource Rule #41. Your ad should make a shopper feel that calling you will be a safe and pleasant experience.

Your yellow page ad is not supposed to be a personal statement about what you have done in the past or your ranking as a top caterer. Most buyers, including yourself, do not take these claims seriously. Shoppers realize that most ads are filled with hard to prove statements.

In the 1990's, with the vast number of ads in the yellow pages, the primary goal of your yellow page ad is to get shoppers to make your company one of the five or six they will call. A caterer needs to be careful about designing an ad that only makes their own ego feel great! Your ad needs to be seductive to the reader and cause them to take action!

It also seems that the best color to use for your yellow page ad is white! It stands out very well. Many caterers seem to like blue ink for the type or design work.

Still More Yellow Page Ads

You've probably already read the ads below. They are different... aren't they? That's just the point. It's important to always "push the envelope" when it comes to making marketing decisions. In EXAMPLE 1, you should notice that the ad sells the two main strengths of this caterer. The uniqueness of the six points is different than all other ads you would see in the yellow pages... that's what makes it great. It reads and looks different than any other ads the buyer sees. EXAMPLE 2 highlights the concept that, unlike other caterers, you will get prices over the phone when you call. Yes, this could be dangerous for some caterers, but it may be wise for others. In both examples you will notice that the actual name of the caterer is not the biggest thing in the ad and that the reader is given a name of someone to call. Remember: CaterSource has to bring you alternative ways to do things.

EXAMPLE 1

We do great WEDDINGS!
We do great COCKTAIL EVENTS!

1. We know this because our customers keep coming back for more!
2. We love working with people who really want a great party for their guests!
3. If you wish, you may inspect our licensed kitchen and talk with our chef!
4. We can arrange for you to speak with some of our very happy customers!
5. We won't rush you, unless you're in a hurry!
6. Prices are always fair... they get lower as your number of guests go up!

ABC CATERING

CALL (555) 555-5555
To get our free menus and estimates!
Ask for James Doe, *owner*

EXAMPLE 2

PRICES GIVEN OVER THE PHONE

ABC CATERING

We do it ALL! Call Us Last! Great Food! Great Service!
We Want To Be Your Caterer!!

CALL (555) 555-5555 Ask For Jim!

69

A Different Type of Yellow Page Ad

After you get over your giggles... what's the sense of putting money into the yellow pages if our message is just like all the rest? Well, while this ad is not suited for all caterers, it is different. When was the last time you saw any catering ad with the picture of the person in charge, or the chef?

It's because no one has done it... that it might work! You will have better luck with your responses if you use the word "casual" somewhere in your ad. Also, even though most will disagree, saying "prices will gladly be discussed over the telephone" will get your phone to ring!

So, it all depends on what type of catering you sell and how you view your public commitment to your marketplace. What do you think about the 100% satisfaction guarantee? Caterers will have to deal with this sooner or latter. Maybe you should be a leader in your marketplace and be the first.

Feel free to call Mike Roman to discuss other concepts for yellow page advertising.

Ad for a Business Journal

FOOD!

It's An Important Part of Business.

And, for Over Ten Years,
ABC Catering Has Been in the Business of Food... For Business.

Use Your Imagination. We Can Bring Food and Business Together
Under Almost Any Circumstance, and Help You Accomplish
Your Objectives Easily.

For Further Information On This Topic, We'll Hand Deliver Our
Full-Color Brochure and Menus Upon Request.

Your Logo
Here

ABC Catering
(555) 555-5555

1. This ad will work best if placed in the business section of the newspaper or in other business type media.

2. It also makes a great postcard promo which is the least expensive type of direct mail.

3. The headline "Food. It's An Important Part of Business" could become an entire marketing theme for your company. You could place it on your business cards and stationary.

4. Future ads could draw on the concept "Use Your Imagination" to develop new ad messages about what they could be using your catering for.

5. The concept of "We'll Hand Deliver Our Brochure and Menus" sits well with buyers. They feel that you are committed to building your business.

Also, it separates you from the rest of the caterers who mail stuff. By the way, many buyers know that even though they call for info it often doesn't get to them. You don't need a color brochure to make this ad work.

6. If you have a logo, place it in your ad. Logos are not necessary and often lose a sale because they are wrongly interpreted by the buyer.

7. Make the phone number easy to find.

Ideas for Better Direct Mail Success

1. Do a press release at the same time as you mail.

2. Send multiple mailings to the same list.

3. Don't rush your project.

4. Use a lick-on stamp.

5. Follow-up with a personal phone call.

6. Use an 800 number and make it easy to find.

7. Caterers should not make their address easy to find.

8. Don't mail a small format.

9. If using pictures don't just show food. Instead show people using your services to entertain and enhance their lives. (WIIFM)

10. Use serif typeface for the majority of your copy.

11. Use quality paper with little show-through.

12. Double space between paragraphs.

13. Add handwritten notes for impact.

14. Don't end a letter on the back of a page.

15. Don't use coordinated paper and ink colors.

16. Don't make your type too small.

17. Underlining important lines builds sales.

18. "YOU" is the most important word to the reader.

19. Start your sentences with power words such as: ALSO... WHAT IS MORE... IN ADDITION... AND

Ideas for Better Direct Mail Success

20. Make an additional offer using a postscript (P.S.).

21. Write your copy in the present tense whenever possible.

22. Tell the reader what to do and how to do it.

23. Never lie. In most cases they don't believe you in the first place.

24. Demonstrate proof of your claims.

25. People expect you to say that your product is the best... so make yourself believable.

26. Use hidden offers when possible.

27. Whatever you offer must be on every piece in your envelope.

28. Use headlines to show the benefits.

29. Take it away from the reader... "Our catering is not for everybody".

30. Remember that readers often look at and read the P.S. first.

31. Use the reader's name whenever possible

32. Don't be afraid of long headlines or copy.

33. When writing about catering let the reader involve as many of the body's five senses as possible... seeing, hearing, touching, tasting and smelling.

34. Keep it personal and use action verbs whenever possible.

35. Refer to other parts of your copy to keep them reading.

Buying Mailing Lists

Direct mail has at its root the names to which you mail. Where do you get these names? Can you purchase them? This article will help to answer these questions... and it will probably raise more.

The best lists are ALWAYS the ones that you create yourself from present clients, shoppers or referrals. The important concept is to keep them separate because you might wish to send a different message to those who have already purchased from you and those that haven't.

With the use of a simple data base program, which often costs under $300 at any software store, you will be able to capture and manage your lists of names. Because you can easily code these names, you will be able to keep them separate, with respect to the kind of buyers they are.

If you wish to find new names you might wish to buy some from a vendor in your area. Look in the Yellow Pages under "mailing lists" and you will be surprised at how many exist.

You will notice that many have 800 numbers to call. This is because many are located hundreds, or more, miles from your city. In one way this is all right. Technology allows them to keep their lists in great shape with a total satisfaction guarantee.

On the other hand, a local company might have some advantages since they understand the nature of your area first hand.

Whoever you decide to shop with to purchase mailing labels ask them these questions:

A. How new, or fresh, is the list that they are selling? When were the names entered into their data base? Do they purchase their names form someone else, or have they secured and built the list themselves?

Don't be afraid to ask for some samples of the list. Tell them that you just want to see the types of names they have. A reputable vendor of lists will always let you have fifty, or so, names free for you to review. You should check these names to see if they really exist.

B. When was the last time that a caterer, or similar competitor, has used the list? How many names did they purchase? How many times did they mail to the same prospects?

Sometimes it's wise to use the same list that a competitor has used and sometimes it's not! There is really no right answer that's easy. If they've mailed several times to the same names you're thinking of buying, then you might be considered a "follower" rather than a leader in your marketing.

C. How often are the lists updated. (old names removed) How are they removed?

After you ask this question listen to "how" they answer. Are they unsure? Do they sound vague? Well, follow your instincts on this one. CaterSource can only advise you that a list is only as good as it updating process. In other words, if you are spending postage for mail going to people who no longer are located where the list says, then.... you're wasting money!

D. What results have other venders had when buying their lists? Can you speak with any other vendors that have used their mailing lists?

Once again you see that we need to make contact with others who have already used their lists. When talking with these past customers ask if they mailed using first class or bulk postage. Remember: only first class postage permits the sender to receive those that are undeliverable back. So, if they have used first class postage they can tell you how fresh the list was, based on returns. You always get returns ... people move constantly. If, however, the returns are over 10% of the total mailing, you are at a disadvantage with a stale mailing list.

E. What is the frequency of duplicates in the list? What constitutes a duplicate? Are the duplicates only purged by name or is address taken into account?

There is no sense in having two letters going to the same home or business. However, people in large apartment type buildings all have the same address. So, does the list identify single unit homes and does it have apartment numbers?

F. What variables can you use to sort the list? (Age, Sex, Size of Income, Education, etc.)

Your list is only as good as the information it represents. In the case of corporate names, how many people work at the company would be an important element in your decision to mail or not.

In closing, remember that the direct mail business is a multi-billion dollar industry. Help is as close as your nearest book store. You will find lots of books on the "how" and "whys" of successful direct mail. The concept is to realize that you just can't randomly buy names and mail out your marketing materials.

Great Direct Mail Phrases

1. A successful event starts with...

2. We just don't cut corners.

3. One of the best kept secrets at our company is...

4. There's no substitute for...

5. You'll swear by us... not at us!

6. Catering doesn't need to be expensive.

7. Think of us as your partner in ...

8. You can taste our difference!

9. ... is our middle name.

10. That will be extra money in your pocket.

11. We will provide you with what you need when you want it ... where you want it!

12. The only way to...

13. The proper way to...

14. The best way to...

15. Perhaps you shouldn't gamble with ...

16. Now, more than ever, you need...

17. Can you afford not to...?

18. It's great to take care of the special people in your life.

19. Once you work with our company, you'll want to stay with us!

20. You can't lose!

21. When every dollar counts, it's good to know that...

22. I'm ready to meet every challenge...

23. Who you use for your event is just as important as what you order for the event.

24. We've got total commitment to your success!

25. The two key thoughts going through my mind are quality and professionalism.

26. One of the things we're offering you is peace of mind.

27. Isn't it worth paying a little extra for...?

28. When working with us, you chart your own course... and we follow it.

30. You're in for a pleasant surprise.

31. I believe we have the solution to your concerns.

32. With entertaining it's pretty much agreed that...

33. If you are like many of my customers, you probably...

34. What is your opinion...

35. How do you feel about...?

36. Please explain why...

Postcards: Dinner Parties

As we often say at CaterSource, Inc., "Postcards are God's gift to caterers!" The 6 x 9 four-color postcard below is from Cuisine de France (New York, NY).

1. Obviously, this is a great picture. It shows quality and style. It is clear from the picture that this is a very high end catering company.

2. "Truly French Cuisine" is making a marketing statement that will appeal to a certain type of buyer. It is a logical extension of the company's name.

3. This paragraph lets the buyer understand that this company is interested in both large and small events. This is usually a good idea and results in more selling opportunities.

4. You can see in this paragraph that the caterer continues with the "quality" and "taste" issues. It is wise to restate your main marketing themes in several different places and in several different ways.

5. We like this a lot! Calling a catering company is scary enough for many buyers... now when they call they can ask for Remy by name. This will relax many buyers.

Cuisine ✦
*de*FRANCE INC *Caterers* 212 **289-1230**

Dear Sir/Madame,

Entertaining family and guests in the privacy of your home is true living!

Cuisine de France will accommodate you! Whether a luncheon for 10, a cocktail party for 100, or a sumptuous buffet for 500, we take pride in meeting all of your special needs.

The menu selections of Cuisine de France are tailored to meet your wishes. Always prepared with the freshest of ingredients and attractively presented, this truly French cuisine is sure to please both the eye and the palate.

I would enjoy meeting with you at your convenience to discuss how Cuisine de France can be of service in designing a most memorable event for you.

Call today...Ask for Remy...Thank you!

Sincerely,

Postcards: Change of Name

We just love this! It's great marketing and it is "neat" or "cool" at the same time! It was sent to us by subscriber, Leanne & Susan Catering (Inglewood, CA).

It was produced on card stock: size 8.5 x 5.5

COVER →

*F*AME

IS A

CURSE...

INSIDE COVER →

...*So*

WE CHANGED

OUR NAME.

BOTTOM INSIDE →

LeAnne & Susan was a catchy name. You'd probably never guess how we came up with it. But every once in a while, you have to spice things up in this town. So...you can still call LeAnne...and you can still call Susan....but you can't call us LeAnne & Susan Catering anymore.

We're L.A. Spice now, thank you very much.

We just couldn't stand the constant recognition and overwhelming adoration that the personal attachment to our image caused. We couldn't walk into a grocery store without being bombarded with requests. We would be begged for just a nibble of our renowned brownies or a spoonful of our salacious soup. Then the wanna-be's began. Kids began to show up to school in chef's coats wielding wooden spoons and rolling pins. When we had to hire publicists, we knew things had gone too far.

We were in danger of being over-exposed but we thought that if we acted quickly we might be able to dodge any negative backlash and come out clean.

LEANNE

& SUSAN

CATERING

is now

Hence the new moniker. No major changes really, just a slight diversionary tactic. Hiding behind the corporate veil.

L.A. Spice: Adventurous Custom Catering. Doesn't it sound a tad more serious? Considering 81% of our clientele is made up of major corporations - names too big to mention here - it's about time we appear intimidating.

Of course, we'll still offer the same personal service (don't tell anyone, but when you call you can still talk to LeAnne or Susan) and we will still plan every detail of your functions from beginning to end.

The down side to all of this is some people won't be able to tell their friends that they're being catered to by pop icons. But hey, the food's the thing. And our service remains unbeatable.

Do us a favor, though - don't spread this around town. You know how L.A. loves a secret. And we're thankful for our 15 minutes of fame.

We really just want to plan your next event and add a little of our secret L.A. Spice. Call us at **310-670-5697.**

Postcards: Unique & Unexpected Mailer

This is a great idea for restaurants who cater. But, Wizard Catering & Special Events (Elizabethtown, PA) is not a restaurant!

What's interesting is that according to Phil Landis, President of Wizard Catering, "After someone asks us if we can lower our prices, we tell them that we can offer a small discount if they permit us to place a few of these cards out during their catered event. It's amazing how many clients will take this opportunity."

While this marketing concept may not be the most agreeable for some caterers and their buyers, you need to consider some of the excellent concepts contained in Wizard's offers.

They are marketing their picnics, indoor events, parties at their on-premise location and the slower season in the dead of winter.

Also, notice the great marketing line "The Larger the Order, the Lower the Price!!!" This is probably a great concept for many caterers to get across to their buyers.

Notice that the buyer reads such lines as "Short Notice Is Possible", "Four Trucks, One Refrigerated" and "Licensed & Insured". All of these marketing thoughts add strength to this concept.

CaterSource, Inc. wishes to suggest that marketing for your slower seasons is wise and can add greatly to your bottom line.

Everyone knows that your catering business is slower, slow or dead in certain months, so give them a reason to plan an event around these "off-season" value times.

Don't underestimate the power of off-season discounting. Your marketplace is full of this type of marketing from travel agencies to realtors!

Some caterers give clients bonus points as they purchase catering that can be used during the slower months.

In closing, we can say that most buyers of catering will not think you're in trouble just because they see you discount for off-season. Instead, they will look upon it as a valid business move. In fact, they will consider you a great business person for taking a step towards more business!

5% off
a Catered Picnic
Not valid with any other discounts.
Must be mentioned when placing your order.

Free Gift
with Catering
at Cool Creek Country Club
Must be mentioned when placing your order.

5% off
any Indoor Event
Not valid with any other discounts.
Must be mentioned when placing your order.

10% off
any orders in
January, February or March
Not valid with any other discounts.
Must be mentioned when placing your order.

1680-A South Market Street
Elizabethtown, PA 17022

Elizabethtown (717) 361-8190
Lancaster (717) 653-6182
Client Line (800) 564-3836
FAX (717) 361-8248

WIZARD
CATERING
& SPECIAL EVENTS

"The Larger the Order, the Lower the Price!!!"

Corporate Catering • Lunches (Buffet or Box) • Picnics and Bar-B-Ques
Wedding Receptions • Open Houses • Reunions • Hors d'oeuvre Parties
Served and Buffet Dinners • Self-Service Catering • Short Notice is Possible
Four Trucks; One Refrigerated

"Serving Excellent Food to Groups of 2 to 1000 people"
"Since 1985, Fully Licensed and Insured"
"Member Elizabethtown Chamber of Commerce"

Postcards: On-Premise Weddings

As we often say at CaterSource, Inc., "Postcards are God's gift to caterers!" The 6 x 9 four-color postcard below is from J.M. Scott Catering (Morrisville, PA). What's really great about this card is the sense of variety and romance!

1. "Estate Weddings" becomes the product name that is asked for when they call the caterer. This is good because it is easier for a buyer to ask for a product line than about catering.

2. These three picture insets give the buyer a message that these locations come in various prices and styles.

3. A wedding is not food... it is a gathering! By showing people in this photo you show what your catering does... not what it is.

4. More pictures of locations that give the buyer confidence that they will find something they will like and afford.

5. Here's the call to action. The buyer is given a directive to "call" one of the numbers to get information on "Estate Weddings". This outstanding promotion is giving this caterer a lot of "bang" for the dollar!

Postcards: Direct Mail Mailings

Postcards are a low-cost, high impact way to advertise your catering. Here are two examples of excellent postcards. The top example is from Festivities Express Catering in San Diego. The second is from Catering Works in Raleigh, NC. They both do the job of grabbing the attention of the reader.

NEED YOUR NEXT OFFICE MEETING CATERED?

Festivities Express
Self-Service Catering

CALL 858-586-2121

YOU HAVE THE MEETING, WE'LL CATER IT!

FREE DESSERT WITH YOUR FIRST ORDER!

From business meetings to training sessions, sales meetings, or for out of town guests.

Festivities Express
Self-Service Catering

Breakfast Meetings • Box Lunches • Buffets • Salads

SELF-SERVICE CATERING!

For a complete listing of all your menu options visit us at

www.hospitalityinc.com

OR CALL KATHLEEN AT 858-586-2121

tasteful hospitality.

Catering Works serves the hospitality needs of corporations. From boardroom brunches to VIP receptions, we've got the works for you. Call for special event consultation and our complete corporate brochure. Watch the mail for an exciting special from Catering Works!

Catering You The Very Best
828-5932
905 - 106 Tryon Street • Raleigh, North Carolina • 27603

We believe the simplest, oldest, most effective tool of business is...

Postcards: Action Sales Generators

THE PICNIC BASKET (COLORADO SPRINGS, CO) USED THIS EYE CATCHING POSTCARD TO REEL IN NEW BUSINESS!

"CATERING FOR SUCCESSFUL HOLIDAY EVENTS"
CALL 635-0200 FOR MENUS & IDEAS

- Hor d'oeuvres & Trays
- Holiday Buffets
- Gift Baskets
- Casseroles & Side Dishes
- Servers & Bartenders

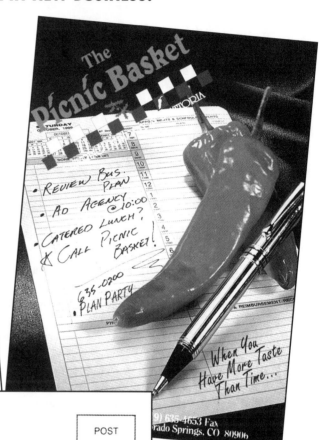

The Picnic Basket

- REVIEW BUS. PLAN
- AD AGENCY @ 10:00
- CATERED LUNCH? & CALL PICNIC BASKET!
  635-0200
- PLAN PARTY

When You Have More Taste Than Time...

(9) 635-4653 Fax
rado Springs, CO 80906

SUCCESSFUL EVENTS START WITH A CATERKART™

CATERKARTS™ An opportunity for new profits! CaterKarts are delightful, casual, colorful, and beautifully crafted in every detail. Select from numerous colors and theme styles. For elegant affairs, casual picnics, corporate or retail promotions. Chafing dish inserts for hot food and washable laminate tops for cold foods, erature, floral and other display.

CATERKART CUISINES™ The foundation a successful event is food! CaterKart Cuisi offers theme style menus for every occasi Italian Festival, Hot Dog Snack Karts, Chu wagon Barbecue Karts, Art Deco Karts, M ican Fiesta Karts, New Orleans Mardi G Karts, Hawaiian Luau Karts and more! A fre creative idea for catering and promotions. . .
.... **CALL (302) 888-4583**

y Bill Lindsey Studio

POST
CARD
RATE
83100692
Litho in U.S.A

POSTCARD

CATERKART *Cuisines*™

CATERKART CUISINES EXPLORES A UNIQUE SALES GENERATOR!

CHAPTER 2  QUESTIONS

1. What is the overall purpose for marketing a catering business?

2. What are some of the ways to determine what marketing a caterer should do?

3. Why is it important to consider "WIIFM" when creating marketing messages?

4. Where are some locations that "demonstration marketing" could be done?

5. Which of the marketing ideas did you like the best?

6. Why is it so hard to market catering?

7. What should a caterer be concerned about with respect to their image?

8. What type of names work best when naming a catering business?

9. How is marketing for corporate clients different than marketing for social ones?

10. What are some marketing ideas for corporate clients?

11. How do corporate buyers view catering?

12. What are some emotional instincts that shoppers think about when buying?

13. Is it proper to spy on your competition?

14. When creating a yellow page ad, what should a caterer be concerned about?

15. What are the rules of doing direct mail marketing campaigns?

BROCHURES

CHAPTER

3

TABLE OF CONTENTS

CHAPTER

3

*"Pack your orders early
or you will stay late!"*

To-The-Point Facility Advertisement

This advertisement is crisp and filled with what advertising people call " white space". In other words, this ad is not crowded and there is a lot of space between the information. It is easier to read by the eye, and provides a simple approach to giving important info. A great job by Catered Elegance of Bedford, OH!

Welcome...to our newly remodeled facilities

...comfortably seating up to 400 guests

...menu selections from traditional to contemporary

...choose from sit-down, full buffet, stations & appetizer parties

...certified entrée & pastry chefs prepare everything fresh on site

...featuring a polished maple hardwood 35' x 40' dance floor

...conveniently located in a picturesque, wooded setting

...large, raised stage for bands, disc jockeys & presentations

...well lighted parking lot with valet services available

...offsite catering also available for 2 to 2000 guests

Catered Elegance

1160 Broadway   Bedford, Ohio 44146

Call today...(440) 232-5039   1-888-409-4664

Slow cooked Prime Rib is one of our specialties

Our famous Ice Sculptures

Our beautiful granite fountain

The Classic 3 Fold Brochure

This is the front panel of this three fold brochure. The entire brochure was done in four-color with green and red being the dominant color used for type.

1. Just below the logo, and a great picture, is the reason for using El Burrito Catering... "Mexican Food Specialists". This tells the buyer that they are in good hands if they wish Mexican foods.

2. Again this section tells the buyer how to use El Burrito Catering.

3. This is small, but important because it reminds the buyer that this company's catering is great for both at home or at work... either inside or outside.

4. Great... phone number loud and clear!!

5. This is the area where the mailing label will go. Some may wish to place a marketing message on this panel i.e. "Attention: Anyone who loves outstanding catering!

6. CaterSource loves this idea...not only do you see the name of the person in charge, but you get to see her picture. Michaele Ann is a popular restaurateur in Tucson... so, people will know her when they see her picture.

7. Notice how the round shape draws your attention!

The Classic 3 Fold Brochure

We wish to share this unique three-panel catering brochure that was sent to us by Michaele Ann Melton of El Burrito Catering (Tucson, AZ). While it's a simple 8.5 x 11 inch format folded down into the three panels, it contains many unique and wise marketing ideas.

1. The entire opening paragraph gives a very positive spin on their catering. Words like "successful", "guests", "quality", and "fair prices" are great.

2. Easy to read phone number!

3. This paragraph deals with the fears of the catering buyer. It also opens doubt about other caterers who don't speak about these fears.

4. In a brochure it's important to tell the buyer how to use your catering.

5. "New" the single most important marketing word!

6. Let's the buyer know that they can ask for less expensive menus!

7. People want to know what your staff look like... great photo!

8. Testimonials sell catering! The inside panels of this menu are great!

A successful event starts with

El Burrito **CATERING**
& Your Special Guests!

El Burrito has been a catering leader in Tucson for 3 important reasons: convenience, quality and fair prices.

We're here to help you!

We can do just about anything that you want at any location. Helping others has allowed us to build our company into one of the strongest catering businesses in the area. We know Mexican food and we know the secrets of turning your gathering into a real **FIESTA!!!**

Phone 744-2225

At El Burrito Catering you can always be assured of fresh foods, sanitary preparation, on-time delivery, generous portions and an attractive, appealing presentation . . . truly an event you'll be proud to host.

CATERING POSSIBILITIES

- mini chimis
- mini tacos
- chili con carne
- birria
- barbacoa
- enchilada casseroles
- tamales
- frijoles
- arroz
- guacamole
- salads
- hors d'oeuvres
- fruit or veggie trays
- salsas and more . . .

NEW Biggie 6 Foot **BURRITO**
for your next party

Since we demand only the freshest, quality ingredients, you can count on tasty selections every time!

Catering doesn't need to be expensive. With El Burrito custom-catering, we will provide you with what you want, when you want it and where you want it! You'll be delighted at our affordable prices!

Our friendly staff is committed to 100% customer satisfaction. The team of professional servers can assist you so your catered event will be fun for YOU as well as your guests. One of the things we're offering you is peace of mind.

How Our Customers Feel

"Arizona Portland Cement has counted on you for ages, whether our function is for a dozen or 50 employees, at 6:30 a.m. or noon! It's nice dealing with a business that's more like friends next door".
Dave Bittel
Plant Manager
Arizona Portland Cement

"Both of us deeply appreciate your caring in helping us plan a very beautiful and special day in our lives. Knowing that you were "next door" taking care of all the reception details really made it possible for us to totally relax and enjoy our wedding celebration".
Tim Wernette

2-Sided Picnic Brochure

This is a tri-fold direct mailer created and used by Cater Inn (Peoria, IL) to promote their exclusive use of a private picnic grounds. The mailer is printed on a shiny, heavier stock paper using black ink plus yellow and red. Notice that the red backgrounds, or screens, are gradient fill to give the piece a simple design feeling. Remember, that one of the more important concepts in marketing picnics to corporations is not to look too expensive. This marketing pulls that off!

1. The two most important words in marketing are "new" and "easy". This is a great opening!

2. The buyer is treated to all sorts of reasons, or benefits, for using their location.

3. Phone number is a winner. In this case, we would suggest that the area code might be useful, especially if the brochure is sent to a home office or a relative in a different area code.

4. Love, Delight, Cheer, and Feast are all emotional in content. Successful marketers know that people buy what the product or service will do for them... not what it is. So, if you use this caterer for your picnic you will get love, delight, and cheers from your staff! Great message!

5. This section will not be read by everyone, but it will be read by those who want "more" information or reasons to have a picnic with Cater Inn. Thanks to Jim & Richard Barrack of Cater Inn!

Self-Serve High Impact Menu

Deli Trays — Our cool and refreshing deli trays feature an array of fine meats and cheeses that will satisfy all appetites ——from the lightest to the heartiest!

Italian Lunch Meat Tray — Volpi genoa salami and prosciutto, Carando capicola and mortadella, provolone cheese, artichoke salad, black and green olives, and pepperoncini

Small (8 - 10 servings) **$24.95**
Regular (14 - 16 servings) **$36.95**
Large (28 - 30 servings) **$54.95**

Signature American Meat and Cheese Tray — Krakus ham, smoked ham, premium smoked turkey breast, imported swiss and American cheese, mayonnaise and mustard, sweet pickles, black and green olives.

Small (8 - 10 servings) **$24.95**
Regular (14 - 16 servings) **$34.95**
Large (28 - 30 servings) **$54.95**

Krakus Ham and Cheese Tray — Krakus ham and swiss cheese garnished with sweet pickles, olives, mayonnaise and mustard.

Small (8 - 10 servings) **$24.95**
Regular (14 - 16 servings) **$32.95**
Large (28 - 32 servings) **$54.95**

Wisconsin Cheese Tray — Muenster, provolone, American, brick and swiss cheeses with black and green olives.

Small (8 - 10 servings) **$19.95**
Regular (14 - 16 servings) **$26.95**
Large (28 - 30 servings) **$39.95**

Gourmet Meat Tray — Smoked ham, imported Krakus ham, smoked turkey breast, Volpi genoa salami, mustard and mayonnaise, pickles, black and green olives.

Small (8 - 10 servings) **$26.95**
Regular (14 - 16 servings) **$37.95**
Large (28 - 32 servings) **$56.95**

Orders are accepted as far in advance as you desire, but we appreciate a minimum notice of 24 hours. When needing something on less than a 24-hour notice, just stop in our deli and order your favorites. On less than 24-hours notice, availability of some items is limited.

To place your order, call:
The Buona Beef Ordering Center
(708) 749-BEEF

Monday - Saturday: 8:30 a.m. - 6:30 p.m.
Sunday: By Appointment Only

Buona Beef Deli Locations:
Berwyn 6745 W. Roosevelt Rd.
Oak Park 7025 W. North Ave.
Monday - Saturday: 10:30 a.m. - 7 p.m.
Sunday: 10:30 a.m. - 6 p.m.

Party Subs — For a more casual gathering, your guests will rave about our super-sized subs!

Super Italian Party Sub — Made with genoa salami, provolone cheese, Carando capicola and mortadella, topped with garden-fresh lettuce, tomatoes and dressing.

2-foot, makes 10 - 12, 2-inch slices **$32.95**
3-foot, makes 18 - 20, 2-inch slices **$47.95**
6-foot, makes 38 - 40, 2-inch slices **$79.95**

Signature American Party Sub — Made with imported Krakus ham, smoked ham, turkey breast and American cheese, topped with garden-fresh lettuce, tomatoes and mayonnaise.

2-foot, makes 10 - 12, 2-inch slices **$32.95**
3-foot, makes 18 - 20, 2-inch slices **$47.95**
6-foot, makes 38 - 40, 2-inch slices **$79.95**

IF A PICTURE IS WORTH A 1,000 WORDS, THEN THIS IS A GREAT EXAMPLE OF WHAT TO DO WITH A PICTURE.

On-Premise Banquet Info

Catersource wishes to thank chef-owner Ron Stytzer for permitting us to re-print the following items from his company's marketing and menu offerings. About 35% of our subscribers operate on-premise banquet facilities, so it's great to have focused information that they can use. Thanks, Ron!

Catering at *Antun's* of Westchester

The Atmosphere...
A spectacular site in Westchester. Our luxurious facilities offer exquisite weddings. Have your wedding in the setting of your choice. A rolling lawn by the babbling brook, a romantic lily pond with Japanese bridge, Victorian gazebo, or an elegant indoor ballroom with a working fireplace and spectacular garden views are all available for your wedding day.

The Food...
Antun's enjoys a four-star rating which indicates excellent cuisine prepared individually. Our award-winning chef owner, Ron Stytzer, heads a European trained staff offering a variety of dishes that are incredibly delicious. Non-traditional, customized menus available. Brunch, garden parties and much more.

Another location available for your use, a Hudson River Mansion Spectacular Sunset Views

The Price...
You might think all this luxury would cost a fortune, but you will find that our prices are much more moderate than expected. Call the Banquet Manager or Ron Stytzer for details.

35 Valley Avenue, Elmsford, N.Y. 10523 (914) 592-5260
(Where the Saw Mill River Parkway meets Route 119)

Banquet Facility Wedding Insert

Selling romance is one of the goals of Windows on the Lake (Lake Ronkonkoma, NY). They developed, and use, this four color 8.5 by 11 inch promo piece to give brides when they visit their facility. They tell us that the photos really create a wonderful situation for everyone!

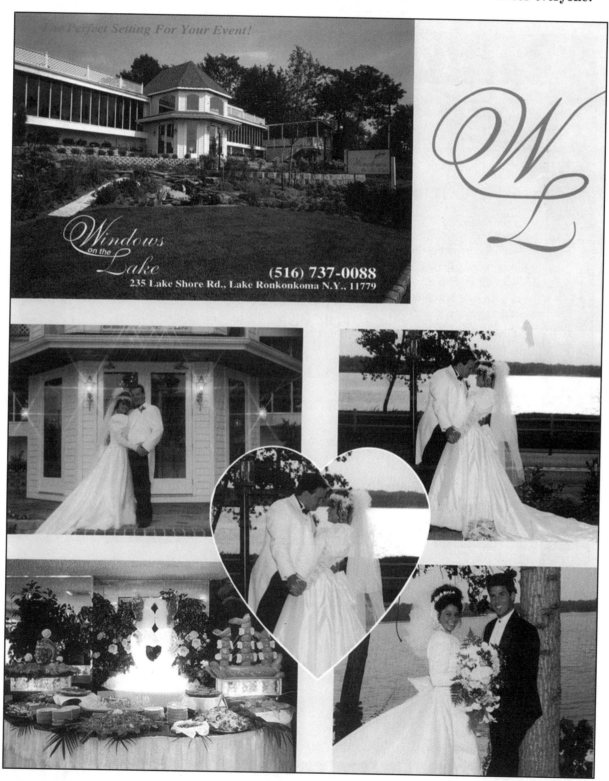

2-Page Inquiry Generator

Sharon Snuffin (Snuffin's • Gig Harbor, WA) has been one of the CaterSource Journal's most consistent contributor. She has sent in some more of her ideas to share with other caterers. On these two pages you can view her newest marketing winner that is built around a coupon and a response card. We believe this to be a winner.

Snuffin's

CATERING WITH STYLE AND ELEGANCE... AT AFFORDABLE PRICES

Snuffin's Catering offers a full range of catering services for everything from corporate functions to wedding receptions.

Let us make your next event both gracious and successful by providing our expert planning, food service, decorations, location selections and on-site hosting.

Snuffin's specializes in large and corporate events. As your premier catering source, you can relax and leave the work to us!

THERE'S ALWAYS ROOM FOR MORE...

From bountiful buffets to fanciful feasts, private parties to corporate events...

Every event is exceptional when you let Snuffin's do the work!

Open Houses
Picnics
Grand Openings
Cocktail Parties
Theme Parties
Trade Shows
Cruises
Fundraisers
Dessert Buffets
Wedding Receptions
Buffet Dinners
Private Dinners
Retirements
Anniversaries
Bar & Bat Mitzvahs
Rehearsal Dinners

(253) 851-2900 • 1-800-940-5989 • FAX: (253) 858-7211

SAVE THIS VALUABLE COUPON

Save 10%

Snuffin's Catering extends this special offer of 10% off (*a $300 or more value*) on any order over $3,000. Party must be booked 30 days in advance. This offers expires April 30, 1998. Call for quote today!

Yes

❑ Please fax me your party planning worksheet.

❑ Please fax me your menu sampler of appetizers and meals options.

❑ Please have an event coordinator call me about our next event. (date of event:_____)

Name: _____ Title: _____

Company:_____

Address: _____

City _____ Zip _____

Phone: _____ Fax: _____

Simply Mail or FAX back this request: (Our fax# is: (253) 858-7211)

FOR THE BEST CATERING IN TOWN ~ AT AFFORDABLE PRICES

2-Page Inquiry Generator

$\mathcal{L}$OOK AT WHAT OTHERS ARE SAYING...

" We have events that cater to a very sophisticated, international client base. We need upscale and class all the way. Snuffin's food styling and professionalism are exceptional. They've been our caterer for over 20 years. "

Joetta Cook,
Meeting Services
The Frank Russell Company

" The October Fest theme was a great hit for our annual customer appreciation event. Everything from tents to oompah bands — Snuffin's handled it all! "

Evette Bailey,
Community Relations
The Port of Tacoma

Catering with style and elegance since 1974

" The receptions Snuffin's catered for a Catalan Masters Exhibit were fabulous! The flavors of the authentic tapas were amazing! Everyone is still buzzing about the events. "

Barbara Neeb,
Special Events
The Tacoma Art Museum

" All we need to do to plan an event is to give our personal event planner a call. She knows our style and budget, and each time we have just the atmosphere we're looking for. Plus, their wait-staff is so incredibly wonderful to work with! "

Anna Pearce
Seattle University School of Law

Place
First Class
Postage
Here

Catering with style and elegance since 1974
6745-A Kimball Drive
Gig Harbor, WA 98335-1231

SAVE THIS VALUABLE COUPON

Catering with style and elegance since 1974
Call: 1-800-940-5989

2-Color BBQ Promo

This 8.5 x 11 marketing piece is from Meier's Catering (Salt Lake City, UT). The following are some of CaterSource's observations.

1. Great emotional opening .

2. Use of red as a second color adds to the message.

3. Giving the marketing a special name helps the buyer know what to ask for when they call.

4. Something new for those who have bought before.

5. It's good to give specific products and services that you offer.

6. Today, clip art abounds. You can get clip art from graphic designers or you can purchase it yourself from software catalogs. In this piece the clip art adds to the country, outdoor and fun feeling.

7. Easy to find telephone number is great!

8. This is a wise way to make the reader remember how important it is to book early so they won't be disappointed.

American Roadhouse Catering

AMERICAN
ROADHOUSE

CATERING

PHONE 404.266.1177 FAX 404.266.3757

ENTREES

Individually served, minimum delivery 20.
Buffet set up available - 25.00 fee. Pricing based on 20 or more.

Texas Style BBQ   7.95/person
• Shredded BBQ pork sandwiches
• Shredded BBQ chicken sandwiches
• Cole slaw   • Potato chips   • Rocky road brownie

Executive's Choice   8.95/person
• Choice of dijon chicken or maple glazed salmon
• Fresh whipped potatoes   • Broccoli with herbed butter
• Corn muffins   • Rocky road brownie

Roadhouse Rotisserie Chicken   7.95/person
• Half of a rotisserie chicken   • Cole slaw
• Fresh whipped potatoes   • Rock road brownie

Georgia Cookout Combo   11.95/person
• BBQ baby back ribs   • Rotisserie chicken
• Cole slaw   • Potato chips   • Rock road brownie

BACKYARD BBQ'S AND COOKOUTS

Starting at 8.95 per guest

The hassle-free way to have a backyard cookout!
We'll cook up hamburgers, hot dogs and chicken breasts
along with cole slaw, potato salad, chips and fresh brewed tea.
Or we can bring over our famous baby back ribs, BBQ chicken
or BBQ pork loin. You name it and we'll work out a package
that is perfect for your event. We can even grill up some
14 ounce New York Strip Steaks, jumbo shrimp skewers,
and marinated vegetables for a more distinguished menu.
Just call our catering number for more information.
We'll visit your site, plan the menu, furnish names of some of
our very satisfied customers and you can leave the rest to us.

ABOUT US

Mission Statement
To serve the highest quality experience of food and service to each and every guest. Maintain an enjoyable and safe work environment our staff feels proud and confident to be a part of and grow with. To ensure a highly profitable organization for purposes of continued quality and opportunity for our guests and staff. We started this company because we know we can serve great food at a reasonable price and have fun doing it.

History
American Roadhouse has been providing corporations and their guests with catered events for the past ten years. Owners Ed Udoff and Martin Maslia are on hand everyday overseeing operations. We have two convenient locations in which we prepare breakfast, lunch and dinner for more than 1200 guests daily. Our menu targets relaxed comfort foods. We use only the highest quality products and pride ourselves on a variety of items we can offer and still maintain flavor and quality in each dish. We are committed to serving you a quality event beyond your expectations every time.

Ordering
Please call or fax orders 48 hours in advance. We gladly accommodate orders with less than 48 hours notice, but please call directly. Delivery is available for orders of 20 or more and a 10.00 delivery fee is added. Orders of less than 20 may be picked up at either location or delivered for an additional fee.

Utensils
All orders include high quality disposable dinnerware, napkins and plates. Disposable utensils are provided when needed at no charge.

Policies
American Roadhouse endeavors to serve only the highest quality product. Our food has continued to evolve over the past decade as demand and trends change. Our service is warm, professional and above all personal. We understand that we must earn your business on every event. We guarantee every event. Should you not be completely satisfied, please inform the driver immediately. The driver is empowered to do whatever it takes to correct the situation.

Payment
Payment is expected at time of delivery. For larger events, a 25% deposit is required. We accept company check, cash, American Express, Visa and MasterCard. Billing may be arranged with proper credit.

For more information visit our Web Site at www.ARH-Catering.com

BREAKFAST

Each breakfast below serves 10 to 12 people.
Chafing dish, china and silverware provided for only 25.00.

Continental Breakfast   42.95
• Fresh baked blueberry and glorious morning muffins
• Fresh baked sesame, cinnamon raisin, and plain bagels
• Buttermilk biscuits   • Fresh seasonal fruit
• Assorted bottled juices   • Cream cheese, jellies and butter

Biscuit Sandwich Breakfast   52.95
• Bacon biscuits   • Sausage biscuits
• Ham biscuits   • Fresh seasonal fruit
• Assorted bottled juices
• Jellies and butter

Executive Breakfast   69.95
• Roadhouse scrambled eggs
  (scrambled with peppers, onions, tomatoes and cheese)
• Thick sliced bacon or country sausage
• Cheddar cheese grits
• Fresh seasonal fruit
• Assorted fresh baked muffins, bagels
  and buttermilk biscuits
• Assorted bottled juices
• Cream cheese, jellies and butter

Light and Healthy Alternative   54.95
• Assorted individual yogurts
• Crunchy nut granola bars
• Fresh seasonal fruit
• Assorted fresh baked muffins, bagels
  and buttermilk biscuits
• Assorted bottled juices
• Cream cheese, jellies and butter

Coffee Service
Self-serve coffee station. Includes cups, sweeteners and cream.
Up to 25 guests - 25.00   Up to 50 guests - 50.00

BOX LUNCHES

Deli sandwich box lunches include choice of overstuffed deli sandwich, salad, chips and rocky road brownie. Condiments served separately.
Sandwiches served on jumbo egg roll except where noted.
Minimum order of 10. See grid below for appropriate pricing.

C.F.O. Luncheons
• Honey roasted turkey, swiss, lettuce and tomato
• Rare roast beef, cheddar, lettuce and tomato
• Lightly smoked ham, swiss, lettuce and tomato
• Rotisserie chicken salad, monterey jack, lettuce and tomato
• B.L.A.T. - bacon, lettuce, avocado spread and tomato
• Albacore tuna salad, lettuce and tomato
• Vegetable Pita - grilled garden vegetables and
  Monterey Jack Cheese rolled into a whole wheat pita

C.O.O. Luncheons
• Grilled Tuna Steak Sandwich - grilled tuna steak
  topped with oriental sauce
• Grilled Chicken Club - grilled chicken breast,
  cheddar, bacon, lettuce and tomato
• Roadhouse Club - turkey, ham and roast beef. and
  cheese with bacon, lettuce and tomato on sourdough

C.E.O. Luncheons
• New York Strip Steak Sandwich - served medium rare,
  open face with vine ripe tomatoes and bermuda onions
• Fresh Jumbo Shrimp Salad Sandwich - jumbo shrimp
  tossed in fresh dill mayonnaise

Kosher lunches available upon request

quantity	10-19	20-34	35-100	101-200	201-300	300-499
C.F.O.	7.50	7.25	6.95	6.75	6.50	6.25
C.O.O.	8.50	8.25	7.95	7.75	7.50	7.25
C.E.O.	9.50	9.25	8.95	8.75	8.50	8.25

DELI PLATTER

Corporate Sandwich Platter   62.95
Serves 12. Choice of three meats and two cheeses.
• Rare roast beef   • Honey roasted turkey
• Lightly smoked ham   • Rotisserie chicken salad
• Albacore tuna salad
• Swiss   • Monterey Jack   • American   • Cheddar

Served on a tray loaded with lettuce, tomatoes, onions and pickles.
A second tray holds an assortment of breads, rolls and condiments.

Side Items and Salads   18.00
Each item serves 12.
• Tossed Salad   • Pasta Primavera Salad
• Potato Salad   • Roadhouse Cole Slaw
• Fresh Fruit   • Chilled Cucumber Dill Salad
• Caesar Salad   • Assorted Potato Chips
• Rocky Road Brownies

LUNCHEON SALADS

Entree salad box lunches are served with a rocky road brownie.

Entree Salad Box Lunch
• Grilled Chicken Caesar Salad - grilled chicken breast
  atop crisp romaine leaves with creamy caesar dressing.
• Cobb Salad - chopped turkey, ham, bacon, tomatoes,
  shredded cheese atop a bed of mixed greens.
  Choice of dressing.
• Roadhouse Club Salad - grilled chicken, mixed greens,
  bacon, cheddar, tomatoes, and pecans tossed in honey
  mustard.
• Rotisserie Chicken Salad - made from fresh rotisserie
  chicken and olive oil served on a bed of mixed greens.
• Albacore Tuna Salad - made from all white meat
  albacore tuna, celery, onions, and mayonnaise.

quantity	10-19	20-34	35-100	101-200	201-300	300-499
price	7.50	7.25	6.95	6.50	6.25	5.95

A Great One-Sided Business Builder

It tells like it is... great food by the great caterers. This straight forward 8.5 x 11 inch promo is a great example of a marketing action tool. The reader gets the information they want quickly and it has the element of "fun" in it. Great work by Hess Barbecue Catering of Schuylhill Haven, PA!

Unique 4-Color Menu

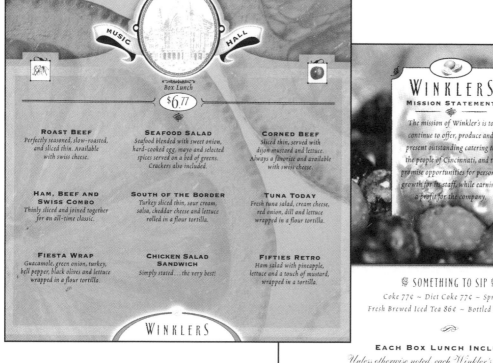

WINKLERS

TEL 242-4567 JUST CALL US — WE DELIVER! 242-3555 FAX

PROFESSIONALISM ✦ QUALITY ✦ SERVICE ✦ OUR TRADEMARK

When ordering our box lunch or planning a catering event for... you can depend on Winkler's for service and quality... we listen to you and take care to help you succeed with your... the freshest of ingredients and take pride in the quality of our... Custom Catering is where unique menus and plans are... Originality, quality and years of experience go into each... Give us a call if you have any questions, or special... on our promise to provide you with high quality food and... dependability.

~Jim Thullen, Proprietor~

WINKLERS

HELP US SERVE YOU BETTER

...ase place your order at least 24 hours in advance ☺
...your order, please call us before 9 A.M. on the day to be delivered ☺
...ive 12 hours advance notice to decrease your order ☺
...d the same day may require an adjusted delivery time ☺
...y effort possible to deliver at your requested time or earlier ☺
...at time of delivery, unless credit terms are prearranged ☺
...We accept Visa and American Express ☺

(MINIMUM ORDER OF SIX)

TEL 242-4567 JUST CALL US — WE DELIVER! 242-3555 FAX
4923 Paddock Road   Cincinnati, Ohio 45237   www.winklersmenu.com

---

MUSIC HALL

Box Lunch
$6.77

ROAST BEEF
Perfectly seasoned, slow-roasted, and sliced thin. Available with swiss cheese.

SEAFOOD SALAD
Seafood blended with sweet onion, hard-cooked egg, mayo and selected spices served on a bed of greens. Crackers also included.

CORNED BEEF
Sliced thin, served with dijon mustard and lettuce. Always a favorite and available with swiss cheese.

HAM, BEEF AND SWISS COMBO
Thinly sliced and joined together for an all-time classic.

SOUTH OF THE BORDER
Turkey sliced thin, sour cream, salsa, cheddar cheese and lettuce rolled in a flour tortilla.

TUNA TODAY
Fresh tuna salad, cream cheese, red onion, dill and lettuce wrapped in a flour tortilla.

FIESTA WRAP
Guacamole, green onion, turkey, bell pepper, black olives and lettuce wrapped in a flour tortilla.

CHICKEN SALAD SANDWICH
Simply stated...the very best!

FIFTIES RETRO
Ham salad with pineapple, lettuce and a touch of mustard, wrapped in a tortilla.

WINKLERS

WINKLERS
MISSION STATEMENT

The mission of Winkler's is to continue to offer, produce and present outstanding catering to the people of Cincinnati, and to promise opportunities for personal growth for its staff, while earning a profit for the company.

❧ SOMETHING TO SIP ❧
Coke 77¢ ~ Diet Coke 77¢ ~ Sprite 77¢
Fresh Brewed Iced Tea 86¢ ~ Bottled Water $1.26

EACH BOX LUNCH INCLUDES...
Unless otherwise noted, each Winkler's box lunch includes fresh fruit salad, Winkler's salad and dessert of the day, an after lunch treat, flatware and napkin.

CHAPTER 3  QUESTIONS

1. Which type of photos work best in brochures?

2. What is the most powerful word to use when marketing?

3. How should a caterer use their phone number in a brochure?

4. How important is the use of color printing when selling catering?

5. Can a brochure make the sale by itself?

6. What type of brochures do you think will work best?

7. What type of brochures will you want to use?

8. What are some great headlines for a brochure?

9. How would you use humor in a brochure?

10. What would be wrong to place into a brochure?

KITCHEN

CHAPTER

4

TABLE OF CONTENTS

CHAPTER

4

"On the busiest day of the year the wedding cake always slips off a table or falls in the truck!"

Executive Chef Job Description

ABC CATERING EXECUTIVE CHEF — Job Description

85% of time spent in kitchen

- cooking as the primary chef for all event orders
- overseeing all food production
- setting up daily prep plan
- scheduling of staff (to be approved by John Doe) allocating hours and days of work
- assisting management with hiring/firing responsibilities
- adhering to labor cost control guidelines
- dispatching parties
- menu development
- recipe development and testing
- working with sales staff on updating menus, concepts, and event themes
- food ordering
- working with operations department to forecast equipment needs
- training of field staff, holding regular training seminars for all new employees
- holding regular "refresher" seminars for old employees
- inventory control, responsible for taking of physical inventory
- upkeep of storage areas includes rotation of all items in storage areas (dry storage, liquor, refrigerator and freezer)
- training and guiding part-time cooks and chefs during heavier cooking periods
- constantly keeping labor and food costs as proper as can be
- formulating weekly/monthly/yearly production and costing goals
- establishing and maintaining proper and firm sanitation policies
- developing and implementing new methods of serving food at banquets
- ordering all supplies and raw food materials for banquets and catering
- helping in daily maintenance procedures in kitchen

15% of time spent on non-production situations

- hiring/firing of kitchen personnel and involvement with other key personnel
- checking weekly schedules processing employee paperwork
- tracking employee records and probationary periods
- placing employment ads in newspapers
- costing food items and menus, reviewing labor & food cost, and help in cost control
- reviewing menus/menu development with owner
- assisting in writing proposals
- working with food and equipment sheets

Possible extra responsibilities

- going on sales calls with salespeople
- networking with clients and potential clients
- Working at off-premise events (earning extra dollars)
- attending and overseeing banquets

Important Kitchen Tips

What is consulting? To me, consulting is evaluation and comparison. First you evaluate what conditions exist, then you compare these conditions with those that exist elsewhere.

This is why the world has consultants. Not for their expertise, but for their exposure to diverse conditions. Most caterers have never been to many other catering operations to see what is happening. I've been fortunate to have personally visited more than 900 catering companies over the last 20 years.

That's what this new series of articles is about. I hope to give our readers some guidelines for "self-consulting".

It is important that catering businesses receive ongoing evaluation in order to continually reach for higher levels of success.

Concepts For Kitchen 101
(Basic)

Catering kitchens are difficult, at best to operate! In most catering companies, the kitchen (commissary) is supposed to be error free and "all knowing".

While this is often the case with many caterers, the pressure on the culinary staff is overwhelming and causes most to be under constant stress and tension.

Here are some of my thoughts regarding tips and strategies that will hopefully permit the kitchen to become the true "heart beat" of the company!

1. Never assume anything when working in, or managing, a kitchen.

I had my desk in our catering kitchen for 14 years. The first thing my mother made clear to me when I was learning about catering was "never assume anything".

My mother would say, "Don't assume that we have enough broccoli in the cooler. Just because the linen company says that there's red linen in that package ... don't assume it to be true. Don't assume that the delivery elevator at that company operates on a Sunday."

I think you get the idea. It's not a matter of not trusting others. Instead, it's a matter of taking responsibility.

> ... THINK OF THESE TIPS, TACTICS AND IDEAS AS A STARTING POINT FOR DOING SELF-CONSULTING FOR YOUR OWN BUSINESS.

In this age of delegation, the error rate in catering kitchens has been increasing dramatically. From a consulting point of view, it is important that every measure of effort be given to establishing systems for overcoming the assumption that something is as we expect, even though we haven't really confirmed it for sure!

2. Kitchens work against constant deadlines.

There are at least two deadlines for most caterers .... today and tomorrow! Well, this is fine for some, but not for anyone who really wants to get in touch with a tension free workplace!

One of the earlier deadlines for a kitchen is knowledge of what normal menu items have been sold. The earliest deadline is knowledge of any abnormal, harder to find, menu items that have been sold.

The next deadline would be the final discussion with the salesperson who sold the event followed by the ordering deadline from the vendors to get the stuff in on time to prepare.

While their are other deadlines to consider, the most crucial would be the deadline of when food needs to be done for either delivery or serving in a banquet facility.

Anyway you cut it, deadlines can lead to tranquilizers if taken seriously.

3. Organization and checklists are the rule in the kitchen.

In my opinion, the kitchen is the "heart" of the business. It is also my opinion that a kitchen needs to have a professional "plan" of operation.

These "plans" need to be prepared ahead of time and followed like a road map. Launching the kitchen into a day's operation is as complex as launching the Starship Enterprise!

If a caterer starts thinking about an operational plan on the same day as an event, then they deserve what they usually get ... disorganized chaos. What we really want to achieve is "organized" chaos!

An operational plan goes hand in hand with a checklist. Think of an airline pilot who sits in the cockpit with a checklist methodically going down the items to make sure that the results are perfection!

Important Kitchen Tips

Don't laugh at this thought... I've met caterers that have developed a checklists for their checklists! They have checklist that deal with food, equipment, sanitation, meetings, pick-ups, purchasing, amounts of food, staffing, and just about anything else that one could possibly think of!

4. A daily kitchen meeting is always advisable.

The most frightful words that can be heard in a busy kitchen are "I didn't know....". It is absolutely imperative that each, and every day, a casual "directional" meeting be held in the kitchen for all staff.

This meeting usually is held just before the official start of the kitchen workday. All should attend, i.e. chefs, packers, drivers, clean-up crew.

The meeting should be casual. Most caterers simply have the culinary team stand near the wall, or door, where the day's order sheets are posted.

The kitchen leader then carefully goes over each of the orders, concentrating on certain aspects that could cause a problem because they are not the "norm".

Here's some types of directions they might receive from the kitchen manager:

- "Let's pay attention to the Smith box lunch... they want butter on only half the sandwiches.

- "Chef, remember that we need the sauces put into an iced travel box."

- "Fred, the picnic order needs to be delivered to the West park entrance.

I think you get the idea. Remember, the important thing is to permit your staff to have access to the team leader's thoughts.

5. Standardization holds down errors.

This concept deals a lot with the factor of not assuming anything. In some of the kitchens that I've seen, caterers tend to place certain types of menu items into certain types of packaging. For example, frozen hors' d'oeuvres are always placed in a 9 by 12 inch foil pan with a foil lid. This standardizes this type of menu item which permits quicker identification of what it is both in the freezer and at an event.

It might also be helpful to standardize your packing boxes to the point where everyone has a better idea of where "things" might be. Many caterers use color tape or dots to help standardize their packing and shipping efforts.

6. The best philosophy in a kitchen is "In this kitchen we use, or sell, everything we buy!

What a nice thought! It didn't happen when I was in charge of my catering kitchen... but I didn't have a CaterSource Journal to read during the eighties!

We're, of course, dealing with the concept of waste. From a consulting point of view, waste is an "attitude" that exists in the body of all kitchen staff. They learn from observation more than a "rule" book or policy manual.

When they see others, and especially those in management, not practicing elimination of waste techniques, their attitude is poor.

Eliminating waste is not a simple program of saving cans for recycling. It is an all out attempt at creatively using everything that the company buys.

Recently I observed a kitchen where the staff was saving the cores that were left after making cabbage ready for slaw. Most kitchens simply throw out the cabbage cores. In this kitchen, the cores were saved to use in a special chopped menu item called "South of the Boarder Firehouse Slaw".

Its really a great feeling when everyone learns to think about eliminating waste through the creation of new uses for items that are usually thrown out. One company saves strawberry pint baskets and washes them to hold filled with tiny muffins for continental breakfasts.

My main message in this article is to remind you that the kitchen can't be overlooked in the total management of your business... as it often is. It is so easy to take the kitchen for granted. If you do this , you will be increasing the opportunities for trouble down the road. The kitchen is the lifeblood of your business!

Evaluating Your Kitchen

Since I earn part of my living from consulting with caterers, I've gotten to know about 45 companies intimately. I've watched companies grow from $300,000 in sales to $2,500,000 in four years. In several cases, I've had the privilege to consult, on an on going basis, with catering businesses that have added three million dollars in sales to when I first started working with them.

I'm not suggesting that I've made those caterers successful. That just isn't true, but, I've become part of their management team. I've been able to add the combined observations that I've witnessed in other companies, to help these growing companies stay on track.

That's what this new series of articles is about. I hope to give our readers some guidelines for "self-consulting".

Beginning Your Kitchen Evaluation

Let's begin with an understanding of evaluating your kitchen. From a consulting point of view, your kitchen is either out of control, or working well.

The symptoms of being out of control in the kitchen are: lack of inventory controls, tardiness of staff, lack of written recipes and procedures, poor sanitation, sending too much food, orders that are mispacked, food and equipment not leaving for events on time, and a chef, or kitchen leader, that is not cooperative with the entire culinary, sales and management team.

Your evaluation begins with a rather simple action ... you need to sit in your kitchen. That's right ... just sit and watch. That's all I do as a consultant.

What do you watch for? Just use your common sense and measure your kitchen against the "out of control" symptoms listed two paragraphs above. The problem is that many owners believe that it just isn't "cool" to sit and watch their kitchen. Often the owners think, "My staff will think that I don't trust them."

Well, from a consulting point of view ... you shouldn't trust them! At least during your evaluation process. What would happen if the airlines felt it wasn't cool to evaluate their pilots?

As you sit in the kitchen watching your team at work, have some paper and a pen to take notes. Jot down your observations as you see things happen or not happen. The amount of time you sit should be at least an hour at a time.

Walk around from time to time, and get close to the action. Ask to taste some of the food being prepared. Just the way in which your staff gets you the food samples tells you a lot about how they respect their food and their sanitation level.

For example, if they simply get a kitchen utensil, load the sample onto the utensil and then give it to you, you know that they are not as concerned than if they put the sample onto a disposable or china, plate (or other container) and gave you a normal piece of metal or disposable flatware. I also take note if they also give me a napkin with the sample.

Does this seem strange to you? It should. However, this is what consulting and evaluating is all about. You need to look at the small details.

Other Things To Watch For

Here's a free-flowing list of things to watch for in your kitchen evaluation:

> ... THINK OF THESE TIPS, TACTICS AND IDEAS AS A STARTING POINT FOR DOING SELF-CONSULTING FOR YOUR OWN BUSINESS.

1. How are the kitchen leaders sitting? Is anyone facing the back door? Is anyone sitting close to the back door to watch what comes in and out of the kitchen?

2. Do your chefs kick the oven door closed, or otherwise "rough house" your equipment?

3. Does your staff eat freely from the foods that are being prepared? Do they eat while they are working?

4. Are there signs of smoking in the kitchen proper?

5. Does your hand sink really work? Are there soap and towels at the sink?

6. In the walk-in cooler, is everything shelved together... or are there flats of strawberries here, there and over there?

7. Take a food package from the garbage. Is all of the food out of it?

Evaluating Your Kitchen

8. Take a pan of food from an order ready to go out and check to see if the food sent is in the same amount as requested on the order or packing list. In other words, if the order calls for 42 chicken breasts... how many are really going?

9. Watch and see if anyone is failing to wash their knives each and every time they move from one food group to another.

10. Try to determine whether there is a fear of asking questions in your kitchen.

11. Moving fast in a kitchen is often a good thing, but it often tells us that the timing is not correct.

Well, these concepts will give you a good start towards evaluating your kitchen. Now lets look at some other concepts that will help you evaluate your team.

Over a period of a couple of weeks, call each member of your kitchen team, one at a time, into your office, or other space away from the kitchen, for a private interview.

Your purpose is to seek information about the attitude and atmosphere in the kitchen. Here are some of the questions that I would ask:

1. "What is your job in the kitchen?"

2. "Have you received enough training for your job?"

3. "Are you happy with your job?"

4. "What do you think of our food?"

5. "Who do you like to work with the most in the kitchen?"

6. "Who is the hardest worker in the kitchen... other than yourself?"

7. "Who isn't carrying their load in the kitchen?"

8. "If you could press a magic button, what equipment would you want to have in the kitchen that would help you do a better job?"

I hope you're getting a feel for the purpose of these interviews. If done properly, you will soon learn who, if anyone, should be trained better, or removed from your kitchen staff.

Two More Ideas

If you wish to quickly tell if your kitchen is in control just make the announcement that you've decided to put a pay phone in your kitchen for all staff non-emergency incoming and outgoing calls. Next, announce that you're going to put in a soda vending machine with sodas selling for .25 cents to cover the costs. If all hell breaks loose call for the consultants!

I hoped these thoughts have helped you. Feel free to call me and discuss, critique, or elaborate on any of these ideas. Remember, it's just a guide. Yes, they are rather negative in nature, but that's the way an owner gets to the bottom of problems that might exist. It's important to move out of our comfort zones if we wish to make our business better. Your kitchen must be in control in order to achieve the best that you can achieve as a caterer! If you invest some time... you will get better!

Tips for Larger Events

1 Have the right equipment to do the job. The oversized mixing bowl above with it's matching floor stand on wheels, will increase your ability to produce larger batches of menu items.

When matched with the use of plastic gloves, this system can be a real labor saver with the kitchen worker mixing by hand. Plastic gloves also come in elbow length. Making larger batches also allows for a uniform level of flavor.

Other large batch handling equipment such as Vertical Cutting Machines and Tilting Skillets are favorites of high volume caterers.

2 Just the thought of delivering certain items to a large job site like these croquembouche can give you nightmares!

When planning your ordering for large events, it is best to find purveyors who can deliver right to the event site at a specific time.

Such items as desserts, ice, liquor, beer, soda, rentals should be arranged to be delivered right to the job site.

Some items like dessert should be delivered after the start of event to limit the problems of little or no refrigeration.

This brings up the concept of "staggered" deliveries from your own kitchens. As long as you have control over your nerves, a better event can be created, for example, if the 60 gallons of coffee arrive at a time closer to when you are using it.

In fact, it might be best to subcontract out things like the coffee to others who have the proper equipment to do the job better.

3 The sheer size of bigger events can get the best of any caterer. The cart above holds foil pans with foil lids that contain 900 slabs of pre-cooked bbq style ribs.

This caterer is using foil because of the savings in weight over using stainless pans. Also, if stainless were used, less product could be placed on this cart.

The use of the rolling cart is also a trick of high volume caterers. It is important to handle foods as few times as possible. By using these oversize rolling carts, the caterer can pack, store in the cooler, and roll right out to the truck all in one motion!

The cost of the foil pans is offset by the possible loss of just one stainless pan while at the job site. The workers at the event will also be grateful for the lighter foil pans as they carry them across the fields at the job site. (Continued)

Tips for Larger Events

By requesting oversized casters (wheels) when purchasing your rolling carts, you just might be able to use them at job sites... even on grass!

Many caterers are rolling carts right onto trucks that have special docking features that allow the carts to be held in place for transport.

4 Learn to rely on outside grilling when possible for larger events. With five to ten charcoal grills, a caterer can cook and reheat food for thousands.

Depending on price, always try to steer your clients of larger events to menu items that have a higher yield with respect to grill-top space.

For example, the tenderloin of beef above has a higher yield than strip steaks. This single grill can yield tenderloin for 180 persons. You would need several grills for the same number of strip steaks.

Grills can also be used to cook coffee using the stock pot cooking concept developed by the military.

Other items that do well on grills are tenderloin of veal, whole NY strip, boneless and bone-in chicken, salmon steaks, and vegetables.

Caterers also use outside grilling during the winter months, even in snow conditions. Grills can be used in alleys of big cities as well as in open fields!

5 When designing large event menus, always attempt to sell some items that can be thermalized and delivered hot to the job site.

Like the steamship round of beef in the above photo, foods will stay hot in plastic carriers between three to six hours depending on the brand of carrier and the tricks the caterer uses in packing.

One of these carriers could hold enough pans to yield 350 to 400 servings of most starches and vegetables. Also, many caterers bring these carriers to events empty. They then fill them with food as they cook fresh at the event site. The trick is to stay ahead of ones needs!

6 As events get bigger, the need for spread out work space increases. This is especially true for large plate served dinners. In this photo, the caterer has taken advantage of a large outside area to set-up long assembly surfaces in order to create the first course and the dessert.

Be concerned with the health department in this matter of working outside. But, when the job has to get done, the caterer needs to be creative!

Mobile Kitchens

Here's a neat promotion that Commonwealth Caterers did to promote their new kitchen on wheels. They created a printed and die cut promo in the shape of the kitchen on wheels. It was then mailed in a #10 envelop. I would take note if I were to open an envelop and find this promo inside... wouldn't you? NOTE: When we scanned this piece into the Journal we needed to place a grey background behind the die-cut in order to see the full shape.

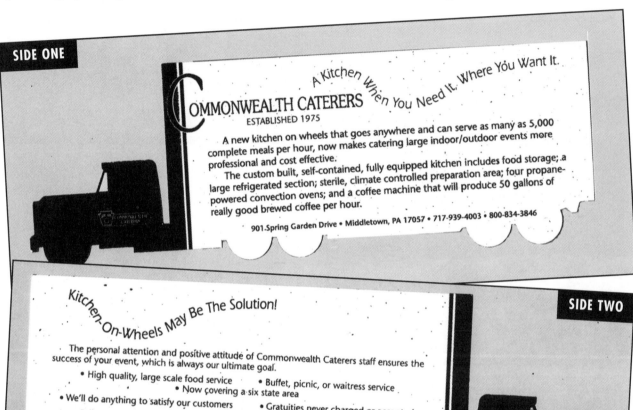

SIDE ONE

COMMONWEALTH CATERERS
ESTABLISHED 1975

A Kitchen When You Need It. Where You Want It.

A new kitchen on wheels that goes anywhere and can serve as many as 5,000 complete meals per hour, now makes catering large indoor/outdoor events more professional and cost effective.

The custom built, self-contained, fully equipped kitchen includes food storage; a large refrigerated section; sterile, climate controlled preparation area; four propane-powered convection ovens; and a coffee machine that will produce 50 gallons of really good brewed coffee per hour.

901 Spring Garden Drive • Middletown, PA 17057 • 717-939-4003 • 800-834-3846

SIDE TWO

Kitchen-On-Wheels May Be The Solution!

The personal attention and positive attitude of Commonwealth Caterers staff ensures the success of your event, which is always our ultimate goal.

- High quality, large scale food service
- Buffet, picnic, or waitress service
- Now covering a six state area
- We'll do anything to satisfy our customers
- Gratuities never charged or accepted

Call us for more information or a free estimate. Ask for Clarence or Wendy Riley or fax event specifications to 717-939-6520 for a professionally prepared proposal.

901 Spring Garden Drive • Middletown, PA 17057 • 717-939-4003 • 800-834-3846

Mobile Kitchens

It's 46' in length and cost $200,000, but it has created an incredible number of catering opportunities for Commonwealth Caterers (Middletown, PA).

According to founder and president Clarence Riley, "Our kitchen on wheels has provided us with a competitive advantage and the opportunity to cater larger functions".

With more than $2 million in annual sales, Commonwealth is poised for rapid growth due to the new kitchen.

The trailer that houses the kitchen, was purchased used, and converted into the power cooking facility that it is now... it has 4 convection ovens, coolers, steam kettles and a coffee system.

The kitchen also has almost unlimited electric generating capabilities to hook-up to other equipment outside. It carries several 250# propane tanks and ample amounts of water.

The kitchen allows Commonwealth to cook from scratch right at the job site. Serving 2,000 guests has become routine for the team of six to eight that work inside the kitchen.

They've decided not to do any frying in the kitchen to keep it grease free. Also, the kitchen is not for rent, but Commonwealth is ready and willing to do joint-ventures on larger events.

Building a New Kitchen

his was a dream come true! A caterer got a chance to build their own building to house their own catering business. CaterSource wants you to see what they did to create, without question, one of the most logical and useable kitchens we've ever seen!

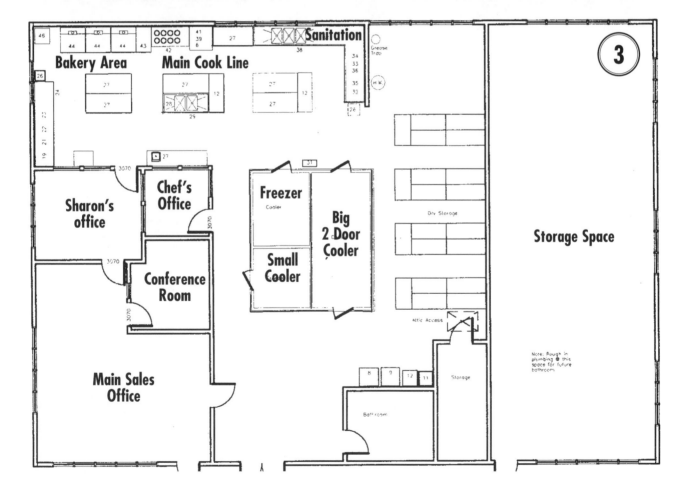

Building a New Kitchen

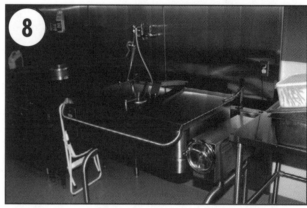

1. Snuffin's new kitchen and sales office is 3800 sq feet of the second floor. **2.** Care was taken so trucks could be loaded with the least amount of walking and effort. **3.** Here's a blueprint that will help put space in perspective. **4.** Sales offices have a simple modern modular design with each work station having it's own computer. **5.** This is the view from the Presidents office. She can easily see what is going on in the kitchen and the sales offices. **6.** Four convection ovens, some old and some new, along with a kitchen range make up the main cooking line. **7.** A view looking back to the left of picture #7 above. This is the baking area. **8.** To cap off the cooking line they've installed a tilting skillet.

Building a New Kitchen

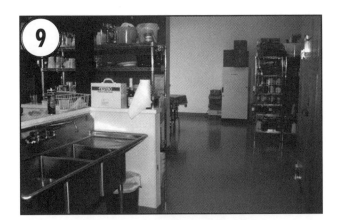

9. They knew they wanted space for storage and future growth so they built it into the plan. **10.** Storage of equipment and other stuff has become much easier to manage. **11.** One of the real treats in the kitchen is the undercounter refrigerator near the baking area. In this way the chef doesn't need to make the long walk to get some eggs, milk, etc. **12.** A little trick that they picked up along the way was to send some electric outlets down from the ceiling. In this manner the floors are kept clear of cords and it is easier to get power. **13.** The freezer is 8 x 8, one walk-in cooler is 8 x 10 while the other is 8 x 16. Each of the coolers were built with extra height to store as much as possible. **14.** The larger walk-in is designated the "finished" cooler. Only foods that are ready to travel are placed into this cooler. This cooler has two doors in it... one on each end. The photo is being taken while standing in one of the doorways. **15.** Using this method food can be kept in walk-ins and rolled directly to the vans for loading. This concept creates a circular motion of food coming in and going out. **16.** Here's the shopping list of what equipment Snuffin's bought. It's a great kitchen... one that any caterer would be proud to have!

Building a New Kitchen

16 Equipment List For Snuffin's New Kitchen

Hood (used)	$12,000
2 Coolers & 1 freezer	$18,000
1 Convection Oven	$4,000
Tilting Skillet	$7,800
Heating & Air	$3,300
Dishwasher (used)	$3,000
Washer/Dryer	$1,100
Shelves, tables, etc.	$15,000
Phone System	$4,000
Office Equipment & Computers	$8,300
Office Furniture	$9,000
Misc. Stuff	$5,000

Total: $90,500

Kitchen Food Safety Tips

The following Kitchen Food Safety Procedures were sent to us by Great Performances (New York, NY). This should give you a foundation for creating the same for your own business. You may wish to show this to your health inspector for review to make sure that the rules and codes are similar to New York City.

I. These rules apply to all employees working in the food prep areas.

1. Employees must wash hands — After using the restroom — Before Beginning work — When changing from one prep task to another — After eating or smoking — After sneezing or coughing— Towel cabinets and soap dispensers must be kept full at all times.

2. Gloves must be worn when handling food which is in its final stages of preparation. Gloves may be worn when handling uncooked food, though this is not required.

3. Employees must wear head covering and /or hair restraints at all times when handling food.

4. Employees who are ill or who have an open wound may not handle food. If you have a wound on your hand which is bandaged, you must wear a glove on the wounded hand at all times.

II. These rules pertain to preparation and cooking procedures.

1. All food prep utensils must be cleaned and sanitized in the dish machine.

2. Do NOT ever use a cutting board which has been used and is dirty, without sending it to the dish area to be cleaned and sanitized.

3. Pay attention to your work space - do not ever set up where there is any possibility of cross contamination. As an example, do not ever cut raw vegetables next to someone who is cutting raw chicken.

4. All machines must be cleaned daily if they are being used - this means they must be taken apart, cleaned with hot soap and water, and the removable parts sent to the dishwasher. Merely wiping the machines down with a towel is not adequate . If you notice any part of a food prep machine which is scored or damaged, please do not use - bring to the attention of the people in charge so it can be discarded or replaced.

5. Practice clean-as-you-go habits. Clean up your area from one task before you move one to the next.

6. When preparing hot food, use an instant read thermometer to determine if the temperature is correct. Be extremely familiar with the hazardous temperature zone - above 44° (or 40° to be very safe) and below 140° degrees F. Remember that ground meats are particularly hazardous - much more than solid muscle meats - so particular care must be taken with these.

7. Once a hot food item is finished, it should be put in the cooler as quickly as possible. This is particularly true of high protein items.

8. When reheating a finished item, it is very important that you reach a high enough temperature to kill all possible bacteria - 165°F is the temperature point to reach for the greatest degree of safety.

9. Do not ever mix older food items with newer food items in the same batch.

10. When in doubt throw it out!

Kitchen Food Safety Tips

III. These items relate to the storage of food in the dry areas, coolers, or freezer.

    1. Nothing should ever be kept directly on the floor of any storage area.

    2. When items are put away they must be rotated and dated and if they are not stored in their original container they must be labeled.

    3. Because of the hazards of cross contamination, it is extremely important that we pay attention to how things are kept in the cooler.

        A. Because of seepage or dripping, no raw item of a hazardous nature should ever be stored above or next to a finished item.

        B. All items must be covered while they are being stored.

        C. All staff should pay attention to the thermometers in the various coolers to make sure they are staying well within the safe zone of 44° F or below.

        D. Special care must be paid to highly hazardous items such as ice pack chicken. These items should always be transferred to lugs or other containers which do not leak.

    4. The walk-in cooler and freezer doors must be kept closed at all times except when being used. Any food which is being packed out for a party should be kept in the cooler until it is ready to go on the truck. All perishable foods should be transported in coolers or thermalized containers whenever possible. These policies apply at all times.

    5. Food from metal cans, or from broken cases is not acceptable for use. Any vendor delivery which looks substandard should be refused! Spoiled food should be disposed of as quickly as possible.

    6. In the dry storage area, it is very important that food items are kept completely separate from cleaning supplies, which should also be kept away from any toxins.

We are all individually and collectively responsible for food safety. All of our jobs depend on it.

More Kitchen Tips and Tactics

Another aspect of the kitchen's well-being is it's relationship with the sales staff. As most are aware, sales staff and kitchen staff don't always see eye to eye! Here are some views in favor of the kitchen staff:

1. The kitchen should provide guidelines of when to sell certain food items that offer purchasing value.

2. The kitchen should be able to request reporting from field staff about amounts of leftover items.

3. The kitchen should always be involved in approving unusual menu items... before they are sold.

4. The kitchen should have meetings with the sales staff to answer questions about a pending event.

5. The kitchen should be able to request that the sales staff also research recipes for new menu items.

6. The kitchen needs to be involved with setting prices.

7. The kitchen should be able to make a site inspection for all mega events before they prepare menus.

The Tilting Skillet... A Caterers Dream!

The tilting skillet is one piece of equipment that many caterers swear by! It's versatility stems from its ability to quickly handle a multitude of cooking tasks... all in rapid succession.

Subscriber, Michael Miraglia of Miraglia Catering and Event Planning (San Leandro, CA) sent us his list of uses for his tilting skillet.

- vegetable saute
- steam mussels
- blanch beef
- braise beef or veal
- deep fry chicken
- poach salmon
- cook pasta
- pan fry breakfast potatoes
- cook scrambled eggs
- prepare fried rice
- make stocks
- make all gravies
- prepare risotto
- cook potatoes for potato salad
- prepare soups and chili
- sear beef tenderloin
- and... just about anything else!

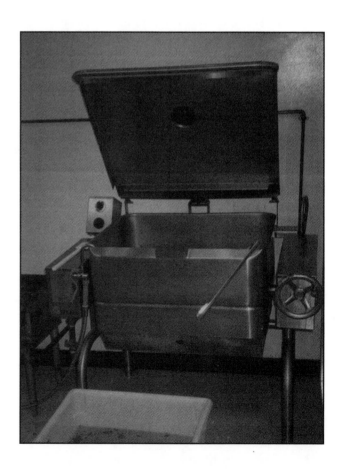

CHAPTER 4  QUESTIONS

1. When running a kitchen, what is the role of checklists?

2. What is meant by "In this kitchen we use, or sell, everything we buy!"?

3. What are some of the ways to control and lead a kitchen staff?

4. Should kitchen staff be involved in setting prices for catering?

5. What are the main points in an Executive Chef job description?

6. What are some of the more useful pieces of equipment in a catering kitchen?

7. What would be your dream mobile kitchen?

8. What are the best concepts in building a new catering kitchen or commissary?

9. What are the concerns for sanitation in a professional kitchen?

10. What is the role of an Executive Chef in a catering kitchen?

SALES

CHAPTER

5

S·A·L·E·S

TABLE OF CONTENTS

CHAPTER

5

"A catering company can't stay in business unless someone sells something!"

Unwise Sales... How to Decide?

What is an unwise sale? How can any sale be unwise? Sometimes it's important to keep my staff working? We're here anyway... so why not take the smaller orders?

No sale is unwise if you want to take it. After all it is your business and you have the right to do with it what you want. The question is why you're taking a particular order. So, once again we ask the question...What is an unwise sale?

An unwise sale is one that causes you loss of profit or lessens the quality of your life. An interesting answer... don't you think?

How can a sale lose profit? Simple... it is either not priced correctly, or it is too small. This is the first point that needs to be addressed on this subject. An unwise sale is created when the price is incorrect and/or the number of guests is too few.

To put this another way, the problem rests with the price being too low and the number of guests also being too few. A $7.00 box lunch for 9 guests is probably an unwise sale. However, the same $7.00 box lunch for 40 guests is a better sale.

On the other hand, a $1.22 per person charge for a day care meal for 100 is probably unwise even if it is a seven day a week order. However, a $1.22 for 800 per day is a great sale.

A caterer's quality of life is also affected by the unwise sale. Imagine coming in on a Sunday for an order that generated only $63. You need to understand that we're taking a "catering" view in this education. Other forms of foodservice, like restaurants, might find it well to take any order that comes along. Catering, however, is different.

Many have learned that a great day can become a bad day simply by taking that one order that turns out to be the "order from hell"! So, it is important to have some kind of policy as to which are unwise orders.

Another reason a sale becomes unwise deals with the product line mix on a particular day. When a caterer has three weddings leaving their kitchen on a busy Saturday, it is unwise to also have a drop-off cold buffet for 25 on the same day.

The Saturday cold buffet, on a busy full-service day, will create real, or false, problems for the culinary and delivery staff. When all attention should be focused on the importance of high volume orders, the kitchen staff is taking the all consuming time to create the smaller cold buffet. By the way, the host that gets the drop off cold buffet will probably call you to tell you to bring over some additional mustard because they don't think they have enough!

For those caterers who still say "An order is an order" or "A sale is a sale" or "A dollar is a dollar" we can only say... that is not necessarily true.

Some sales cost the caterer more than others. Say, for example, that you have an absolutely packed day and you take one more order. Chances are that this last order you took will create some additional costs for your company that you hadn't thought about.

These costs would include overtime, extra personnel, the rental of an extra delivery truck, and so on. Each of these costs seems innocent. Unless you ask the person who placed the last order to help pay for these extra costs created by taking their order, the only way you can cover these costs is by taking some of the profit away from the other sales for that day!

"I'm sorry, but we've closed off that date because we've got a full-day. If you would like to place an order for that day, we would need to add an additional charge to cover the additional costs that your order would create for our kitchen. Or, perhaps you can arrange for your catering on a different day?"

While this may seem like a "fantasy" script to many reading this, we can assure you that many caterers have realized that it's crazy to take certain orders under certain circumstances.

So, we can now ask another question. With respect to your business, are you a "dog wagging its own tail" or a "dog that's being wagged by its tail?" The answer is a crucial one for all caterers. As one caterer told us recently "If I'm making a clear profit... I book it. If I'm not going to make money with it... I tell them unfortunately I'm totally booked on that day."

Have we confused you? Great! That's what education is supposed to do... make you think and re-think your ideas. Remember, complacency is a danger for any business and doing things "just because that's the way we've been doing it" is also foolish, especially if you don't stop once in a while to rethink the validity of your actions.

Many caterers have more unwise sales than they think. While it's very hard not to take a particular order, often it's the best, and wisest, course of action if quality profit and less hassle are your goals.

What Buyers Expect From Caterers

As each selling situation becomes more competitive for caterers, the selling element of customer expectations with respect to the salesperson becomes more crucial.

Buyers of catering expect the sales representatives from catering companies to be able to recommend solutions that are both cost effective and that provide the buyer with the level of impact and results that are desired.

Customers are looking for value from caterers, and the person that is expected to present this value is the catering salesperson. In addition, many buyers expect the caterer to give them an advantage over their previous caterers.

Of equal importance, buyers are expecting the salesperson to be at the same level of knowledge and sophistication as they are. On the one hand, this means that a sixty year old corporate president, who's traveled the world, probably is expecting a salesperson that comes close to his experiences.

This may seem unfair, but it is the basic rule of selling expensive products. Catering is an expensive product. So, as you build your team of professionals, it might be best to have sales talents with varying degrees of experiences, as well as ages.

To meet your buyer's expectations of what they perceive a salesperson to be, you should keep these three areas of knowledge in the forefront of your thinking:

1. Total knowledge of your buyer's own industry and company.

If your buyer, who is planning a holiday party, is part of the insurance industry, then, you need to better understand the joys and sorrows of selling insurance.

It's really quite simple to do. You can talk with your own insurance agent and tell him, or her, that you need to gather some instinct information about a client that you're going to see. Or, you could go to the library and look into the Reader's Guide to Periodical Literature under insurance. You will find lots of articles on the state of the insurance industry.

While this may seem excessive to some, it is certainly wise if you're going to bid on an important event.

2. Total understanding about your catering companies full range of abilities.

When you understand what your company really sells, you will be able to better sell your buyers because they wish you to really make them aware of what you can, and can't, offer them. They simply don't have time to learn your business

from you. They are expecting to hear from you what they should probably do for their catering.

This is where a buyer gains confidence in the enthusiasm and knowledge of the salesperson before them. Also, the buyer is expecting the catering salesperson to understand, and be able to talk about, the various competitors who the buyer is also talking with.

Buyers don't wish to buy from a salesperson who only knows about their own catering!

3. Total awareness of entertaining etiquette and protocol

A buyer expects the salesperson to keep them from embarrassment in front of their guests. If they sense that the salesperson is unsure of the engineering of an event , they will give the order to a different caterer.

This means that you need to continually provide them with ideas and words that demonstrate your knowledge of the flow of events.

The buyer wishes to view their salesperson as a resource of information and skills. They will give the order to those who are best able to project this important feeling!

Additionally, buyers are expecting trust, rapport and respect, on a mutual basis, from the caterers sales representatives.

More than ever, the buyer wishes to get to the sale quicker, so they don't expect a long relationship before getting to the decisions of "buy" or "no buy". In other words customers wish to buy more today, but shop less in the process.

TEN ELEMENTS OF SELLING SUCCESS

1. Be a giver... not a taker!
2. Be able to laugh at yourself.
3. Make buyers feel comfortable.
4. Continually search for new business.
5. Remain positive and optimistic.
6. Have total confidence in yourself.
7. Always stay on the buyer's side.
8. Practice your presentation skills.
9. Develop mentors to learn from.
10. Be a team player.

What Buyers Want From the Salesperson

Each buyer of catering is certainly looking for food, beverage and entertaining ideas from their catering salesperson. In addition, they are listening for other information that deals with non-food elements of the buy-sell process.

In other words, the buyer buys you first. Also, most buyers usually buy catering from the salesperson who gives them the idea that they (salesperson) knows what's really on their (buyers) minds. This is really as important to them as a great menu is!

Here's some of the non-food concepts that need to be provided to the buyer:

1. That you're truthful. This is not as easy to do as you might think. The most important thing to remember is to look your buyer in the eye when you're responding to their questions. Don't be afraid to say "I'm not sure." Also, you'll find that a small vocal pause before you answer a question often gives the buyer the correct feeling that you are not just reeling off a script. Again, the eyes are probably the most crucial here.

2. That you'll listen. One of the best concepts here, is to say to a client just after they make an important statement "Mr. Smith, I wish to make sure that I really understand what you're saying, so, please take a moment and restate your point so I will be sure I understand."

3. That you'll take them seriously. One method that works, especially for on-premise caterers, is to take time to introduce your buyers to other people in your organization. While doing this you mention "I've promised the Smiths that ABC will work very hard to insure that we meet all their expectations."

4. That They'll be part of the process. Take the direct route on this one. "Mrs. Smith, it's important to me that my clients help me make their events the best they can be, by making me aware of what they really wish to do and then providing me with constant feedback as we move towards creating a great party."

5. That they'll get a fair price. The easiest way to demonstrate to the buyer that you're being fair when it comes to printing is to give them "odd-ball" pricing. Instead of rounding your prices to an even plateau i.e $12.00, $11.95, etc., use price points like $12.17 and $11.86. Many of your buyers will perceive that you really took time to calculate the correct and fair price.

Here's some of the emotional concepts that the buyer will need to experience before they buy:

1. Get the recognition they deserve. Call it stroking the buyer. Everyone loves to know that they are great, or better than the average person. With this in mind, mention "Mr. Jones, I speak to a lot of customers each week, but you are really one of the most aware people I've met with respect to menu design."

2. Be made to feel important. Once again, it is important to let the buyer know that they are special. Feeling important is a nice feeling. Try some simple phrases like "I like the way you think..." or, "I've never thought of it that way before, I'll suggest that to my future client."

3. To feel free of risk. Risk is very scary for anyone. It's important for you, and your company, to decide in what ways you might be able to relax the buyers fears. All buyers wish to be free from feeling that they made a poor choice. Some businesses provide clients with a refund of deposit for 60 days, while others offer a 100% refund if not satisfied with the catering. While these may seem drastic, they are examples of how to take the risk out of the sale.

4. To have someone else to blame. A tricky, but valid, goal to achieve when selling corporate catering. One of the more intriguing methods of doing this is to secure the name of your contact's boss, and then write them a letter praising the "cooperation" you received while working with (your contact) and that you have assured (your contact) that the event will be a huge success. This action on your part will enhance your success in selling larger events.

5. To have some fun. Why not? This could be as simple as you telling a fun story about catering. Be careful of political jokes etc. Food is also fun, so let them taste some foods while you sell them. Deliver some foods when you send your proposal. Get them to talk about funny things that have happened to them.

6. To work less at this task. When you determine that your buyer does not want to spend a lot of time in creating the event, let them know that you are prepared to do the whole thing for them. "I want you to know that many of my clients like to get involved with the work that goes into creating this type of event, while others want me to do all the work... which do you want?"

Twenty-Three Ways to Sell Better

Selling catering is a constant battle to keep inventing something new to try. While a salesperson should never stop doing those things that have worked in the past, they need to continually look to enhance their understanding of what they do.

What follows is a random listing of ideas, tips, and tactics that might help you sell better:

1. Don't procrastinate. What can we say... don't put off what can be done today. Also, be sure to take quick action when it comes to important moments in the sale. Get the proposals out on time and gather the information that the buyer requested quickly.

2. Listen. Tough to do. Let the ear of your ears take part in the selling situation. Don't be afraid to ask the buyer to go over their point one more time because you want to make sure you heard them correctly. All buyers want to be heard!

3. Become an expert. Don't be a know-it-all. Just be a person who beams credibility and an overall understanding of catering. Remember: Experts really don't know all the answers, they just know where to find them!

4. Ask more questions. Its no secret. Questions leads to sales. The person who asks the questions stays in control of the situation. There are three types of questions. Refer to Back Issue 13. Questions will help you understand more about what your buyer is all about.

5. Celebrate your victories. Winning is wonderful. Enjoy your wins. Reward yourself. If a team of salespeople worked on the sale, then the team should celebrate!

6. Work for referrals. Finding new cold customers is not as good as finding warm ones that have been to one of your events or who have a friend who can't stop talking about how great a caterer you are. Referrals are the foundation of any great salesperson. Without referrals one can not reach their full potential!

7. Stay focused. Selling is a profession. It takes total commitment and concentration towards its goals of bringing a buyer and a product together. You need to stay focused on your goals at all times.

8. Qualify your customers. Too many salespeople waste their time by speaking with shoppers who really can't buy from them today ... or anytime. Be sure that the person you are speaking with has the authority to purchase today. Be sure that they have the financial ability to purchase from you today. If you don't qualify them then you often will be wasting your time. Refer to Back Issues #4.

9. Think like a buyer. If you wish to sell more catering, you need to decide what buyers are thinking when they sit in front of you. Remember, most catering salespeople are selling services that they have never bought themselves. This leads to a false selling situation. After all, could a non-pilot sell jets to pilots?

10. Follow through. Say what you do and do what you say. If you make a promise, you need to keep it. If you set a date to have something ready, you need to have it done. You already know this, but you also know how hard it is to do... especially during your busier times of the year.

11. Get up earlier. If you've never tried it, early morning hours are some of the best opportunities for getting your work done. Get to work at 5:00 am and you will be amazed at what you get done with no phones ringing or other distractions, to keep you from creating

12. Analyze your competition. Do you know your competition? Have you watched them in action? Have you tasted their foods? Do any of your present customers have experience with them? You need to know as much about your competition as you can. You shouldn't be obsessed by them, you should just know what their strengths and possible weaknesses might be!

13. Touch your clients. Handshakes, pats on the back are examples of physical actions you can take. But you can also send a gift, letter, or make a phone call to touch them. The thought that you just speak with them once or twice during the year when they are placing orders makes you an order taker... not a salesperson!

14. Learn about the internet. Yes, its scary at first. Take a class, read some magazines, look at some of the computer programs on t.v. You need to take some steps towards getting involved, or it will leave you in the dust. This is a tool that we will all be using in the next three years. Give us a call at CaterSource and we'll help you get involved.

Twenty-Three Ways to Sell Better

15. Value your time. Think about it for a minute. How much real time does a salesperson have on a given day for selling? Remember, the salesperson also needs to do paperwork, talk with the chef, etc. We figure that a salesperson has approximately four hours a day that can really be used to sell someone their catering. That's 240 minutes... not very much time... so, use it wisely.

16. Encourage change. Be a leader in your company when it comes to doing new and exciting things. Preach for change. Don't throw away all that you've learned, but seek new ways to do old things. This will not make you very popular with the rest of the staff, but change is what we all need to do better!

17. Know your batting average. How many sales did you make last month? How many buyers did you speak with? What is your closing percentage? How many home runs did you hit? You get the point. All salespeople need something to measure themselves by and goals to reach. Some even want records to break!

18. Sell yourself. A buyer shopping for catering is just as interested in the person who they will be working with as in the chef or the menus. It is important to take time to sell the buyer on you! This is done with scripts and providing them with a clear understanding of what you believe in. Remember, clients are looking for someone they can count on; someone who will keep them free from embarrassment.

19. Have more fun. Selling catering is a tough business. Salespeople work hard and long. It is wise to have some fun along the way. Look for the humor in our business wherever you can find it. Don't be afraid to loosen up with yourself, your peers and your clients. Everyone enjoys a little fun.

20. Do your homework. Before each selling situation take time to think about what you might encounter in this particular selling situation. Also, for major bids take time to research the company that you are making the bid with. Check the trade journals to see what others think of them. Your party rental dealer knows a lot of gossip about some clients from what other caterers have shared.

21. Expand your range. As a salesperson you have a chain of contacts that have helped you grow your business. Now its time to expand your areas of contact by joining other professional organizations, going to community meetings and luncheons (that you don't cater), and making new personal friends. A salesperson is like a fishhook, the more it is in the water the more fish will be caught!

22. Don't be afraid of mistakes. This doesn't mean that you can goof when ever you wish. It means that mistakes do happen in our type of business. We have problems with communication, customers keep changing their minds, staff has different levels of skills etc. It is important to keep mistakes at a minimum, but when you make them consider them learning opportunities for everyone.

23. Don't forget the basics. Successful catering salespeople take the basic principles of selling and advance them. These "advance basics" become the foundation for their success. Success starts with believing in the basics.

16 Ways to Increase Your Selling

1. Always say..."Thank you for calling"... or, "Thank you for coming in"... or "Thank you for seeing me".

2. Send thank you notes before you see the buyer.

3. Talk about why you "choose" to work for ABC Catering.

4. Never use the phrase... "They're in a meeting".

5. Never walk past anyone without introducing them and explaining what they do for the company.

6. Never ask a client..."What is your budget?"

7. Offer, or bring something to taste each and every time you meet with a prospective customer.

8. Live by the motto... "It's easier to resell happy existing customers than it is to keep finding new ones!"

9. When selling an event through a proposal format, always involve the five senses of the buyer.

10. Make the buyer understand that you're more concerned with their event's success than you are in making a sale.

11. Always offer three options... the Cadillac, Buick and Chevy.

12. Find excuses to see your new, and past clients, in person.

13. Stay in control by asking questions.

14. Explain to the client when they are making a mistake.

15. During a closing situation, it's best to give the buyers some time alone.

16. Never apologize for what appears to be higher prices... just explain what they do for the buyer.

Script for Qualifying the Shopper

CATERER: ABC Catering, may we help you?

CALLER: *I wish to get some information about giving a party?*

CATERER: **Thank you for calling.** My name is Bob Jones... If I may ask you a few questions I will be able to serve you better or place you with the right person. **Please tell me...** what is the date you were looking to reserve for your catering?

CALLER: *June 25th*

CATERER: For approximately how many guests?

CALLER: *About 125 guests*

CATERER: And...what type of event will it be?

CALLER: *A wedding.*

CATERER: **Thank you.** Please allow me to check our reservation book to make sure that June 25 is still available for your wedding of 125 guests.

CATERER: Thank you for waiting...Yes, June 25 is still available. May I please have your name?

CATERER: Mr. Smith, from what you've told me so far I'm convinced that you should be speaking with Mary Stevens our Sales Manager. Mary specializes in weddings. I'll get her for you right away. (or, Mary is with another client at the moment...May I have her call you later in the day?)
Mary must not break the mood of professionalism...so when she begins with the client she welcomes him and asks a question. She should never ask for the same information that the caller gave to Bob.

MARY: Hello Mr. Smith, Bob tells me that you are planning a wedding for 125 guests on June 25th... **Have you ever been to one of our catered events?**
(Mr. Smith can answer three ways: Yes, no or I'm not sure? But Mary is still controlling the time clock!)

MARY: Well...let me tell you a little about our company... or Well...I guess you already know...

THE **BIG** QUESTIONS

1. **What will it cost me?**

2. **Is the price a fair one?**

3. **Will they let me participate in the planning?**

4. **Will they run out of food?**

5. **How much extra food do they send?**

6. **Will they ask me difficult questions?**

7. **What does their staff look like?**

8. **Will they embarrass me?**

9. **Is the food good?**

10. **Will they show-up on time?**

11. **Is their kitchen clean?**

12. **Has anyone gotten ill eating their food?**

13. **Will they still be in business on party day?**

14. **Who else has bought from them?**

15. **What are the things that might go wrong?**

16. **How will our place look after they leave?**

Evaluating Yourself as a Salesperson

Every salesperson needs to take inventory of their skills, energies, tactics, etc. from time to time. Think of yourself as a "mental athlete" who needs to measure themselves from time to time.

The job of selling catering is a very lonely job. When one sells catering it's just them and the buyers. Because of this, catering salespeople often go for a long time without coaching or serious critique.

This simple list of questions below will give you a simple starting point to help you coach and critique yourself. If you take the information below in a positive manner amazing growth may take place.

What every salesperson should be asking themselves

1. Am I getting the sales volume I should?

This question assumes that you have been keeping a record of your sales results and that you have a firm belief of how much you can or should be selling for yourself and the company. When you make your sales target don't go too high ... but don't wimp out either!

2. How many sales does my company expect of me for this year?

Does your company give you a sales quota to make? If not you can use the 10% rule as a guide. Whatever you are being paid, it should be at least not over 10% of what you sell. So, if you are paid (with benefits) $25,000 per year, you should be selling at least $250,000 in sales.

3. Do I have a consistent and proven sales script for qualifying the caller?

In order to achieve the best evaluation for yourself, you need to really think about this one. A quality salesperson always uses a script for getting through the process of deciding if these potential buyers are ready to be worked with. This script always includes three questions.... what is your event date... how many guests... and what type of event is it? This is followed by some attempt to decide if the buyer has the money necessary to purchase your catering.

4. Do I always talk to the right person when selling catering?

Two concerns with this one. First, am I wasting time because this buying unit is incomplete... a parent is missing etc. Second, while giving the sales presentation, am I favoring one of the buyers over the others?

5. Do I spend too much time with clients who really can't buy?

CaterSource believes that during an average day, a catering salesperson has about 72 "real" minutes to spend with a real buyer. Why waste these valuable minutes on a person who can't buy today.

6. Do I spend at least two days a week out of the office prospecting for customers?

Only about 25% of all catering salespeople cold call. This is sad because so much can be won by going out and touching potential buyers... especially corporate ones.

7. Have I set my three-year income goal?

If you are normal, you haven't any goals for next year let alone three years out. If you are a winner, you have a five year master plan!

8. Have I read at least three books on selling in the last 24 months?

Any major book store has hundreds of books on all aspects of selling. If your company doesn't already have a "selling library" for you to utilize demand that they do at once! Then go back to school and teach yourself something!

9. Have I spent time analyzing my competitors?

If you wish to be a winner in the war, you need to be a student of what, and how, the competitors sell!

10. Am I aware of my closing average?

Do you close two out of ten or eight out of ten? You need to know. This is your batting average and is one of the most crucial elements to your evaluation.

11. Have I spent time during the last 30 days talking to the chef about the foods I sell?

Your culinary department and chef are most crucial in your growth as a better seller of catering. They can be your best allies or worst enemies. The choice is yours.

12. Am I having some fun when I sell?

Well... are you? Is it just a job? Can you understand the humor of what we do? Are you thrilled with joy when you make a sale?

Checklist for Professional Salespeople

You really can't be sure of what characteristics determine who will be the better salesperson. Nothing takes the place of talent, timing and luck when it comes to making sales.

However, here is our list of some of the elements that seem to be possessed and practiced by many of the better catering salespersons:

A. Speaks clearly and precisely at all times, particularly during a selling interview.

B. Answers typical buyer objections before they arise.

C. Plans sales calls in advance... and really makes a plan for each day!

D. Decides ahead of time what they are going to sell to the buyer.

E. Asks good, probing questions.

F. Is always honest in their approach to selling.

G. Uses sales aids while selling. Involves all of the buyers senses i.e. smell, hearing, seeing, touching and tasting.

H. Sells the concept of "not embarrassing" the buyer in front of others.

I. Takes the risk out of buying when possible.

J. Uses time properly. Isn't afraid to stop a selling situation to move on to someone else.

K. Listens to the meaning of what the buyer is saying... not just the words.

L. Acts professional at all times.

M. Never apologizes for price... only explains what the price does.

N. Understands why the sale was missed.

O. Is in constant search of competitor data.

P. In theory, is ready to sell twenty-four hours a day!

Q. Isn't afraid of making mistakes.

R. Is always honest and user friendly to the buyer and those influencing the purchase.

Great salespeople know that when they are selling a product or service they need to try to unveil what the buyers real "hot buttons" are.

These "hot buttons" ar not necessarily logical or even part of the reason for the event. They usually deal with deep psychological reasons that are in the buyers mind and nervous systems.

Here are some examples of these "hot buttons":

1. **Achievement** - having an event will demonstrate to others what they've been able to accomplish.

2. **Independence** - a recently divorced person may give a party to establish their new status to peers.

3. **Exhibition** - this is the "be better than the last party" syndrome.

4. **Recognition** - a parent giving a graduation party or a Bar Mitzvah.

5. **Dominance** - a particular buyer may need to be in total control of the situation.

6. **Affiliation** - this is branding. A buyer wants your name on their event which puts them in the same league as peers.

7. **Charity** - this buyer would wish to give the leftovers to the needy.

8. **Self-fulfillment** - buyer may wish to be told how "forward thinking" they are to give this particular event.

9. **Sexuality** - this buyer would be concerned for the romance of the event and the look of the staff.

10. **Stimulation** - buyer wants to engage the salesperson on a combative, but friendly, basis.

11. **Education** - buyer has the "Martha Stewart Complex" and wishes to learn all that they can.

Buyers do come to the sale with specific prejudices, needs, and concerns. During your next selling opportunity, make an attempt to put a few labels from above on your buyer. It won't always make you a winner, but it will keep you thinking!

How to Be a Winner at Selling

We're not trying to be pretentious, but it's good to get refocused from time to time. Here's some reminders of what it takes to be a winner in selling catering in a competitive marketplace.

1. Be enthusiastic at all times.
Is this too obvious? Well, so what! Selling is a twenty-four hour a day job. You never know when, or where, a sale will be coming. You need to be "UP" twenty-four hours a day.

Enthusiasm is contagious. If you offer it to your buyers, you will get them doing it also. Enthusiasm is not just being positive, it also is beaming confidence in your food, team and company.

2. Never make excuses.
Don't use these for excuses: "Our prices are too high." "It's the slow season." "The chef doesn't really care about us". "This is the third time this caller has come to us for a bid and I know she won't take us."

Excuses are serious and create losers. To be a winner, you need to keep your mind clear of any negative thoughts. Yes, this is hard to do... but, it needs to be done if you wish to sell more catering.

3. Put the buyer first.
Buyers can sense it. They know when a salesperson is in it for only the commissions. They also know when a caterer is concerned for the successful outcome of the event they are planning. Putting the buyer first will always win more sales.

Demonstrate to your buyer that the information you give will help them do a better party no matter who caterers it. Let them realize that they have finally met a salesperson who cares more for them then they do for themselves. Remember, you are selling yourself to the buyer as well as your catering. In fact, you are going to become involved in their personal, or corporate, goals, so, it is great if they sense that your motives are based solely on their goals and happiness.

Imagine saying this to a buyer after they said they wish to think about it for a while:

"Mr. & Mrs, Jones, if after you think about it for a while, and you decide to use another caterer than us, don't hesitate to call us for an opinion on what the other caterer is offering. Also, if you like one of our menu items, and the other caterer doesn't have the recipe, please have them call me and I'll gladly give it to them. I just want your party to be the best it can be!"

4. Take the blame.
Leaders take the blame when things don't go as they should. In the real world of catering, things don't always go as planned or promised. Therefore, it becomes crucial to understand the importance of letting your buyers understand that you are mature and confident and can take blame when necessary.

5. Standout in the crowd.
Be the opposite of everyone around you! Be more, or less to achieve a position of uniqueness. We don't mean to be "strange". We are suggesting that the way you dress, walk, speak, act, etc, adds to your ability to sell more.

With the exception of a "conservative" buyer, most want a salesperson who will help them standout in front of their invited guests. So, being unpredictable and different is often a valid strategy for selling more catering.

6. Take some risks.
Yes, it's dangerous to take risks. Risks can turn out bad for the salesperson. Still, risks usually make you first and a leader.

The concept of getting out on the ledge is often misunderstood by a salesperson. We suggest that you take simple, or little risks, that will lead to better sales. Don't take risks that will hurt you or your company.

7. Don't run the company.
Stop worrying about who's doing what to, or for, whom at your company. Run from gossip. Let the owners and managers be owners and managers. Don't lessen you energies by participating in second guessing what you can't control.

8. Keep learning.
This is important. How many books, audio tapes, magazines, etc. do you have around you right now that deals with selling? A salesperson can't become the best only from practicing with, or selling, real buyers.

In order to attain greatness as a salesperson, you need to read about what other salespeople have done to get better. There is an amazing body of "selling knowledge" in the stores. Purchase what materials you can, borrow from your peers, and spend some time in the library. Learning is the cornerstone to success!

Handling an Unhappy Client

The list below was sent to us by subscriber James Barrack of The Cater Inn (Peoria, IL), a frequent contributor to the Journal. It might be the basis for a great training session.

1. Talk to the guest away from the other guests. This is especially imperative when the complaint is serious.

2. Let the guest know you are sincerely interested in his complaint. Always be friendly. In some situations, thank the customer for telling you the problem.

3. Listen to the problem/complaint. Never interrupt or argue with what they are saying - maintain eye contact and remain clam. Always ask the guest for all the details.

4. Speak clearly and calmly, so the guest can understand you.

5. Apologize and solve the problem yourself immediately whenever possible. Tell the customer that you will take care of the problem immediately. When time permits, notify your supervisor. If you cannot solve the problem, notify your supervisor or manager, A.S.A.P.

6. If the solution is not satisfactory to the customer, let them know that you will inform management A.S.A.P. of the problem.

7. Document the problem on the contract or moment sheets. Provide the guest's name and the telephone number so management can contact the guest.

8. Proper handling of a complaint could turn an irritated customer into a satisfied one!

Objections... They are Needed for Success

Objections are required to make a sale! In fact, the caterer should encourage them and be suspicious when a buyer is not stating any objections! They are the foundation of most sales.

Here's some tips on the whole process of handling objections:

1. Make sure that both you, and your buyer, really understand what the objection is.

A. "Mr. Smith, I'm not sure that I understand what you mean... are you saying that..."

B. "Mr. Smith, please repeat your last comment, I apologize, I don't think I heard you correctly."

2. Provide a safety net for your buyer to raise or state the objection.

A. "Jim, is there anything you need clarification on?"

B. "Fred, do you disagree with anything I've talked about?"

C. "Ms. Jones, it would help me greatly if you made me aware of any concerns you have about the information that I'm presenting today?"

3. The salesperson needs to decide if the objection is really valid or just the result of a nervous buyer who realizes that they are getting close to buying your catering.

A. "Mr. Smith, does your concern really have great weight over whether you purchase our catering, or is it something we can fix after we reserve the date for the wedding?"

B. "Yes, that is a valid concern... but I really don't think that will happen... do you?"

C. "Let me share with you what one of my clients did to insure that..."

4. Try to overcome the objection before it arises.

A. "Mary, let me take a few minutes to share with you why I decided, after interviewing with most of the other caterers in town, to work for ABC Catering. In this way you will understand why ABC is the top company in town."

5. Most objections assure you of a sale... or, it's very difficult to make a sale without objections. Use them to move to the close.

A. "Jim, if that answers your concern... which color linen do you wish for the event... the yellow or the light blue?"

B. "Now that we've agreed on how to solve your concern, which menu do you wish to go with for the event... the veal or the salmon?"

6. Always listen to the meaning of the words the buyer uses not just to the words themselves!

A. "It seems to me, Mary, that what you're really saying is"

7. Rush towards objections... accept them as your challenge!

A. "Mr. Tompkins, I like the way you put that... what I'd like to do is explain how we'll eliminate your concern and then I'd like to hear about any other concerns you might have."

8. Remember the 5 Cs of Catering: Clarify, Confirm, Convince, Confirm, Close.

9. Professional salespeople always get back to the sale and close after the objection is overcome or neutralized!

Using the Guarantee to Get the Sale

The guarantee, in catering, is the number of guests that the buyer will pay for, whether all these guests actually come to the event or not.

In other words, if a client tells us that they are having 225 guests to a wedding and only 200 show up, they are still obligated to pay the caterer for the full 225 they originally ordered for.

From the caterers point of view, the guarantee is extremely important. It is the basis of how much food, equipment and staff we bring. It is the "rule of order" that is required for catering to be a professional business.

Now that we all agree on the importance of the guarantee to the caterer, let's look at the guarantee from the buyers point of view.

It's scary. Think about it for a moment. A buyer is told by the caterer that even though they are spending $10,000 for a wedding, if Uncle Charlie can't make it at the last minute due to his health, they are still being penalized by the caterer for the cost of his empty chair. This is how many buyers of catering hear our tough and unkind "rule" concerning the guarantee.

Our point is not whether this "rule" is a good one or not. Our point is that the guarantee becomes an excellent place to offer a buyer advantages over your competition.

"Mr. & Mrs. Smith, please let me explain how our company handles the guest guarantee for the wedding. As you both know, most caterers require that the host and hostess provide them with a final number of guests so the caterer will know what to prepare and charge for, whether all of these guests come or not.

At our company, we realize that when inviting several hundred guests to a wedding, even after they confirm by mail that they are coming, a few often still don't make it for reasons of health, missed airplanes, etc.

So, we handle the guarantee differently than other caterers. We have made it more flexible and realistic for our clients. Let's say that you give us a final guarantee of 225 guests for the wedding. Even though we will be prepared to serve the full 225, we will permit you to have a leeway of five guests. This means that if only 220 guests come to the wedding, you would only be charged for the 220, not the original guarantee of 225 that you gave to us. We feel that this is a wiser way to treat our clients. Don't you think that our more liberal guarantee policy is an advantage for you?"

This may seem too much work for some reading this page, but we feel that it is the little things that separate one caterer from another in the buyer's mind. Here's another unique way to create a win-win situation between the caterer and the buyer.

"Jim and Mary, let's take a moment and explain to you how our company deals with your guaranteed number of guests for the event.

You've mentioned to me, several times, that you are planning for 150 guests for the event. One of the advantages of using our company is that we give you our "cushioned guarantee".

The "cushioned guarantee" provides you with the opportunity to be less worried about whether all of your invited guests will be coming. In your case, the "cushion" will be seven guests. This means you will only be responsible for paying for 143 guests, or the actual number, if higher than 143, that come to the event.

The "cushioned guarantee" is one of the reasons for our exciting growth as a caterer. It just takes the pressure off our customers. Don't you agree with me that this is a great idea?"

In both of these examples, the caterer is using their more liberal guarantee policy to achieve a selling advantage over the competition. Hopefully, the shopper realizes the economic and psychological advantages that these different policies offer them.

The scripts above have been tested with actual caterers and with real buyers. They work! They work especially with the corporate buyer or those that believe the caterer, and others in the hospitality industry, are robber barons. They work because they go right to the buyers nervous system. They impact on your sales because they offer your shoppers an opportunity to win one for a change.

Thoughts on Closing the Sale

Successful closing of a sale means continued success for the salesperson and the company! Without a sale, the company cannot survive!

So, why is closing such a mystery to so many salespeople? If you have a great product to sell, it really is a shame when a buyer buys catering from someone else!

Closing can happen at any time before, during or after your presentation to a shopper. Your good judgement, based on the circumstances, added to your gut feeling should tell you when and how to ask the buyer for their business.

In general, a close can be started when:

1. You've finished your presentation.

2. You've just completed a very strong point in your presentation.

3. You've just answered a question for the buyer.

4. You've just overcome a major objection of the buyer.

5. Your buyer has just asked you a question about the cost of the catering.

6. You've finished your presentation and answered all of their questions and they have a "what's next" look on their face.

Below are some sample questions that a buyer might ask at some point during your presentation. They are "closing questions" that permit you to start your close.

A. "Do you take credit cards?"

"Yes we do. We would need $500 to reserve your date with ABC for the 15th of June. Do you wish to use your MasterCard, Visa or American Express?"

B. "Do we need to give you money now?"

"In order to give yourself the piece of mind of getting the date you really want, it would be wise to place a small deposit with us. For example, we can guarantee your date and menu price with either a $600 or $300 deposit. Which would you prefer to go with... the $300 or $600?"

• If they answer in a positive manner, ask:

"Great, do you wish to use a check or credit card for the deposit?"

• If they don't answer in a positive manner:

"Is there anything else you wish to ask or discuss about the deposit or catering costs... or may I continue with my presentation?"

C. "Is it possible to take the salad from menu three and change it for the one in Menu 2?"

"It's possible, but it probably would raise the price of menu 2 about $1.25 per person. However, if menu 2, with the change of salads is the one you would like to use for your wedding... and you can make your decision now, I'll be happy to give you the special salad for just .50 additional which saves you $150! So, would you like to take advantage of the $150 savings and get the menu you want or do you wish to wait and pay the extra $150?"

The most important point in this last example is that the salesperson pursued the buyer's wishes and forced himself (not the customer) to move into a closing situation.

For those readers who believe that this is pressure selling, you can be assured that it is not! Even if you think that saying words to a client that makes them have to make a decision is pressure, and you don't do it, then they will eventually buy from the caterer that gives them the opportunity to make a decision... not you!

A salesperson is not supposed to be an order taker and wait for the buyer to tell us that they are going to use us. The job is to give our buyers the information that they need and then to stop them from shopping anywhere else.

> **... OUR JOB IS TO STOP THE BUYER FROM SHOPPING ANYWHERE ELSE!**

SPECIAL INDUCEMENT CLOSE

"Mr. Smith, I've got a suggestion. I know that you wanted Saturday night for your dinner party. However, we're really busy on that Saturday. I can offer you a 10% discount off this menu if you have the party with us on Friday or Sunday. Is that possible?

"Mary, we've got a unique program for first time users. If you reserve with us for this event, we'll give you a certificate worth $150 off your next event with us. In this way we make first time users into regular customers. Would you like me to issue one of these certificates to you?"

Six Rules When Closing the Client

CaterSource has attempted from our beginnings to bring our subscribers a variety of do's and don'ts pertaining to the act of closing a sale.

The reason we like to offer so many varieties of tactics and scripts is because of the great diversity of both the salesperson and the buyer.

Here's six guidelines that might be helpful to you when you've presented a close to the buyer:

1. Questions keep Control

Most professional salespersons agree that during a critical closing situation, the person who wishes control needs to ask the questions for the other person to answer.

> SALESPERSON: *"Mrs. Smith, would you prefer to use a credit card or a check? Buyer: "I'm not sure?" Salesperson: (wrong/not a question) "Use whatever one you think best." Salesperson: (right/question) "Do you get any travel miles when you use your credit card?"*

When the salesperson says a non-question "Use whatever you think best" to the buyer, it gives them an easy way out to say, "Well, let me check my bank statements at home... I'll call you tomorrow". It just makes it too easy for them to block you from continuing on to get the sale.

2. Don't talk at the wrong time

This may sound absolutely stupid, but ... once you ask your buyer for the order, the person who speaks first usually loses!

What we're suggesting is that the moments immediately after the salesperson asks the buyer to buy, need to be silent moments from the salesperson's point of view.

No talking! We mean it. By the way, thirty seconds of non-talking will seem like a hundred years to even the senior sales staff! If you must talk, it must be in the form of a question!

> *"Jim and Mary, you've been rather quiet. I wonder, is your silence resulting from an error in my selection of menus or prices... which is it Jim and Mary, the menu or the price?"*

This keeps you in control of the sales flow!

3. Don't forget to smile

Is this too basic for you? It's so important to remember. Who wants to buy from an unfriendly salesperson? If you have a pleasant smile on your face while you're closing, you will win more sales and friends!

4. It's o.k. to leave the close to answer all the objections

The most important thing about closing is to remember that starting is the most difficult and the most important. Once you offer a close to your buyer, they realize that they need to take you seriously.

In other words, the buyer knows that you're doing all this work for a purpose... to build your company and permit the buyer to have the best caterer in town!

So it's o.k. to settle back in your chair and stop your current close... if that's what your instinct tells you to do. You might go back to answer some objections or even start selling again. The point is, it's up to you to decide what you want to do next.

5. Leave the buyers alone

This might tickle your fancy! So often, a salesperson works so long and hard to get the buyer to make a decision before they leave. The problem is that one needs to sell smart also.

Most buyers promise themselves, and each other, before they walk in, or open the door for you, that they will not buy today no matter what. They even tell each other to be firm with each other in case one of them weakens.

So, the only way you'll make a sale today with these buyers is to make an excuse to leave them alone so they can mutually agree to break their promise to each other about not buying today!

Go to the bathroom. Check with your secretary about something. Ask to be excused to call your spouse.... or, something!

6. Agree... then show leadership

> *"Jim and Mary, I really agree with you that it will be less costly if you don't have the tent, but have you really thought about what will happen if it does rain... especially during the meal? Here's how I see it...."*

Hope these concepts get you thinking about how to do better in your selling strategies!

Sample Trial Closes

A TRIAL CLOSE ASKS THE BUYER FOR THEIR OPINION.

Think about it for a moment. When you give your clients a close... you're asking for the order. When you ask the buyer a trial close... you're just asking them "How am I doing?"

1. "Mrs. Smith, I noticed that beautiful wood table in the family room. On the night of the party, may I move this table to the foyer and use it for place cards?"

2. "Mr. Jones, from what you've heard so far, is my company going to be one that you consider using for your event?"

3. "Mary, would you like me to put my ideas in writing?"

4. "Jim and Alice, our presentation is about two-thirds completed. Usually, at this time, I make my clients aware of the different pricing packages we have. This will also give you the information that explains how our deposit policies work. May I present this important information to you now?"

5. "Ms. Franklin, I'm concerned about the date that you've selected for the Christmas party because it's such a busy one for us. Would you like me to take some shortcuts in giving you my sales information so you are able to decide quickly if you like our policies and menus?"

Closing the Sale is Our Job

Closing the sale is the moment of truth. It is the moment, or moments during a sales presentation, when the salesperson culminates all her energy into getting a "yes" from the buyer.

Without a successful closing, both the buyer and the salesperson lose! Does this statement seem too strong to you? Well, let's think about it.

If the buyer doesn't buy, then they will not get the benefit of your great food, service and overall hospitality. Also, if the buyer doesn't buy, and the sale was built around proper profitability, you won't be as successful as you could have been. So, from this point of view... both lose if a sale doesn't take place!

In other words, if you have great products, outstanding service staff and stand behind your catering with a 100% guarantee, then it's a shame when a buyer decides to purchase catering somewhere else!

Closing techniques will vary depending on your buyer's needs at a given time. Some buyers are easier to close than others. To be a successful closer of catering sales, you need to practice both on real buyers and, also, when you're alone.

In simple terms, closing is just a collection of well selected words infused with the salespersons own enthusiasm and belief in their products and services.

> **"... IT'S A SHAME WHEN THEY BUY SOMEWHERE ELSE"**

Here's some things to remember about closing:

1. Great closing techniques can make up for weak presentations and other shortcomings.

2. Most salespeople are reluctant to ask for the order.

3. To be a great closer, be a great opener!

4. Closing is a natural step that is part of the entire selling process... it is not separate!

5. A salesperson needs an array of different closes to fit the array of different types of buyers.

6. The decision to buy is first made in the mind of the salesperson!

7. Ask for the order several times during the sales situation.

8. A pleasant smile is a crucial part of closing.

So, what are your beliefs on closing? Is closing an uncomfortable... or even an unnatural act for you? Does your stomach feel "fear" when you know that a closing opportunity is coming up in your presentation?

If you answered "yes" to the above questions, you have the potential of becoming a super closer! Remember, Barbara Streisand gets nauseous each and every time she performs

Now you're thinking "...but Barbara is performing not selling". Are you sure? Also, that's what a good close is ... a performance. It's just a selection of well chosen words presented to the buyer using a well written sales script:

> *"Mr. and Mrs. Smith, it seems that you both feel comfortable with our company, so I'd like to suggest that we come closer to deciding which of the menus you wish for the wedding. You both like the menu with the tenderloin and chicken breast as well as the menu with the cornish hen and salmon. For the wedding do you wish to have the beef and chicken or the cornish hen and salmon?*

or

> *"Bob and Mary, it's time to decide on whether you wish to have the large dunk tank or the smaller one for the picnic... remember, as I've showed you, they both work well ... so, for the picnic did you wish me to reserve the large or smaller dunk tank?"*

The above examples of "choice closes" hopefully demonstrate what we mean by sales scripts. It's a collection of words that help the salesperson gain the framework to launch and then say the closing words.

Closing is not an "art" alone... it is also a "science" of procedures and techniques that help both the buyer and the salesperson win! You just need to practice your "art" and keep thinking about the "science"!

Assorted Scripts for Closing

Learning to close sales is an ongoing process filled with a lot of trial and error. CaterSource will, from time to time, bring information on closing to our readers.

REMEMBER: closing is not waiting for the buyer to say "yes" or "I'm ready". The salesperson needs to set the tone and provide the buyer with the opportunity to complete the sale.

The following are an assortment of closing scripts that might be of help to beginners and old timers alike. It is important to remember that these scripts can be changed and molded in any fashion you wish. We've provided both ON-Premise and OFF-Premise scripts.

1. Assumptive Close

OFF-Premise Versions

A. "On the night of the party, may I move this cocktail table in front of the windows?"

B. "Are we going to cut the wedding cake?"

C. "Do you wish any of our staff to stay after the event to help you?"

ON-Premise Versions

D. "Let me give you the address and contact for packages you will be shipping ".

E. "Should we have the first break start at 8:30?"

F. "We'll hold the room cut-off till just one week before your event... will that help get more registrations?"

2. Impending Event/Need - Immediate Action Close

OFF-Premise Versions

G. "Mr. Smith, you've selected dates that are very popular with other clients and it seems that you are going to need a few days to discuss your important decision, but I'm concerned about our owner closing off this date... how would you feel about providing me with a credit card number so that I can guarantee your thinking time for about ten days. In this way you will be able to create a win-win situation for both of us. Remember, we will only use your credit card if you decide in the next week to come on board with us. Do you feel this will help us?"

ON-Premise Version

H. "Mr. Smith, I'm concerned about our event space for your time period. We've only got two rooms left that would fit your present needs. It will take a few more days for me to get you the contracts and then you will need a few days... how would you feel about providing me with a credit card number so that I can remove this space from our inventory for about ten days. This will give us both the small amount of time we need. Do you feel this will help us?"

3. Special Inducement Close

OFF-Premise Version

I. "Mr. Smith, you're in luck. We've got light bookings for those dates. February is one of our slowest months. In fact, we've got a promotion during the time you've selected. Our company is offering a 10% discount on all catering for February. Would you like to take advantage of this promotion?"

ON-Premise Version

J. "We've got a unique program for first time users. If you reserve with us for this event, we'll give you a certificate worth $150 off your next meeting with us. In this way we help turn first time users into regular customers! Do you wish to take advantage of this promotion!"

4. "Why not?" Close

K. "Ralph, it seems to me, from what you've shared with me, that our facility is the one best suited to cater for your reception. But, there seems to be something that is still causing you some doubt. Please share with me your concerns so I'll be able to clarify them for both of us or put you in touch with the person at our company that will have the answers."

L. "Fred, it seems to me, from what you've shared with me, that our banquet center has got everything you need for a successful meeting. But, there seems to be something that is still causing you some doubt. Please share with me your concerns so I'll be able to clarify them for both of us, or put you in touch with the person at our company that will have the answers."

The 3 Tells... The Close That Works

1. Tell what you're going to tell.

It's really quite simple. The script below would be told to your buyers before you started your official sales presentation. It comes right after you have the buyers relaxed and ready to listen. The amount of time it takes to give the "first tell" is between two to three minutes.

> *"Mr. and Mrs. Smith, I wish to begin by taking a moment to tell you about what I'm going to cover during the next forty minutes.*
>
> *"First, I'll you about our owners and why they started ABC Catering. Then, I'll tell you about myself and the other ABC staff that will be assisting you in making your event one that all will agree is memorable!*
>
> *"After this, I'll show you a variety of menus and explain the different ways in which we can present the food to your guests. If you wish, I'll even tell you what the hottest foods are this year with our other customers.*
>
> *"Next, we'll go over in great detail our prices and other costs so you will be able to know exactly how much you will be spending. Then, I'll explain how our deposit policy works and about what you will want to do to reserve your date for the event. Does this seem to be the type of information that you are looking for?"*

2. Tell your sales information

This "tell" is the simplest. This is where you tell your customers your sales information. During this section of your sale, you offer them all the information on your goods and services as you need to to get them ready for the close.

Obviously, you need to discuss all the elements mentioned in the "first tell". This "tell" takes the longest amount of time ... usually between 45 minutes to two hours.

3. Tell what you've told

When you begin to realize that you're about to finish with your "second tell", you need to get your mind ready to take the critical actions necessary to launch your first close. It is nothing but a rehash of the "first tell" and takes between two to three minutes to do.

> *"Jim and Betty, let me take a minute to review what we've covered so far. I've explained about our owners and other staff... I've made you aware of the incredible menus that we have to offer you and some of our hottest themes... I've discussed some realistic prices and costs with you. It seems that you both like our Oriental themed buffet very much."*
>
> *"I need to make you aware of our deposit policy so you will be able to reach a decision."*
>
> *"It's quite simple. We request that our customers provide us with a $500 deposit to reserve the requested date. Some use a check for the deposit while others use a credit card. Which would you like to use for your reservation, a check or credit card?"*

Fixed Day Tastings

It is a way of life for many clients... "We wish to taste your food before we make a decision." Caterers have different views on the question of letting people have tastings.

Some believe that it's o.k. for all potential buyers to have a tasting. Others believe that only buyers who have given a deposit are eligible for a tasting. Still others have their unique rules of when to permit tastings.

CaterSource would like to offer some thoughts on a style of tastings that combines marketing and sales energy to create new clients. This type of tasting is called the "Fixed-day tasting".

This solution to the "tasting" debate has proven to be very successful for both on and off-premise caterers. The caterer sets aside two, three, or more days a month to hold group tastings for prospective buyers, or for those that have given deposits.

Why? As you know, scheduling a tasting for a single buyer, even if they have a large committee or family, is filled with problems. First, it is often difficult to capture the same taste when cooking food for two, or three, people. Second, the energy during the tasting is usually one of non-excitement.

With the fixed day tastings, a variety of buyers are invited in for a group tasting of your latest and best menu items. You can offer both buffet, station, or plate served samples.

Another advantage of the group tasting concept is that a "buyer frenzy" is established with a variety of strangers, all with a common goal, begin "ooowing" and "ahhhing" your food!

"Yes, we do offer tastings Mrs. Smith. However, we do them in a very special way. We discovered a long time ago, that giving tastings to just a few people didn't allow our culinary team to shine, since all our recipes are for larger groups.

So, now we offer group tastings three times each month. These tastings usually have between fifteen and thirty people, who like yourself, need to decide on their menu, and permit our culinary team to offer an incredible range of menu items for all to try.

This month we can offer you a group tasting on Saturday, the 10th at noon, or Wednesday evening the 14th at 6:30 pm, or Tuesday morning the 20th at 10:30 am. Which of these tasting times is best for you?"

If you are going to offer these group tastings, you need to offer one on a Saturday... even though this is a "bad" day for most caterers.

On-premise caterers will find the fixed-day group tasting to be great business builders. Many caterers have reported to CaterSource that more and more clients don't want to have private tastings because of the "added pressure to buy" it places on them.

Some on-premise caterers hold their tastings in their kitchens, while others use their banquet space. The off-premise caterer can use their offices or kitchens for the tastings. Often caterers use one of their venues to hold tastings. Most private, or public party facilities will permit a caterer to hold a tasting at no charge to build mutual business.

These fixed-day tastings can also be utilized to increase the sales of your corporate catering when used as a marketing tool. Instead of using the tasting in response to a client request, you market your group tastings to corporations as an opportunity for them to taste you foods and see your style in the low pressure group situation.

You can market these tastings by direct mail or through in-person or telephone cold calling programs. Using direct mail will give you an excellent response, but cold calling, especially in-person, will offer you more chances to learn more about the needs of the potential client.

"Hello... my name is Fred James and I'm from ABC Catering. I just wanted to stop in to give you an invitation to one of our group tastings so you might be able to taste some of our foods. We've got some tastings scheduled next week so here's an invitation to attend with five other people from your office.

When you come to the tasting, you will be able to sample everything from a box lunch to cocktail appetizers. Do you think you might have more than six people who would like to come?"

No one tasting method is perfect, but the fixed-day system does offer some controls for a fast paced caterer. The important thing is to test it quietly before you launch it in a big manner. Many caterers, both on and off-premise, have had great luck with the energy and excitement it creates for those attending. In other words, people often buy better when they are in an atmosphere where other people are buying also!

Only 72 Minutes to Sell Each Day!

How important is one minute to a professional salesperson? Probably not too crucial. But, what about seventy-two minutes?

This page of education could be a life changing experience for those reading it! The simple truth is that time is everything to a catering salesperson! What's even more crucial is for salespeople to realize, once and for all, that during any given day, a salesperson really has only seventy-two minutes of selling time available to them.

But, what about the other eight, nine or ten hours during the workday? In most cases, these other hours and minutes are used for things other than speaking with a potential buyer.

It is our opinion that for most catering salespersons, the amount of time they have during a normal selling day to sell is... seventy-two minutes. The other minutes of the day are used to get back to old clients, calling to check the status of a proposal that was sent out, speaking with the chef, spending time in meetings, traveling to site inspections, writing bids and proposals, attending more meetings, etc.

Does this seem like what you do? If it is, then you are just like most other salespeople who are involved in our crazy profession! So, now you can understand why we say that during a normal sales day, the best of catering salespeople only get seventy-two minutes of quality selling time to make new sales.

Managing your time

First, a salesperson needs to make the best of the brief selling time they have during a normal catering day. This entails a predetermined plan on how to manage your daily routine.

Starting early is probably the best choice. Make phone appointments with clients for early in the day... even 7:00 AM. Many clients you are trying to sell are just as busy as you are, so they might actually enjoy an early phone appointment.

"Mr. Jones, I would be happy to have one of our sales associates give you a call tomorrow. Bill James, who has been with our company for eight years, specializes in the type of catering you're looking for. He really enjoys speaking with people in the early AM ... are you available to speak with him from home, or in your car between 7:00 to 8:00 AM?"

Why not? If you think this is rude, or uncalled for the problem might be with you. If our job is to manage our time to maximize selling "time zones" than this is a great "time zone" to be speaking from.

Managing time for maximum sales means that you need to make some changes to keep control of your day and get the desired sales results. It won't be easy. Once the phones start to ring in your office your time for selling is harder to get into. Once others in your company begin to need your "time," it becomes more difficult to sell correctly.

Selling ten minutes at a time

When you start to sell a new prospective buyer, think of only giving them ten minutes of your allotted selling time. Make them earn the next ten minutes by demonstrating to you that they are really the type of person with whom you should invest twenty minutes of your time.

Remember: they don't know what you are supposed to do or say to them... or how much time you are going to spend with them. If they don't seem like you should continue to give them part of your seventy-two minutes you need to move away and be ready to sell the better callers who may call at any time. Here's some scripts:

"Ms. Smith, I really believe that I understand what you're looking for. Let me speak with our chef and then I'll send you some ideas of what you might be wishing to do."

"Jim, I need to get into our kitchen for our weekly meeting with the chef... I wonder if I might be able to get back with you later in the week?"

The concept is to remember that the salesperson owns their time and should not even think of wasting any of the seventy-two minutes they have to sell a new caller on giving them a deposit check!

If you feel that this is too bold, rude, or pushy... then, you're probably feeling that you need to give each and every caller as much time that they need to understand what you are selling.

On the other hand, your time is golden and you should only use it when a caller has demonstrated through your qualification process that they are in a position to purchase from you "today!" The salesperson needs to stay in control of the selling situation at all times... each and every minute!

Questions to Challenge Your Readiness

1. Is your facility clean?

2. Are your best people answering the phones?

3. Are your proposals getting out in a timely manner?

4. Do you give information over the phone instead of just taking it?

5. Are you talking to the clients or sharing your thoughts with them?

6. Are you listening to the clients or hearing what they're saying?

7. Are you speaking proudly about your company and team?

8. Do you call clients back in a timely manner?

9. Do you send clients who had a second party the same thank you letter as the first?

10. Do you get excited in front of the client when they tell you "yes"?

11. Are you giving everyone you talk with the same amount of your valuable time?

12. Have you given your best clients a special telephone number, or way, to get in touch with you?

13. Are all your thank you letters typed?

14. When is the last time you took any of your best clients out to lunch?

15. Have you ever had a disagreement with a client?

16. What does your company do when they receive a "bad" letter, or call, from a client?

17. Have you ever turned a shopper over to another salesperson?

18. Do you get excited when you make a sale?

19. Are you promising less than you deliver?

20. How long does it take you to call a client after an event?

Are They Really Buyers?

A professional salesperson has an obligation, or duty, to ascertain whether or not a person is a buyer or not. It's part of the job! It is absolutely true that after a salesperson has given freely of their time, energy and information they have earned the right to have a better answer than "I'll get back to you!"

It is better to shake hands and say good-bye then risk the waste of personal and company time and money just because you are unable to let it go! Everyone will not, and cannot buy from us!

We are looking for a positive action on the part of the potential buyer that says "Yes, at this point in time you are the caterer that we're going to use!" The salesperson's job is to take the buyer out of the marketplace and stop them from continuing to either search for other caterers or to change their mind about the whole concept of having the event in the first place.

The hospitality industry revolves around dates and levels of performance.

Because of this a salesperson needs to create the atmosphere and belief that the date that the client wants is in fact being sought by other clients also. Fast action will assure them of getting their first date selection.

"Mr. & Mrs. Jones, it might be best if you consider an alternative date besides the primary one, since most of the best caterers limit the total number of events that they take on a particular date in order to maintain quality."

or

"Mr. & Mrs. Jones, it seems to me that you are pleased with what I've created for your daughter's wedding. It might be best if we call the office right now to put a "temporary hold" on May 15th."

A "temporary hold" absolutely guarantees your primary date of May 15th with ABC Catering by holding it for you for 10 days... no other salesperson can take your date during that 10 day period.

During the ten days I'll have all of the necessary menu and financial proposals back to you so you can make a final decision. Or, you can give us a $500.00 deposit now and have us put a "definite hold" on the date.

Which do you wish to do... the "temporary hold" which gives you another ten days or the "definite hold" with your deposit?

Try to take the buyers out of the marketplace whenever possible!

Another way to look at this concept deals with getting something in return for the time they want to take to think about it. It may not seem easy at first, but in a careful manner you need to paint a picture that they are really lucky to have an opportunity to get ABC Catering to do their event.

"Mr. & Mrs. Jones, when you told me you wanted May 15th, I took a careful look at our "green holds" for that date. We already have two major events booked and our manager tells us that he will only take one or two more.

So, unless we can work quickly with each other and make our decision in the next 10 days, it doesn't appear that the date will be available."

Here's another approach:

"Mr. & Mrs. Smith, the hour that we've spent together has proven to me that ABC Catering is right for your event. I'm going to also assume from your comments that you share my belief. I am, however, concerned with the date that you've chosen because it really is a busy one for us.

So, I took the liberty of putting a "temporary" hold on our best event leader and 6 of her best assistants. I really wasn't supposed to do this, but I know how much your daughter's wedding means to you all and, quite frankly, I always want to have the absolutely best events that I can for my clients, and these 7 people that I've reserved as part of your event team will guarantee that your family and friends will talk about the wedding for years to come!

Let me explain how I can place an official "temporary" hold on May 15th that will give you the time necessary to make all of your final decisions."

Cold Calling: Where to Find Leads

Here's some obvious, and not so obvious, places to search for leads to sell your catering:

1. Visiting office to office.

2. Yellow Pages.

3. Reverse telephone directory.

4. Business newspapers.

5. Customer lists from your suppliers.

6. Customer lists from realtors.

7. Lists from party rental companies.

8. Anyone that you spend money with.

9. List of your past clients.

10. Lists of people who didn't buy from you.

Cold Calling: Some Tips

Here's some tips for getting better results while selling over the phone:

1. You need to be a good listener.

2. Take notes as you talk with your contact.

3. Stay on track.

4. Concentrate on what you say, how you say it and the tone of your voice.

5. Turn a negative response into a sales advantage.

6. Never apologize for calling.

7. Explain your offer in clear terms with "WIIFM" (what's in it for me) to the buyer in the forefront.

8. Write a script or checklist to follow during the call.

9. Smile while you are speaking to the potential client... it really works!

10. Tape record your side of the conversation so you can review it later.

Getting Past the Secretary

It has been a question facing salespeople since the beginning of time! How do we get past the "protector" to see the buyer? This "protector" could be a secretary, receptionist, manager, etc.

If you've made cold calls, you already know how difficult it can be to get around this roadblock. CaterSource doesn't have a magic answer to this situation, but it would like to offer some ideas that might help you with this situation:

1. Be honest and state your business.

When you are facing a "protector" in person or on the phone, remember to state your business clearly and quickly. Don't act like the person who is protecting is brainless. Treat them with respect.

"Hello, I'm Bob Smith from ABC Catering and I'd like to speak with the person who does your ordering of catering. Who would that be?"

2. Watch your attitude.

REMEMBER: This protector gets approached by dozens of cold callers each and every day. They have heard it all. Don't be overpowering. Don't infer that it is their job to put you in touch with the correct person. Be careful of humor or sexist remarks. Show respect for their position. Refer to number 3 below.

3. Ask for help.

Share with the protector what it is you do and what your goal might be for this sales call. Then request her opinion on how you should proceed.

"As I mentioned, I'm from ABC Catering and we have several clients in this area, so I wonder if you could suggest a plan of action for me to make your company aware of the great food we have. What would you do if you were me?"

4. Make the sale to the protector.

REMEMBER: The protector will probably eat your food if you make a sale. So rather than hold back your sales information or marketing materials, sometimes it's a great idea to launch your presentation on the person who has to give you permission to go further in the search of the real buyer.

"Let me share with you why our company has had such success in the area. We specialize in catering for corporations and we are the only catering company to offer a guaranteed "on-time" delivery program. If you don't get your delivery by the time you specify, it's free."

5. Bring something.

The paper salesperson brings pens for the "protector" and the insurance person brings calendars. Pretty boring when you compare them to a freshly made chocolate chip cookie or white chocolate dipped strawberries. Everyone loves to eat and a little snack will go a long way towards winning over a protector.

"On the way out of our catering kitchen today I picked up some freshly made cookies to bring to some of the new potential clients I would meet today... here's some for you... is their anyone else who would like some?"

6. Talk to someone downstairs.

You don't know about the company you're calling on, but someone else does. The security guard, janitor, mailman, candy store operator, etc. all know interesting things about your potential new buyer. They know who does their catering at present, how many parties they have each year, how many meetings they have a week and if they are happy with the present caterer.

"Hi, I'm Bob from ABC Catering and I'm about to make a first time visit to XYZ Corporation on the 3rd floor to talk with them about doing some of their catering. I could use your help... who does their catering now..."

7. Just try to set a future appointment.

One of the easiest ways to gain success with the "protector" is to announce early that you are not there to see anyone today. All you want to do is to make an appointment for a future date with the right person. This relaxes the protector and often makes their "protective shield" come down.

"Hello, my name is Bob Smith, here's my card. I'd like to make a future appointment to speak with the person who orders your larger catering events for sometime in the next three weeks. Who do you suggest I make an appointment with?"

I hope you found some of these ideas interesting. They should help you get your own thinking into high gear. If you wish to get past the "protector" you need a plan and a script. If you take this to heart, you will sell more catering than you did last year!

Answers to... "You're too Expensive"

It is only natural for buyers to either really believe that your prices are too high, or to simply state it in order to see if you will budge on the price.

If you have a great product of the highest quality... you have a right to get paid fairly for it!

Here are some types of answers that can be given to explain your price:

1. "Your prices are much higher than other caterers!"

Yes, Mrs. Smith, we realize that we charge more than many caterers in Clinton... but, when we started ABC Catering we quickly realized that we could charge less by giving less as some other caterers have chosen to do, or we could charge a realistic and fair price that would allow us to maintain a catering business that offers only the finest quality in order not to embarrass our clients, their guests or ourselves. So, Mrs. Smith, I'm sure that you want only the best for your friends... don't you?

2. "Well, I'm not used to paying this much for catering!"

"We hear that from many people... and it's an honest comment! But, because we charge a little more we are able to put a lot more into the order. So, I would think that the extra money is worth your peace of mind because you won't have to worry about the success of the party... what do you think?"

3. "This is the first time that I've called you and I must say that your prices are higher than Fred's Catering."

As you know, as with most things that you buy, you get what you pay for! Since you brought up Fred's let me share with you some of the major and minor differences between the two of us...

Yes, Fred's is somewhat cheaper than we are... but look over this list of our present clients who have already switched to us from Fred's because of what they discovered after they tried us just once.

4. "But, I can get the chicken dinners from down the street for $1.00 less!"

Mr. Smith, if you really want to try us I'll guarantee your $1.00 difference back to you, if you honestly believe that you and your guests aren't happier with our chicken dinners!

or

What would you say to me if I told you that I would sell you the chicken dinners at exactly the same price as down the street... if you let me buy the chicken I use for your dinners from his supplier rather than mine and if you will let me give you the same portions of food he gives rather than our portions?

or

Yes, there are a great number of caterers who are attempting to buy sales by offering prices that any informed citizen quickly realizes are impossible and will not fulfill the expectations of their promises. After all, Grade A chicken costs the same for me as it does for anyone else...so they must be using lower grades. Mrs. Smith, with caterers you always get what you don't pay for!

5. "It seems to me that one caterer should be as good as the next. Your prices are really out of line."

Yes, many customers think that all caterers are the same. Many cars seem the same as the next. But you're not buying a car when you buy catering! Let me explain. If you can decide on a particular car model that you want and then go around to different car dealers and try to get the best price, then that is great! A Cadillac is a Cadillac! But, when you call around and get different prices from different caterers for the same menu, you are buying qualities that you can't examine by "kicking the tires," such as experience, track record, quality of suppliers, cleanliness, people and their overall investment in their professions. So, spending $500.00 less on one caterer over another could be one of your worst nightmares... especially if you are comparing a Cadillac with a Chevy!

or

When a caterer doesn't have any track record, they usually offer lower prices which result in lower levels of experience and quality that foster much more risk for the host and hostess!

6. "You are without question the highest priced caterer in town!"

Yes, but I thought that is exactly why you are here today! You know that we do the best job!

or

Yes, we are one of the more expensive caterers in town, but we also have the most clients... so we really must be doing something right!

or

Yes, Mrs. Smith, we are expensive... but we stand behind everything we do and you won't have any complaints, mishaps or failures.

or

We are very professional, Mrs. Smith, and we really don't expect to sell everyone. We need to charge prices that permit us to maintain the professional staff and high standards of ABC Catering.

> **"NEVER DEFEND HIGHER PRICES... JUST EXPLAIN THEM!"**

Finding New Venues for Events

1. Go out and meet people. The best location to get an exclusive contract with, is one that has never had events before. Car showrooms, office building lobbys, funeral homes, garden stores, carpet stores... anyplace that has good parking and ample event space.

2. Call a florist, as a client searching for a unique place to hold a wedding... ask them for suggestions. You will be surprised.

3. Using your own money, reserve various prime event spaces in advance... even though you don't have a booking yet! Next year, will you need a location for a wedding on a prime Saturday evening in June? If the answer is yes, then you should think about reserving your space before the other caterers.

4. Ask your clients if they know of any places they would like to have an event. Some caterers actually rent their client's homes for other clients!

5. Use tenting on vacant land. Look for vacant land that has a beautiful setting and ask the owners if you could place a tent on their land to hold events. They will earn income and you will have a new event venue!

6. Rent banquet space in hotels! Yes, this can be done. However, if you don't ask, you won't get it! Even some of the larger hotel chains have let caterers in because they haven't booked their ballroom one hundred twenty days out. They usually take over the bar, but they will let you use their kitchens.

7. Use your own facility if it's big enough. Also, don't forget that any warehouse will do if you decorate it correctly.

Cold Call Reluctance

The need for continual prospecting for new customers is a never ending one for the catering salesperson!

When utilizing cold-call selling techniques it is only natural for the salesperson to be fearful of barging into the lives of total strangers.

In fact, the term cold-calling seems to have negative connotations to just about everyone who either tries to do it or has someone do it to them!

So, cold-calling reluctance on the part of the salesperson is a natural occurrence. Accept this and move on.

When salespeople finally make the plunge and participate in cold-call selling, they usually increase their volume. They are never at a loss for new customers and additional business.

There are many approaches to use to begin your sales call, such as the provocative question or referral method. In any case the goal is to get the prospects attention. The real goal of a cold-call is not to make a sale, it is to set an appointment for quality sales time with the potential client.

"YOU MUST BELIEVE"

When you get right down to it, the telephone is a terrific selling tool. It provides the catering salesperson with an easy and flexible method to touch a lot of prospects in a short time.

You must believe to be successful in cold-calling! You need to have the proper attitude. Your attitude needs to be of total commitment to looking at your prospect as one who could benefit from your catering.

You need to be a problem solver. Add this to the right selling attitude and you have a success! Once you believe in your company's catering ability totally, nothing can stop you from getting your share of the cold-calling success!

Here's some tips and scripts that will help you get the attention of your sales prospect during cold-calling:

1. Try to clear the mind of the prospect to give you about 30 seconds to make contact.

2. Don't be afraid to sound like a salesperson. Remember, the prospect needs your outstanding catering!

3. Give the listener a new slant on catering as it affects his life.

4. Use the prospects name as often as possible.

5. Always have a special reason for your call.

6. When possible, talk about a special benefit that your catering provides.

7. "Mr. Smith, my name is Mike Roman of ABC Catering, my special reason for calling you today is to show you how our new "Employee Incentive Catering" will create enhanced morale at your company at very comfortable prices. Do you have about three minutes now or would this afternoon around three o'clock be better?"

8. "Mr. Smith, my special reason for calling you this morning is at the suggestion of Robert Johns of the Johns Company. He's been a customer of our catering company for five years and is pleased with the company picnics that we've done for him. He felt that you would benefit from seeing some of our menus and activities that make our company picnics so successful. May I have an appointment with you later this week for about 20 minutes so I can explain our new value pricing and show you some photos of the picnics we did for the Johns company?

9. "Mr. Smith, thank you for taking my call. I'm Mike Roman with ABC Catering and I really wish to make you aware that I've worked with many companies similar to yours that were amazed at how much money and time they saved using our "FAX BACK" ordering system for daily lunches. Please let me meet with you to demonstrate how you can save money and get great tasting food at the same time. I'll be in your area on Thursday of next week... could I meet with you in the afternoon for about 20 minutes... which is better for you 2:30 or 4:00 pm?"

The single most important aspect to successful cold-calling is to START! Yes, you will make a fool of yourself from time to time. Yes, you will be nervous or afraid of rejection. Yes, you will need to leave the safety of your office from time to time.

Cold-call selling is the best way to achieve more success when selling catering. Reluctance to cold-calling is a state of mind that can be overcome with preparation and scripts that will help you do your job better. Cold-call selling is a privilege that is reserved for those who wish to reach total perfection in selling. catering!

Ways to Cold Call Better

It's no wonder that most catering salespeople don't like to participate in any sort of cold calling! Cold calling is one of the most frightening, but rewarding, tasks that a salesperson can do.

One of the most critical blocks to cold calling is "fear". Here's some general tips on making your experience a more pleasant, and rewarding, one:

"SECONDS COUNT WHEN DOING COLD CALLING"

1. To telephone or not to telephone? Here are some of the advantages of using your phone:

   A. Convenience, speed and ability to cover a geographical area.

   B. Distance is not a problem.

   C. Salesperson gets complete focus from the listener/buyer.

   D. Not travel time, weather or parking problems.

   E. The way the salesperson dresses isn't important.

   F. Usually less expensive.

2. To telephone or not to telephone? Here's some of the advantages of making in-person cold calls:

   A. More difficult to stop you or cut you short.

   B. Salesperson can physically touch the listener/buyer.

   C. Salesperson can watch their body language.

   D. Salesperson can demonstrate the product.

   E. Salesperson is able to show their own personal charm.

   F. The listener/buyer is required to involve more of their five senses.

3. Qualifying your listener...

   A. Do they have a need for your service/product?

   B. Can they afford to buy your service/product?

   C. Is the time allotment that you are about to commit worth it?

   D. Do they fit all your other pre-determined demo graphics?

   E. Is this the right time for them?

   F. Are we talking to the right listener/buyer?

   G. What role will this listener/buyer play in a sale?

   H. Are there other people who should be listening at the same time?

4. Tips for your opening statements...

   A. State your reason for talking with listener/buyer quickly.

   B. Provide them with a clear understanding of who you represent.

   C. Demonstrate enthusiasm.

   D. Use the listener/buyer's name as often as possible during your conversations.

   E. Offer solution/benefits to them.

   F. Talk about what others have done with your product/service.

   G. Remember that you will probably get a no.

5. The first 20 seconds are the most crucial. Here's what you need to do:

   A. Clear the listener/buyer's mind of what they were thinking about when you called them.

   B. Demonstrate the idea that you are for real!

   C. Give them self-justification for taking time to be with you.

   D. Take the risk out of the situation for the listener/buyer!

6. The next 30 seconds are also crucial. Here's what you need to do:

   A. Hit the "hot button" of the listener/buyer.

   B. Gather visual facts by being a detective.

   C. Determine if they already know of your company.

   D. Let them know that you are aware of their concerns.

   E. Get the listener/buyer to start talking to you about something that they really want to talk about!

7. Remember to always be sincere, truthful, appropriate and timely.

EXAMPLES OF STATEMENT-FIRST QUESTIONS FOR ON-PREMISE CATERERS

1. "It's amazing how many people don't like to pay for valet parking. Do you think that our paid parking passes will make them happier?"

2. "I realize that when planning an event the host likes to have constant contact with the banquet facility staff. Would you like to have my home number just in case?"

3. "I find that the way a lobby impacts on a guest coming to a wedding is very important. Do you find our lobby as beautiful as I do?"

Samples of Sales Scripts

Scripts are the heart and soul of all selling. Gone are the days when salespeople just "winged" their presentation on an, as you go, basis.

Today's salesperson realizes that a well written series of scripts will enhance their ability to make more and larger sales.

Scripts give the salesperson the ability to learn from their mistakes by adjusting a word here and a word there.

Here's some interesting examples of some scripts.

A. Closing with a deposit.

I've noticed that you've shown enthusiasm for our menus and the way we do catering. Let me now explain our deposit policy and how using it will guarantee a beautiful event for you.

A deposit of $_____ will guarantee your date and permit me to reserve some of our best staff for your event. Most of our clients use either a check or credit card to provide us with their deposit to hold the date. For your event on _____, which do you wish to use for the deposit a credit card or check?

B. Proposal follow-up.

CATERER: This is _____ calling from (YOUR COMPANY). May I please speak with _____ about the information I sent after speaking with him/her last week.

and/or

CATERER: I need about two minutes of his/her time to clarify some information from the proposal he/she requested from us.

and/or

CATERER: It's important that I speak with her before _____ because the date that he/she has requested for catering has been requested by another client and I really need to know if he/she wishes for me to continue to hold the space.

C. Closing with a deposit.

You know it's very interesting that you've mentioned _____. They are one of the better caterers in (CITY). In fact, I would say that they are probably one of our top three competitors. What's interesting is that some of my best clients who use us on a regular basis also use _____ for some of their parties.

As my customers explain it to me.... they use _____ when less impact is necessary for the event and they select us when they want the food and service to be talked about by their customers or guests in a favorable way. In other words, they rely on (YOUR COMPANY) to make them look great in front of their guests!

For example, (YOUR COMPANY)'s food is always prepared from scratch and is presented in a beautiful and exciting manner. Our staff comes to your event ready to please you and your guests in both large and small ways.

D. Handling objections

I can understand your point since other customers have often made the same point about _____, but, just for a moment, let's suppose that _____, wouldn't it be quite embarrassing to you and your guests if _____.

and/or

It's interesting that you've brought that up because many of my best clients made the same observation the first time they heard it. Let me take a moment and provide you with the same explanation that I gave to them...

and/or

You're right about that, but are you sure that it will be as important on your wedding night as it seems now?

What Promises do the Buyers Make?

"Dear... in a few minutes we're going to meet with the catering salesperson. We need to stick together on this. In fact, let's promise each other not to say 'yes' until we meet with some of the other caterers."

This is an example of the promise that "social" buyers might make to themselves when preparing to shop for catering for weddings, dinner parties, etc.

"The president wants us to make sure that we shop to compare the picnic prices of about five caterers, so let's remember that we're not buying right away... we're only gathering information."

This is an example of the promise that corporate buyers might make as they develop their game plan for shopping for caterers.

In order to sell catering more effectively, a salesperson needs to understand how this basic, yet powerful, "promise not to buy today" stands in the way of successfully closing the sale.

If you take a moment to think about it, you will admit that when you shop you often make a promise not to buy quickly. This is a very normal response for most Americans.

So what can we, as salespeople, do to overcome this "promise to delay the purchase" and make a quicker sale? We can create a potential "sense of loss" for the shopper, if they don't take quick action.

First of all, why would a client be concerned with losing the opportunity to work with one catering company over another. Isn't one caterer the same as the next? The unfortunate truth is that to many clients all caterers are the same. They really can't help themselves... after all, isn't one Cadillac the same as the next?

The salespeople that win are the ones that stop the shopper from going elsewhere to shop. They give the buyer reasons to buy from them... right now! This is accomplished by causing the shopper to think about the reasons why all caterers are not the same. The great caterers book up earliest!

Here's some concepts that salespeople can use during a sales presentation to create excitement about the advantages that the shopper might lose if they don't act quickly to book their event.

1. Price. Price is the most powerful and critical tool to create concern for lost value by a shopper, when thinking about postponing their decision to buy. It is easy to do if you start creating seasonal pricing i.e spring prices 97, summer prices 97, fall prices 97 and winter prices 97. When a buyer is speaking about an event that will happen in the summer of 97, the salesperson can offer spring prices if they make a quick decision.

2. Date. This is especially strong with celebrations like weddings, showers, birthdays, etc. An advantage is gained by the seller when they point out that the day the client has selected is a popular one ... and that most caterers will be getting booked very quickly.

3. Prime space. Banquet facilities use this to create urgency and excitement by offering a special room, on a first reserved basis. If they wait, they might lose this great room!

4. Discount. One needs to be very careful with this one. Some caterers call it an "early bird" discount. It is offered for those who make a quick decision so they can close off a date. It is explained that all caterers like to get their dates filled as early as possible, so they give better prices for those who buy early. If you wait, you usually pay a premium price for the catering.

5. Special staff. In this scenario the caterers explains that by booking quickly, the party can be staffed with their greatest staff. If they wait, they will get just great staff!

6. Menu. Often caterers offer additional menu items for early booking. The shopper is told that if they come on board now, they can get two more appetizers and a special presentation of their dessert.

7. Equipment. Caterers explain to the shoppers that during peak seasons the best tents, chairs, glassware, etc. are rented early, so waiting too long can have an effect on the appearance of the event.

If these seem negative to you, remember that they are all out of context. Also, one would probably not use them all with the same clients. The point is that the salesperson needs to emphasize reasons for the shoppers to make a positive decision quickly.

The only way to break the promise of "not buying today" is to explain that there are wonderful reasons for buying now to gain super advantages!

CHAPTER 5  QUESTIONS

1. What do buyers want and expect from catering salespeople?

2. What are the ways to sell more catering?

3. When qualifying a buyer, what are the ten big questions they want answered?

4. What should every salesperson ask themselves when selling catering?

5. How should an unhappy client be handled?

6. What are the five "C's" of selling catering?

7. What are the six rules of closing a client?

8.   Why is closing a sale the job of the salesperson?

9. What is the third "Tell" when closing?

10. How do you decide if a sale is unwise to book?

11. What are fixed day tastings?

12. What are the main concepts of cold calling?

13. What might a salesperson say when a shopper states, "You're very expensive"?

14. How do caterers find new venues for events?

15. What is your favorite selling script?

PRICING

CHAPTER

6

TABLE OF CONTENTS

CHAPTER

6

"There will always be a caterer who will charge less!"

The A to Z of Pricing

Here are some interesting and thought provoking concepts to discuss at one of your next sales meetings.

Try to ascertain what your position is on these rules and axioms on pricing. You really don't have to agree, or disagree, with them to gain some insight into your beliefs on pricing.

A. Pricing is a major part of your success or failure.

B. Pricing for caterers needs to be carefully thought out. It can not be the same for everybody or every party. Even McDonalds charges differently for a Big Mac in different parts of a city.

C. Using a normal mark-up policy for every event type, such as cost times three, will only lead to trouble in most catering companies.

D. If your price is too high you know because buyers don't buy, if your price is too low buyers will never tell you!

E. The real question to ask is... "How much is this particular client prepared and then willing to pay?"

F. All prices should reflect volume discounting.

G. Prices for customized catering should reflect the value as perceived by the buyer along with what the market will bear. Let's not forget that as caterers we can do a better party with more money to spend from the clients!

H. The definition of fair pricing means that the client has an outstanding event, the guests become future clients of the caterer, and the company prospers greatly!

I. Don't "buy back your business" from the clients. "That's o.k. Mrs. Smith, I'll reduce your charge by $50.00." This is "buying back the business" from clients. If you really want to give the client a break of $50.00 then you should put $50.00 of your own money back into the company!

J. The catering salesperson usually is the one who thinks the prices are too high.

K. "Quick Deals Will Be Bad Deals" for caterers!

L. Balance your costs and then take bookings that exceed these costs.

M. Never raise prices without lowering some.

N. Tell your buyers what others are spending on the same type of functions and why.

O. Don't be mysterious about prices or costs. Let the buyer hear you speak naturally about this important topic of price and cost.

P. Respect the difference between price and cost.

Q. Learn techniques of careful price manipulation moving from a higher starting point to a lower one... with the buyer leading the way!

R. Use discounts.

S. Higher or lower prices are never defended by the caterers... instead they are simply explained.

T. Sell the concept to the buyer that when buying from a caterer one gets exactly what one pays for!

U. Raising prices is a right, not a chore for a business person.

V. You will sell a $10.00 menu more easily to a buyer, if you also have a $14.00 menu for them to compare it with.

W. Options are the key to winning a buyer over. By letting the buyer participate in determining how they are spending their money, you give them a sense of confidence that lets them buy from you more quickly!

X. Always give an answer to a customer who asks what something costs. It doesn't have to be the exact final price, but at least it needs to be a range of prices that the catering might cost. No buyer wants to be put off when asking "How much is it?"

Y. It's best not to ask the buyer about their budget. In most cases they are not going to tell you the whole truth.

Z. If you never ask the buyer to buy more, or higher, they will never buy!"

The Secret Power of Understanding Wants

Pricing takes into account many different elements. One of the most important is the concept of "value" from the buyers point of view.

When you develop, or revise, your company's pricing philosophy, it is important to think from the perspective of the buyer instead of the seller.

Buyers of catering wish for many things. "K-value" is the term that economists give to the begrudging index of buyers with respect to the ratio between the increased price of a product or service and it's perceived (or not) increase in value to the buyer.

Let's start with an easy example. A buyer is trying to choose between two menus sent from different caterers.

Caterer A has event staff that costs $12 per hour, while Caterer B's staff costs $15.50 per hour. To the buyer, is the $15.50 staff better than the $12.00 staff?

If the buyer's event is extremely important from a "show" point of view, the $15.50 staff will have a higher K-value in the buyer's mind, because if you pay more for staff, the staff must be better.

On the other hand, if the event is not deemed important, or special, the buyer may find that the $15.50 staff is a waste, since staff is staff. This means that the buyer isn't accepting the concept that the more expensive staff is better for this particular event.

Let's look at food. A buyer comparing two different menus of chicken curry, each made with boneless breast of chicken, will have greater difficulty believing that the higher priced menu has better chicken curry since chicken is just chicken.

However, if they are comparing the chicken curry with a boneless chicken entree covered with fresh crab and shrimp, they will be expecting to pay more since this menu item has a higher K-value in the buyer's mind.

So, K-value is how the buyer feels about comparative pricing in relation to the purpose and concern for the catering needed.

All American buyers know, for example, that, generally speaking, the more costly a bottle of wine, the better it is. In other words, when it comes to buying wine, the quality and value increase as the price goes up.

Are you getting the interesting difference between value and quality? We tend to think of value as something that is cheaper, or saves us money.

K-value effects the concept of value, because it puts impact into the equation. Buyers are willing to pay more, for the same item or service, when a high impact is required.

So, when a corporation is entertaining a special client, they are willing to spend more for better service or menu items.

On the other hand, if the corporation is entertaining their own staff for a party, the concern for higher prices, and greater impact, decreases. This means that the buyer's K-value is low.

The real problem for the caterer comes when a corporation is going to entertain, for example, the board of directors.

Was it a good year? Was it a bad year? Has the company recently let go 2,000 employees? How is the stock doing?

The answers to these questions will help determine the level of K-value to the buyer. What's interesting is that sometimes we as caterers misjudge what the buyer is thinking.

For example, when a company has just laid off 2,000 workers, we might think that they would have a desire for lower K-value and the lower prices that they bring.

However, sometimes the company needs to build the morale of the remaining staff, so they are thinking in a higher K-value range.

> "CATERERS NEED TO LET THE BUYER DECIDE HOW MUCH THEY WISH TO SPEND"

The obvious answer for the caterer is to offer options on menu and services to the buyer that permit both high and low K-value decisions.

This is really not that hard to do. Besides the obvious option of a boneless breast of chicken with or without a topping of crab and shrimp, some caterers offer K-value options in the style of service and the level of staffing.

Other K-value concepts deal with plastic vs. glass, paper vs. cloth, silver vs. stainless, tuxedos vs. casual, fresh vs. frozen, 8 oz vs. 10 oz, charcoal vs. mesquite, service vs. self-service, 25% deposit vs. 50% deposit and Friday vs. Saturday.

Options are the answer to fulfilling the K-value concerns for buyers. Don't be afraid of options!

Factors That Determine Your Pricing

Pricing is easy at best! So many factors affect how you price. Here's some thoughts on how competitors and customers fit into the decision making process of establishing and presenting your prices on menus and proposals. These are meant as concepts for you to consider when dealing with decisions on raising and lowering your prices.

1. How will competition react to your price?

This may seem strange to you at first thought, but you do not want a price war. So, when considering a lowering of price, be considerate of what your competitors might do to counteract your actions. If you feel that they might also respond with lower prices, then you might wish to rethink your strategy. Perhaps a better method might be to leave your prices where they are and offer private discounts.

2. How similar is your competitor's catering to yours?

This is simple apples to apples. However, you need to decide whether the buyer feels your products are the same as those of the competitors. If so, a lowering of prices would be advised since they would reflect a higher value due to the price advantage over the competitor.

3. Have your competitor's pricing strategies affected yours?

This determines whether you should respond to your competitors lower or higher prices. If you're losing sales to a competitors lower, or higher, pricing, then you need to consider making the appropriate price changes yourself. Changing a price is not a personal decision. It is based on the potential results that might come from your actions.

4. How much are your buyers willing to pay?

This is the big question! Caterers who learn to answer this question win big. The best solution, in search of the answer, is to continually offer your buyers a variety of options that act as a dead giveaway as to what pricing ballpark they are in. This is much more than asking "What is your budget?" This is a matter of giving them multiple menu, service and equipment options that help you better understand what their buying patterns are going to be with this event. Remember, the mother and father marrying off their first daughter usually spend more than when they are marrying off their fourth daughter!

5. Does your catering fill a need?

If your company is the only one with a mobile kitchen in your area, and a client needs a catering situation that demand a mobile kitchen... well, I hope you see what I mean. Your pricing should always be strong when your products and services are superior to other caterers, or when you're the only one that sells that particular item needed by the buyer.

6. How much of your catering do you need to sell?

While it's not always true... "the lower your prices the more you sell" is valid. So, if you are in need of a lot of sales, you should consider softer prices. On the other hand, many caterers have learned that sometimes a buyer will pay more for catering that needs to be special.

7. How much price sensitivity is there?

In general, when you hear your customers tell you "But, I can get it down the street for less" they are just positioning themselves for bargaining. However, it may be more important if you are continually losing your sale to lower price. The solution for having higher prices is to explain them to the buyer. Never defend your higher prices ... just explain them!

So, you can see that more than one factor can, and should, be considered before taking action on establishing your price points in the marketplace. The answers are to be found in your need for volume over profit or profit over volume. While their is no right answer for all caterers, your decisions need to be backed by an understanding of the above seven questions.

What Do You Charge For?

Even the most experienced caterers often ask us for our thinking on what a caterer should be thinking about when deciding how much to charge a client.

Most caterers think about pricing a menu. This is not the same thing as pricing an event. Here lies the problem. Catering is a business of an incredible number of hidden costs. In fact, some of these costs don't seem to become known to us until after the event is over!

The first rule of pricing an event is not to make any decisions until you really understand what the buyer wants to do and where they want to do it! For off premise caterers this means that no significant event should be priced until you've investigated your event site completely!

Caterers need to constantly reevaluate the methods that they use to build their prices. Once your price is in the contract, it becomes very difficult to change it!

While there isn't any "absolutely all inclusive" list of these items that caterers should charge for, here is our attempt to bring the most crucial to you.

1. Food Cost. Everything that goes into the food production for an event needs to be tallied to create the final price. It is a mistake just to take into account the meat, but forget the 1/2 box of parsley that you're sending. Parsley costs money!

2. Labor cost. This is usually considered to be the wages of your kitchen staff that prepare the menus. These are usually hourly wages.

3. Operational cost. These are usually the fixed costs of your business... or the costs of being in business. Rent, truck payments, and other fixed costs tend to get into this section.

4. Profit. That's right. Some caterers actually determine the amount of profit they wish and place it into the price as a non-negotiable item.

5. Cost of sale. These might be as simple as commission to a salesperson or advertising. This is a wide open category. Some caterers place their plastic wrap, sterno and other disposables into this category. If you know that you will need to give gratuities to security guards etc. this is where you can justify it.

6. Delivery. The wages of the delivery staff, gas, maintenance, etc. go into this category.

7. Set-up Cost. Often there are costs in setting up an event that seem to be missing from our prices. This could be wages for staff that physically set-up the event or charges by a rental dealer for doing the same.

8. Pre-Party Cost. Food samplings, parking fees, gas for salespeople going to and from a clients location, are a few examples. Some caterers assign a cost to the production and delivery of the proposal.

9. Insurance. A big one. Some portion of your premium needs to be placed into each and every price you build. Some caterers are actually adding a line item to the invoice for insurance coverage. In some cases they are charging 3% Insurance Coverage on all invoices. The client can eliminate this by giving the caterer a certificate of insurance that makes the caterers the primary beneficiary of the client's policy.

10. Degree of Difficulty penalty. More and more caterers are learning to add just a little bit more for the more difficult types of events, or for more demanding clients. Tent events are a good example of an event where the caterer should charge a little more.

11. Extra meals. The client should pay for all extra meals that will be needed to feed her band, valet parkers, photographer, etc. Often caterers will only put into this section the actual food cost without taking any mark-up.

Mark-up and Price

How much should you mark-up your catering? This is a question that all caterers live with daily!

The answer rests not with a magic formula or rule, but rather with some common sense. Obviously, a caterer wishes to get the most they can for their hard work.

The problem comes when a caterer doesn't remember when giving prices to buyers, different mark-ups need to be considered for different situations.

Here are some of the concerns one needs to address before deciding how to price an event:

1. How big or small is the event?

2. What day of the week is it?

3. What month is it?

4. What else am I doing on that day?

5. Do I need the business?

A caterer who jumps to a quick decision often loses in the attempt to mark-up the catering properly. The mark-up needs to be one that will reflect the answers to the above questions.

Let's look at the chart on the lower right of this page. This will be a simple, but effective, approach to educating ourselves about catering mark-ups.

We've taken an imaginary menu that costs us $7.00 per person to create in our kitchen. Let's say that it also includes the kitchen labor... so we might wish to call this the total, or prime cost for the menu.

Take a look at the chart to see how the margin changes in relation to how many times you mark-up your prime cost.

Many caterers at this point would be thinking that the chart is silly because nobody would sell an event at just a two time mark-up. After all, that gives you a 50% cost of sales which is out of line... isn't it?

Maybe, would be the only answer. The answer really rests in the answers to the questions above dealing with day of week, number of guests etc.

The next thing we need to remember is that a caterer banks dollars... not percentages. This not true in all foodservice cases, but in catering it is. A caterer needs to think more about how much money is left after the event is over, than on how much the food cost percentage is. Don't read too much into these statements. They are simple catering logic. Volume is what caterers search for.

Catering is a numbers business. For example, let's say that we wish to sell our menu that costs us $7.00 per person to produce at a 3 times mark-up for a party of 200. Our selling price is $21.00 per person times 200 guests coming to $4,200 in volume. The margin, or what's left for us, after we subtract our expenses is $2800.

Now let's take the same event at a 2 times mark-up. Our total revenue is $14.00 per person times 200 or $2,800. The margin here is $1,400 left for us.

If this event comes during your busy season, or on a Saturday night you can deal with strength and stay with the 3 time , or maybe even 4 time, mark-up.

However, if this event is being bid for your slow season, or for a Wednesday, you might wish to go with the smaller mark-up.

But now, let's make it interesting. Suppose this menu were going to be used for an event of 800 persons. With a three time mark-up your margin is $11,200 left for you and with the 2 time mark-up your margin is $5,600 left for you.

Now, as the event becomes larger, those questions of Wednesday or Saturday and slow season or busy one take on an added importance.

If you have full time staff to pay, and normal bills on a twelve month basis, it is wise to understand that $5,600 for sure is better than a maybe $11,200. $5.600 is a lot of money for a day's work!

Remember, catering is a bid situation. When you bid too high they go with the other caterer! Play with the numbers and give Mike Roman a call if you wish to discuss it more.

YOUR COST	MARK-UP	SELLING PRICE	MARGIN
$7.00	TIMES 3 33%	$21.00	$14.00
$7.00	TIMES 4 25%	$28.00	$21.00
$7.00	TIMES 2 50%	$14.00	$7.00
$7.00	TIMES 2.5	$17.50	$10.50

Giving Prices Over the Phone?

An age old question in all types of selling... should I try to give prices over the phone when a client calls me, or should I wait till I see them in person?

Each and every salesperson is faced with this decision each and every day of their selling career. If we polled our subscribers, we would find that many of the salespeople believe that giving prices over the phone is perfectly o.k, while others would tell us that it's crazy to give your prices to somebody who's not sitting in front of you.

So, should we give pricing information over the phone? What do you do when you have a caller ask you the questions below:

"Yes, I'm calling to find out how much you charge for a wedding of 200 people?"

or

"What types of menus do you have?"

From the "never give prices over the phone" point of view, the decision would be made to try to set the appointment or to tease the individual calling.

"It's really difficult for me to give you prices without knowing exactly what you're looking for. As a caterer we do a wide variety of menus and themes, so we can accommodate most budgets."

From the "sell over the phone" point of view, the decision would be made to give the caller an understanding of what price range they might fall into.

"With respect to price, I can only give you an example because I don't know the particulars of your event. We have wonderful wedding packages that sell for $28 per guest and some that sell for $39 per guest. The main difference between the two is the type of entree our customers select and the day of the week they wish to have their catering."

Are you starting to see the dilemma? It's really a personal decision by each and every salesperson as to whether they give price information over the phone. Of course, it could also be a management decision.

We wish to suggest that in either case, it's probably better not to treat each and every caller in the same manner. In other words, it's best not to have a hard and fast rule about giving , or not giving, prices over the phone.

Let's take a moment and think about this from the callers point of view. How will they respond to either of your approaches? Can we raise their curiosity, or will it just make them angry?

Think about this... you walk into a jewelry store and begin to look at some watches in the showcases. Do you look for the price tags? When you look at a restaurant menu in a new restaurant do you look at the prices?

Most of us would certainly look. We want to know about prices. We wish to know the type of store, or restaurant, we're in. We don't want to be embarrassed by being in the wrong buying situation.

We're not suggesting that having a policy of giving prices out over the phone will get you more sales. We are suggesting that in certain cases, with certain buyers, it is best to give them an idea of what type of "store" they're in.

On the other hand, we can also share with you, what most caterers have found that when they give pricing information over the phone, they tend to give ranges of price or price examples. In this way, they get the best of both worlds!

Things To Remember When Giving Prices Over the Phone

1. It helps to think about how you would want a salesperson to treat you if you were the one asking the pricing question.

2. Try to develop scripts that permit you to give price ranges or examples to the caller.

3. Don't give a firm, or a final, price till you're sure you've heard all the details of the event!

4. It's never wrong to seem mysterious about price as long as you give believable realistic examples to the caller.

5. The goal is always to make a sale, and it's easiest if you're in front of the buyer.

Thoughts on Raising Prices

When, how and why.... these are questions often asked by caterers when it comes to price increases. In general, most caterers resist making any "waves" in their buyer's minds about increasing the costs of their food, beverage, equipment, staff etc. To many caterers, the fear rests with the concept that their present buyers might leave them for another caterer with lower prices.

While this could happen, the need to maintain proper profitability, which springs from having proper prices, requires price increases. The information below might be beneficial to you as you consider, and then launch, price increases.

1. Raise prices when everyone else does.

It is a basic rule of retail sales... raise your prices when others do. There is nothing to gain by selling your products below market value. Other caterers, who are just as reluctant to raise their prices, wouldn't be doing so if they didn't need the extra margin created by increased costs.

We're not just talking food and beverage. If a competitor of yours raises their staff charges by $2.00 per hour, then, you should also raise your staff charges. This would be especially true if the company that made the increase was considered a leader in your marketplace. This, follow the leader, action often makes the buyers believe that your company is just as good as the other one.

2. Not too much at any one time.

Seems like a simple guideline. However, in the real world of catering, caterers save up all the little price increases they should have taken over a longer period which results in the announcement of a 10% price increase across the board! It is best to take 2% here and 3% there... a little at a time.

3. Not too often.

In general, it would be best to make price increases twice a year. The buyers will understand your actions better if they don't have to constantly think about your ongoing price increases. Many caterers simply coordinate their increases to hit during their slower seasons to stir up less controversy.

4. Lower some prices as you raise others.

This is an important guideline. CaterSource suggests that caterers announce price "adjustments" instead of price increases. You can do this with a simple letter mailed to your buyers. The core of this letter is marketing the fact that your company is fair, and realistic, when it comes to raising prices.

For example, you could say "ABC Catering is adjusting prices for the next six months based on present, and projected, market conditions. Please note that two varieties of foods have increased prices, two have stayed the same and one has been lowered."

What you're demonstrating, is that seafood and beef items have increased prices, chicken and lamb have stayed the same, and pork prices have actually been lowered. This type of logic sounds and feels fair to buyers.

5. Protect your best buyers from the increase.

You've probably heard the axiom "80 % of your profits are in the hands of only 20% of your buyers". Because of this, it might be best to let these buyers have special arrangements with you that limit your price increases with respect to their purchases. This is playing "favorites", but it might be important for economic safety.

6. Communicate your actions clearly and with truth.

Letters announcing your decision to raise, or adjust, your prices are obviously important. However, a personal phone call, or a visit to their company, might be even better when it comes to announcing your increases in price. Pricing is a very personal thing. Increased costs are a very important element of your business. It is important that your regular, and new, buyers believe that your price increases are due to increased costs of labor and raw materials.

Sample Pricing Sheet

NAME:_____

TODAY'S DATE_____

COMPANY NAME:_____

ADDRESS:_____

CITY,ZIP:_____

PHONE - HOME:_____

    WORK:_____

    FAX:_____

TYPE OF FUNCTION_____

DATE OF FUNCTION_____

DAY & TIME_____

OF GUESTS_____

MENUS SENT:_____
☐ PINK   ☐ BLUE   ☐ BBQ   ☐ CREATE
☐ OTHER_____

APPOINTMENT ON _____

LOCATION:_____

MAY I ASK HOW YOU HEARD OF US?_____

MENU PACKAGE: ☐ KOSHER $_____   ☐ OVER ⬅⬅⬅

ADULT $_____   **GTD. MIN** _____   CHILD $_____   6&⬇ $_____

FIXED

SERVICE: ☐INCL   ☐ADD
___ WAITERS @ $_____   ___ MAITRE D @ $_____
___ BAR @ $_____
___ CHEFS @ $_____   **$$**_____

CHINA   ☐INCL   ☐OPT $_____
☐GOLD   ☐GLASS
☐PASTEL   ☐OTHER_____   **$$**_____

STEMWARE   ☐INCL   ☐OPT $_____
☐STANDARD   ☐CRYSTAL
☐WATER   ☐WINE   ☐CHAMP   **$$**_____

LINENS: $_____   ☐INCL ☐OPT
☐CUSTOM   ☐STANDARD
COLORS: TABLE_____   NAPKINS_____
☐ BUFFET OVERLAY_____   **$$**_____

BAR SET-UPS   ☐INCL   **☐OPT ⬇**
$_____   ☐SODA ONLY @ $_____
☐ JUICE ONLY @ $_____   ☐ BLENDER @ $_____
                    $$_____

SUBTOTAL   **$$**_____

$$ WORKSHEET
MENU   _____   PRICE _____
FIXED   _____
RENTALS   _____
T&G   _____

REVIEWED:
OVERTIME   ☐ POTENTIAL   ☐ SERVERS @ 25.00   ☐ 10% OF MENU   **$ PER HOUR**_____
☐GUARANTEE   ☐GRATUITIES   ☐PAYMENT   **☐DEPOSIT REQ** $_____

©The Ultimate Caterer, Inc.   all information contained on this lead sheet remains the property of The Ultimate Caterer, Inc.

Finding a Food Cost

1. Item or Ingredient	5. Expected Shrink or Waste	9. Item or Ingredient
Ham	1#	$2.33 ÷ 16oz = .15¢ per ounce

2. Original Purchase Weight or Unit	6. Real Useable Weight or Units Less Waste	10. Amount Needed Per Person
7 #	6# useable 1# waste	5 oz.

3. Original Purchase Unit Cost	7. Real Unit Cost with Waste Added In	11. Final Cost Per Person
$2.00 per #	$14 ÷ 6 = $2.33 per #	.15¢ x 5 oz = 75¢ per person

4. Total Purchase Cost Before Waste/Shrink	8. Food Cost Measuring Unit	**FINDING A FOOD COST**
$2 x 7# = $14	per ounce	

1. Item or Ingredient	5. Expected Shrink or Waste	9. Measuring Unit Cost

2. Original Purchase Weight or Unit	6. Real Useable Weight or Units Less Waste	10. Amount Needed Per Person

3. Original Purchase Unit Cost	7. Real Unit Cost with Waste Added In	11. Final Cost Per Person

4. Total Purchase Cost Before Waste/Shrink	8. Food Cost Measuring Unit	

Adjust Prices Continually

Never raise prices without lowering some! Your buyers don't understand how all your prices can increase at the same time... without some staying the same or even some going down!

The concept at hand is not really pricing ... it's marketing! You will find that moving from a price increase once, or twice a year, to price adjustments four times a year will help you market your food in a positive manner.

The script is simple. "Mrs. Smith, our chef has just given me our Spring prices, and three categories of foods have increased, four have stayed the same and two have been lowered."

The customer can better understand that the "chicken" or "veal" prices have increased. They can also understand that "seafood" has stayed the same and "beef" prices have been lowered.

To the buyer this is "real life" since they have read about these types of adjustments in the newspaper, heard them talked about on radio and t.v. and experienced them while shopping for themselves at the supermarket.

So, this year, why not make a positive change and send a letter to your best buyers about your new PRICE ADJUSTMENTS.

If you make them logical, and based on fact, your buyers will sense your professionalism on this crucial issue.

Next, give some thought to using these four seasonal pricing situations to price your events.

A buyer coming in during August 2002 for an event in March 2003 would be given both August 2002 pricing and what it will be in March 2003.

Seems too complicated? Well this is marketing ... think emotionally... not logically!

"Mary and Bob, unlike other caterers that just guess at what a menu will cost ten months from now, we've planned ahead and can give you a firm, and fair, price. Based on what our chef has researched, it appears that all our "beef" menus will be going down during the summer of 2002. So, your price will be...."

Still seem complicated? Try this. "Bob and Mary, as you can see on this price list, the summer 2002 "chicken" prices are increasing about 4%. If you can make your decision at this time, I can give you the menu at today's prices."

If you're a salesperson, or a buyer of anything, you probably feel that this sounds gimmicky at best. That's the point ... when you have it down in writing and have a realistic pricing system and blame it on the chef, the buyer is more apt to believe in what you're proposing. This is using pricing as marketing!

Once you have your four yearly price adjustments in place, it permits you to appear different to the buyer from the rest of the caterers who are telling buyers "We reserve the right to raise your prices up to 15% if the market prices increase before your event."

The four yearly price adjustments portray you as a professional company who looks upon pricing in a realistic and fair manner.

"BE THE FIRST CATERER TO GIVE BUYERS FOUR YEARLY PRICE ADJUSTMENTS!"

CHARGE DIFFERENT PRICES TO DIFFERENT BUYERS FOR THE SAME MENU

There is no rule, or law, that says all prices must be the same for everyone buying catering. A caterer needs to try to charge "what the market will bear!"

In fact, if you take time to travel to different McDonald's around your area, you will discover, to your amazement, that at one McDonald's the large drink sells for 30 cents more than at the other restaurant.

You will also notice differences in the pricing for other items. This is based on "what the market will bear" and "what the owner needs to get in relation to rent and other costs."

So, a restaurant in a high rent shopping mall will charge more for the same thing as one in a lower rent situation.

No... don't rip-off your buyers. That will lead to trouble. Instead, don't be afraid to go for that extra dollar, or two, when working with someone who can, or wants, to spend more on the catering.

Most caterers worry about getting caught by the client in this variable charging system. Ask yourself, "what's the worst thing that can happen if I'm caught?'

Depending on your answer you can decide if it is worth it to you to attempt to get better prices in certain situations.

Call Mike Roman and he'll be happy to discuss this selling concept with you.

Showing Volume Price Advantages

In EXAMPLE 1, a caterer was told to plan a menu for 235 guests. On the proposal, given to the client, the caterer gives the buyer the price for the number of guests (235) they are asking for in a range from 225 to 245 guests.

However, because this caterer is concerned about the number of guests decreasing between the booking date and the party date, the customer is also given two additional prices. If their guest list increases by more than ten, the customer saves $2.80 per guest for a larger group. On the other hand, if the guest list drops more than ten, the customer's per person price increases by $2.25.

EXAMPLE 1

225 to 245 - 42.65 per guest

246 or more - 39.85 per guest

224, or less - 44.90 per guest

This means, if the guest list drops by 30 to a final guarantee of 205, the caterer picks up $421.25 of extra volume that he wouldn't have had without the ability to raise the price.

If a format similar to Example 1 is used in your customized proposals you should achieve better profitability when numbers drop. It should also encourage people to begin telling their friends that they know a caterer who gives better prices for larger events.

It is important to note that this range of pricing format needs to be given to the customer as they finalize their menu and/or at the time of booking. A corporation who books for an event of 800 guests and then ends up with only 300 will be less likely to fight it out with you, if they signed off on the price ranges at time of booking.

EXAMPLE 2 is designed for a pre-printed menu like the ones you use for self-service catering to corporations.

Think about it for a moment. Can you think of anything that you buy for your business that doesn't have a price that gets lower as you order more? When you buy meat for 1,000 you get a better price than when you buy meat for 100.

Corporations have the same situation. When they buy copier paper, they get a better price if they buy more cases at one time. So, a caterer would be wise to offer their catering on a sliding range basis.

The exact same menu would cost more when bought in smaller amounts and it would cost less when bought in larger amounts.

In Example 2, a cold buffet for 22 people would cost $7.25 per person, but it would cost only $5.65 per person for 255 guests. The point is that most corporate buyers will understand the concept of volume discounts. Since most caterers resist using anything resembling Example 2, the market is wide open for any caterer who makes a move towards volume discounting.

When a client sees that you have a special price for 1000 in your menu, you demonstrate to that buyer that you must be selling orders for 1000! This results in more confidence, by the buyer, in the abilities of your company to do larger orders, over the other caterers who just show one price for all sizes of orders.

The end result for the caterer is usually more orders over 50 and less orders under 20 guests. Besides, shouldn't a caterer get paid more for the work it takes to put together a smaller order?

EXAMPLE 3 is a method of showing ranges on either a customized or preprinted menu format. Example 3 is for those who really hate Examples 1 and 2, but realize that there may be something to this concept of group discounts!

Pricing techniques may be used by a caterer to solve certain problems and concerns that affect everyday operations. The way you place your numbers in your menus, proposals, or letters can provide you with better profit and more control of the selling situation.

CaterSource Rule #26 - Resist using dollar signs when giving prices to clients. They are not needed and they often scare the buyer!

Above all, remember that if all the caterers in your area are showing prices in the same fashion, then a buyer would like to see an alternative pricing method.

EXAMPLE 2

10-19	20-34	35-59	60-99	100-199	200-499	500-999	1000+
7.95	7.25	6.75	6.25	5.95	5.65	5.30	Call

EXAMPLE 3

Prices for selections on this page are 11.00 to 19.00 per guest depending on items selected and final number.

Pricing Methods

Price, and pricing, are interesting concepts for caterers. How a caterer views the concept of pricing has a lot to do with the success of their business.

The "selling" price is the amount of money which a caterer can obtain from a willing buyer in exchange for the catering. Or, "selling" price is the amount that someone is prepared to pay for the catering.

So often, when deciding what to charge, a caterer thinks only of what they can get by with. In other words, the caterers thinks to themselves "What price can I place on my catering that will insure the least chance that I'll miss the sale?"

Remember, most buyers of catering only tell us when they think we are asking too much for our hard work. They don't ever seem to tell us when we're charging too little! Imagine a buyer saying, "I'll take the chicken menu... but I want you to charge me $2.00 per person more because your price is to low."

What a wonderful day that would be! Until then, the only thing a caterer can do is to attempt to keep searching for the highest "selling" price they can attain without losing the sale.

In educational terms what we're saying is:

> *"The selling price is the right price that enables you to sell your goods, yielding an acceptable margin of profit, at the same time giving the customer the feeling of getting value for their money."*

Pricing to get the right selling price is a combination of both art and science. Also, you need to constantly measure your price by balancing profitability with goodwill and repeat business. This is not an easy task!

There are several aspects to consider when moving towards your "right selling" price. Here are a few of them:

1. What is the buyer willing to pay for your catering?

2. What is the buyer expecting to pay for your catering?

3. How do your competitors price their catering?

4. Is the date of the catering on a prime day or a soft one?

5. How much does this particular buyer want to use your company?

6. The complexity of the actual catering.

7. Your need for volume over profit or profit over volume.

8. The level of quality that the buyer is searching for.

Added to the above thoughts is the matter of your costs in producing the catering. The problem rests with your costs in relation to those of your competitors.

A caterer's costs are peculiar to themselves. In other words, it doesn't cost each caterer the same to create the same menu. This results in a buyer getting both higher and lower priced bids for the same specs from different caterers.

Your catering company does things in a unique manner. You have your own methods of preparation and kitchen staffing. You pay your preparation team by your own standards.

This results in a set of costs that are entirely unique to yourself and different than your competitors. So, your competitor just might be able to produce the same level of quality for less because of a different set of costs.

This results in two, or more, caterers having different prices for what appears to be the same menu. So, in order to neutralize these possible price variances a caterer needs to present the buyer with a set of options that permits them to realize that the price of catering is set not just by the cost of food.

The "selling" price becomes the amount a buyer will pay for the total concept of catering. It includes the caterer's level of culinary skills, the amount of the company's liability insurance, the expertise of the serving staff, the method of safety in transporting the food, the cleanliness and sharpness of the banquet facility, the quality of the air conditioning etc.!

The "selling" price is never defended... it just needs to be explained to the buyer before they encounter the lower prices from a competitor.

Each caterer needs to be in constant search for the correct "selling" price of their catering. It is not easy, but it needs to be respected for what it is... the financial future of your business!

Pricing Methods

Pricing Method #1:
Total Price
All costs including menu, staffing, rentals are given to the buyer in one number.

$32.00 per guest

Pricing Method #2:
Break-Down
Each cost of the sale is given to the buyer with separate numbers.

Menu - $21.00 per guest
Staff - $327.00 for the evening
Rentals - $551.00

Pricing Method #3:
Ranges of Price
The buyer is given both high and low price points. "Your event will not cost more than $35.00 per guest, but could be as low as $29.00 per guest depending on the market changes."

Pricing Method #4:
Cost-Plus
Buyer is given the option of paying a fee to the caterer plus the exact cost of doing the event. If you wanted to get $10.00 per guest you would ask for your margin of 45%, or $4.50 for your fee and then let the buyer pay the rest of the exact costs.

The Matrix Pricing System

What is consulting? To me, consulting is evaluation and comparison. First you evaluate what conditions exist, then you compare these conditions with those that exist elsewhere.

This is why the world has consultants. Not for their expertise, but for their exposure to diverse conditions. Most caterers have never been to other catering operations to see what is happening. I've been fortunate to have personally visited more than 900 catering companies over the last 20 years.

That's what this series of articles is about. I hope to give our readers some guidelines for "self-consulting."

It is important that each catering business receive ongoing evaluation in order to continually reach for higher levels of success.

The matrix selling system

The matrix system of selling catering is built around price and buyer options. It can be used by a caterer either sparingly on a sale by sale basis, or as the normal selling system.

The definition of the matrix system it is... a process of simply offering a buyer multiple levels of choice and the prices that go along with those choices. In short, it is a marketing and pricing system that permits the buyer to participate in choosing the various components that make up the event they wish to cater.

You can also view the matrix system as a package approach to selling your various product lines. At the heart of the matrix selling system is the shopper's opportunity to customize their purchase by selecting the level of cost they wish from your matrix of catering components.

In a self-serve corporate drop off selling situation, the caterer might offer the shopper a choice of three levels for a box lunch.

The first box lunch may sell for $6.95 and include a sandwich, two salads, and dessert. The second level of the matrix would offer a box lunch for $7.45, while the final, and most expensive box lunch, would sell for $8.95.

The matrix in this case could be offering two levels of choice. First, as the box lunch increases in price and impact, the types of food selections could be enhanced. For example, salads in the box lunches could range from a simple potato salad through a pasta salad with baby shrimp.

> **... THINK OF THESE TIPS, TACTICS AND IDEAS AS A STARTING POINT FOR DOING SELF-CONSULTING FOR YOUR OWN BUSINESS.**

On the other hand, the matrix would also work if the food in the three differently priced box lunches were to stay exactly the same, but the box itself changed. For example, the lowest cost box lunch could be a simple white cake box with no frills, while the second and third box lunches could be of "sexy" plastic or have ribbons and other neat packaging elements that provide more impact for the buyer.

The purpose of this type of matrix is to demonstrate to the buyer that the caterer they are shopping with is a source for all levels of impact. So, if the need is for fifty box lunches for a low-level training class, the caterer has an appropriately priced lunch. And if the need is for a managers meeting or customer lunch, the caterer still has the solutions to fit the particular buying needs!

Is this starting to make sense to you? Remember: many buyers of corporate catering keep a list of several caterer's names to call for lunch. The problem is that each of the caterer's names they keep is called for a certain level of sophistication.

For example, one caterer may be called for the more expensive box lunches, while another one would be called to send in the cheaper ones. The consultants view is that a caterer needs to be the total source of all wants and needs of the buyer. The matrix system permits this to happen. In many ways this is the "supermarket" system of selling.

Supermarket selling

When you go to the supermarket to shop you are constantly being offered foods in a matrix system. You can get a croissant freshly baked, frozen uncooked, frozen cooked, day old, bake your own, filled, etc. The same matrix system is presented with the choices of many vegetables, wines, meats, poultry, and even toilet papers!

The managers of supermarkets realize that they really don't know what every shopper's level of desire is for any particular food or product, so they give us a matrix of choices that most often permit the shopper to select from at least three price and impact levels.

Three, or more, choices

I suggest that you make your matrix offerings consist of at least three different levels. You can go with as many matrix levels as you find necessary, but I suggest that you never fall below three choices.

The Matrix Pricing System

For example, one choice a shopper would have that would affect the level of impact they wish their party to have would concern the service rentals i.e. china, chairs, linens, etc.

The caterer offers three different groups of rental packages that carry a price point, and impact, from low to medium to high.

The low cost package offers a simple white china plate, a plastic folding chair, simple linens, etc.; the middle rental package offers a Rosenthal Silver Rimmed china plate, white wood chair and custom linen, etc.; the most costly package offers a Gold Rimmed Rosenthal china plate, Chivare chair, linen overlays, etc. Are you getting it?

Often these packages that form the caterer's matrix are simply called Premium, Traditional and Value to represent the high, medium and low levels of impact. They also could be called Primo, Deluxe and Regular.

Freedom of choice

The reason that the matrix system works well is due to the caterer's low pressure approach to selling their products. The message to the buyer is simply "Buy whatever you want... Purchase what fits the situation... I'll still love you whether you buy my most expensive package or one of the lower cost ones!"

In addition, the matrix for full service catering often breaks each event component into three, or more, levels of choice. The entree might have three selections of chicken, but each has a slightly higher price because it rises in perceived value. This is done with portion size, bone-in versus boneless, a simple rice or a risotto (one with shrimp and one without), and asparagus versus fresh, or frozen green beans.

The selling script for this type of matrix would be the following:

"Mrs. Smith, I've created three approaches to your request for a chicken menu. In all three cases I've used a ten ounce boneless chicken breast.

The first one, which is our Traditional approach, at $14.90 per guest, has a fresh garden salad, baby new potatoes, fresh green beans, and a beautiful lemon tart for dessert.

The second offering is our Premium menu at $19.85 per guest, and includes the Caesar Salad, seafood risotto, fresh asparagus, and our exciting chocolate sampler.

Finally, I can offer you our Chef's Value menu at $13.85 which comes with the garden salad, mashed potatoes, peas and carrots, and a great carrot cake for dessert.

Mrs. Smith, whatever you choose, your guests won't be disappointed!"

In closing, I need to really stress that the matrix system of offering variety and choice to your buyers will bring huge rewards to those who use it. It is the hottest selling and marketing concept that I've been offering to my consulting clients over the last two years. In short, this system has been making many caterers a lot of money!

The final benefit of this matrix system is that the salesperson also offers your more expensive offerings along with the middle priced ones. The result is that the buyer gets a chance to purchase what they really wish to purchase. They can buy up, or down. But, they will buy something!

The Matrix Pricing Graph

ABC	TRADITIONAL	PREMIUM	VALUE
MENU	28.50	32.25	26.95
STAFF	355.00 or 18%	455.00 or 16%	220.00 or 20%
RENTAL	753.00	1,044.00	622.00
FLORAL	550.00	700.00	326.00

ABC	STYLE A	STYLE B	STYLE C
BOX LUNCH	6.25	7.50	9.75
LUNCHEON	12.25	13.05	16.90
COLD BUFFET	8.35	10.50	12.75
COCKTAIL EVENT	16.10	18.95	22.40

Range of Price Method

The terse script below is one that many caterers would really like to say to their buyers, but, obviously, these words would not lead to successful sales records!

"Look... Mrs. Smith, it is very hard to know exactly how much your menu will really cost for an event booked today and then catered 14 months from now. So, whether you like it or not, I'll need to check with our suppliers twelve months from now to see how the marketplace is going in relation to the floods, earthquakes, and cost of labor. Then, and only then, can I give you a final price that will insure that I can make the profit I need to make on your catered event."

But the above words are correct. The truth is that it is unfair to both the caterer and the client to try to guess what costs will be when planning longer range events.

The range of price method uses the above concepts to increase the closing rates of both off and on-premise caterers. It is a method that needs good scripting and the right type of shopper to use it with.

"Mrs. Smith, let me explain how we price our menus for events that have over twelve months of lead time before they are catered. Unlike other caterers who give you what appears to be a firm price up-front and then tells you that they have the right to increase the price up to 15% due to unforeseen and future market changes, we take an entirely different tact.

Let me explain, we provide you with a fairer way to insure that you will get the right price for your catered event. In essence, we provide you with two prices for each menu you create.

First, we give you the current price, based on current costs of the menu ingredients as if it were to be catered in the next thirty days. Then, we give you a price that reflects what we think the correct price will be twelve months from now when we actually cater the event.

By giving you both the present cost and the potential cost we create a range of prices that will reflect what the correct and fair price will be.

In other words, lets suppose the range for your menu is between $17.50 to $19.75. About 30 days before the event, our chef will tell me what the final price will be based on market conditions at that time. The price he gives us will fall somewhere between $17.50 and $19.75.

It could be $17.95, or $18.25, or $19.50, or, for that fact, $17.75 per guest. Mrs. Smith, with our range of price you can budget for the $19.50 menu, it can't go any higher, and, more than likely, save money on the final price. With our range of pricing system you can only hear good news at the end, especially if the price comes in on the low side, so you'll get the fair and correct price."

To gain maximum effectiveness with the range of price method, you need to know what the competition will be charging for a similar menu or catering package.

Think of it this way. Suppose Mrs. Smith was told by a competitor that a similar, or exact, menu would cost $19.50 per guest ... and suppose that this competitor didn't use the same range of price story that you have. It just may be that the shopper realizes that with the competitor's firm price, she is getting the highest price possible based on that caterer's guess about the market prices 12 months from now. Mrs. Smith, realizes that your competitor is being selfish and safe by giving the highest price possible.

Mrs. Smith may look upon your range of prices as the better, or fair, way of doing business. In fact, she might think, that it is sort of like "lotto". If she waits, she might save money. If she likes the idea of possibly saving some cost by taking the range of pricing method, she might be swayed towards your company.

Then again, she might not. However, this is a very successful concept with some buyers and can be used very successfully if you are not the highest priced caterer in your market. Many social and corporate shoppers have switched away from their regular caterer because of this different pricing concept.

Some caterers have used this method as a second chance opportunity with a buyer who balks at the traditional method of giving the price as is.

"Mrs. Smith, I see your point about our price being a little high. Let me explain how we can utilize a range of price so we both get what we need."

The Cost Plus System of Pricing

Don't even think of reading this page if you are set in your ways as a caterer. Don't think of reading this page if you are a salesperson who doesn't like to match wits with a buyer.

Do read this page if you wish to learn about a unique way to move from your normal pricing methods into a bold pricing structure... especially when you're dealing with a difficult customer or a giant company's multi-day catering needs.

Let's begin. It's called "cost plus" in the same manner that contractors tell their clients that they charge "time plus materials". So, a cement manufacturer might tell a customer "I'll need to charge you for the cement you use, plus the labor I need to put it in place".

In other words, in some catering situations, it is possible to tell a potential buyer "I could charge you a flat fee for my skills, as long as you reimburse me for the food and staff that I need to make your event happen successfully."

Here's the foundation of the cost plus pricing system for catering:

1. The buyer pays a predetermined flat fee based on a per person charge.

2. The fee is based on your need to capture your normal profits and gross margin. So, if you normally have a margin of 40% of sales, this is the formula you would use in deciding on what your fee, or plus, will be.

As an example, let's say you normally would charge $10 per person for a particular menu. In the cost plus pricing method, if your margin was supposed to be 40% of sales, you would charge the client $4 per person.

3. Now comes the cost. The client is told that in addition to the fee, or plus, they will need to reimburse you for all of your base expenses pertaining to the event. These costs are not marked-up and are based on the invoices that you receiver from your purveyors.

So, if you purchased $365 from your poultry purveyor the client owes you $365. If you spent $265 with the produce purveyor, they now owe you $265. If you used three bartenders and seven servers who normally get $100 per job, the client owes you $1,000.

One caterer simply takes the customer shopping at a large price club, or at the market, and lets the client pay for all of the stuff that is purchased!

4. Finally, it is important to remember that you are simply packaging your price differently during your sales approach. In fact, the amount of margin you make is the same as you would if you used your traditional pricing systems.

Now, when do you use this cost plus system? When the buyer is a friend who thinks you owe them a huge discount, or one that desperately needs to think that they are getting a "deal".

The cost plus system is ideal for any bid where you need to cater over several days i.e a golf tournament, grand openings, training sessions, etc.

For example, say you are asked by a Fortune 500 type company to bid on a four day golf outing that would include three meals a day, full bar, snacks, and other undetermined food needs. The expected number of guests would be between 450 and 600.

Your preliminary figures tell you that the job would be billed out at between $200,000 to $300,000 when priced in your normal fashion. In fact, all of the other caterer's bids will reflect these figures.

Why not be different? Take your 40% margin, or whatever your margin is, and offer that as a cost plus price. Your projected price of $300,000 times 40% margin gives you $120,000 margin.

You simply type into your bid the price in this fashion:

> *"ABC Catering will be pleased to professionally cater your golf outing for a one time fee of $120,000 plus the reimbursements of all our costs. These costs would be without any mark-up or increase in price. In this manner, you will be controlling all your costs for food, beverage and service. You will pay only for what you use, so you will not need to worry about paying for a guaranteed number of guests."*

Well, what do you think? Are you disappointed or glad that you read this page. Remember, in the example above, once you get your check for $120,000 dollars, why worry about how many people come.

Obviously, you can put in extra safeguards dealing with minimum numbers if you wish. Give it a try!

Thoughts on Service Charges

What is a service charge? Is it used by on and off-premise caterers? Will it lose a sale? What are caterers doing to make money on their staff?

These are just a few of the questions CaterSource gets from subscribers. While the answers are rather simple, the goals of using service charges are complex.

A. FIRST DEFINITION OF SERVICE CHARGE

A percentage, usually around 18%, taken by a caterer on the total catering invoice to capture the money necessary to pay the staff working the event and certain managerial positions.

B. SECOND DEFINITION OF SERVICE CHARGE

A marketing concept that makes buyers feel that they are getting better value from one company over another.

C. GOALS OF SERVICE CHARGES

First goal is to convince more buyers into using your company over the competition. That means that using the service charge for just paying the labor charges of an event is probably not the wisest use of service charges.

D. SERVICE CHARGE VS. SET HOURLY FEES

No contest for off-premise caterers and a draw for on-premise ones. Hourly staffing fees, such as $12.00 per hour, will capture a guaranteed amount of money to pay the staff correctly. The service fee will not get the proper amount, especially on smaller volume events. For example, 18% of a $10,000 invoice, which is $1,800, will not cover the costs for a professional service and production team at an off-premise event.

E. SERVICE CHARGE VS. GRATUITY

In non-legal terms, a service charge is an amount of money that is controlled by the catering company management and can be paid out, or not, in any manner they wish.

The gratuity is an amount of money that is needed to be given to all the staff at an event equally. The ownership cannot hold any back.

F. THE BIG MISTAKE

Most on-premise caterers only use the service charge concept and most off-premise caterers only use the hourly rate. There are times when each could use the opposite of what they normally use.

In fact, when you ask a caterer why they use, or don't use a service charge, they respond by telling you that they do what their competitors do.

G. MARKETING AND PROFIT

The successful caterers of the next five years will be those who discover how to charge both an hourly wage for workers and, in addition, a service charge percentage.

First, whether you're on or off-premise, you need to consider breaking away from the traditional 18% percentage. It's overused and boring to the public. Or to put it another way, whatever everyone else is doing, you should be a little, or a lot, different.

This is important: A buyer of catering would rather spend their money on anything else other than a service charge!

A buyer getting a chance to purchase two identical menu packages from two different caterers, will always buy the one with more value.

Look at this scenario... one caterer is charging $24.00 per guest plus an 18% service charge, while another caterer is charging $27.00 per guest with a 14.5% service charge. Which do you think they buy?

Buyers will always choose to spend money on their guests rather than line the pockets of management!

Here's some other concepts to think about:

1. To be different ask for a 20% service charge.

2. Change the name to Support Fee.

3. Explain that as the menu price goes up, the service charge percentage goes down.

4. Offer a lower service charge on those days that are harder to sell.

5. Add a 3% Catering Support Fee to all proposals. Explain, when asked, that this is for the people that the host doesn't see i.e. the drivers, dishwashers, stock room persons etc.

6. Tell the clients that your chefs working at events get an additional 6% service fee because of their profession.

7. Tie service charges into size of events. As the volume goes up, the service charge goes down.

The point is... that there is no point! A caterer can become as creative as they wish with the concept of service charges. It's your call.

CaterSource can reconfirm for you that whenever a caterer is the first to break away from the pack, to demonstrate creativity and understanding on how buyers think, they earn great success and increased profits. Should you be the first to break away from the rest?... why not!

Discount Pricing Has a Place

If you needed a 26 Sony inch television... would you pay full retail for it? Would you go to Neiman-Marcus to buy it? Or, would you, like everyone else go to one of the major discount appliance houses, that spend millions of dollars to let us know that we are stupid if we pay too much for a television set! In fact, there are people who will be creative enough to get the television set even cheaper, from a third source.

Yes... a caterer should get paid what they're worth! The point is that pricing is also a form of marketing. So, sometimes a person selling a product or a service needs to think about what the buyer wants to experience while they're shopping.

One theory in pricing is based on the fact that a buyer really perceives extra value when they get a discount off the full price.

CaterSource's point is that discounting is not for everyone ... but it seems that we are all moving towards "Wal-Mart" lowest price thinking!

Here are some types of discounts that might be considered:

1. For being a regular buyer.

2. For buying an order over a certain plateau.

3. For buying two orders in one week.

4. For buying two orders in one month.

5. For buying on a certain day.

6. For ordering early.

7. For ordering earliest.

8. For picking-up the order.

9. For using a Fax for ordering.

10. For not using a Fax for ordering.

11. For ordering two orders at once.

12. For giving you a referral.

13. For letting you use their thank you letter as a reference.

14. For paying COD.

15. For paying 50% deposit.

16. For paying the entire amount in advance.

17. When paying with a credit card.

18. When not paying with a credit card.

19. When they give you a reference letter after the event.

20. When they mention you on the invitation.

21. When they get your name mentioned in the media.

22. When they give a certain gratuity to your staff.

23. When they pay the rental company directly using a second check.

24. For an early signing of their agreement.

25. For catering that starts after or before a certain time of the day.

26. For catering purchased in the slower months.

27. For self-service catering.

28. For full-service catering.

29. When they take care of their own bar.

30. When you get the mailing list information of their guests.

31. When they put out a sign or other notice about your company.

32. When you are permitted to send the guests a letter before the party.

33. For using your rental company.

34. For celebrating your company's 5th anniversary in business.

35. Because you are a manager and not one of the regular salespeople who earn a commission.

36. Anyway that they can save the commission.

37. If they are referred by one of your regular buyers.

38. When your company has "made its sales goals for the month".

CHAPTER 6  QUESTIONS

1. What factors help to determine a caterer's pricing?

2. When and how should a caterer raise prices?

3. What is meant by volume price advantages to buyers?

4. What should every salesperson ask themselves before they quote a price?

5. How does a caterer decide on the right selling price?

6. What are the differences between the "Break-Down" and "Total Price" methods?

7. Do you see any advantages in the Matrix pricing concept?

8. When, and why, would the "Cost-Plus" pricing format be used?

9. What are some of the discounts that may be offered a buyer?

10. What is the difference between a "Service Charge" and a "Gratuity"?

PROPOSALS

CHAPTER **7**

TABLE OF CONTENTS

CHAPTER

7

*"If you can do a party for 250
guests you can do one for 500
... it's just two parties of 250!"*

Elements of a Great Proposal

The words you use in your custom bids or proposals are only the first half of what you need to make a successful sale to a prospective buyer. The other half is the impact or "theatre" that you infuse into your package of ideas to the buyer.

Yes... the actual menus and prices are certainly extremely important, but so is the manner in which the buyer perceives your energy, style, and pizazz!

Here's some of our suggestions on how to get more impact into your proposals. Remember: the words tell them and the "theatre" demonstrates your level of sophistication.

1. The weight and quality of paper. Review the paper that you use for your copier. How thin is it? How flimsy does it feel? Does it have a watermark? The best way to judge what paper will do for you is to hold it yourself and ask the questions above. White paper is fine, but off-white often has a different impact. If you haven't seen some of the paper catalogs call 1-800- A- PAPERS and ask them to send you a catalog of what they sell.

2. The length. Some of your buyers want short proposals while others wish to read for hours on what you are suggesting for them. You need to make this call. We suggest that a proposal not be less than three pages in length to include the cover letter, a menu page, and a financial summary cost page.

3. The overall level of professionalism. Correct grammar and correct spelling win more proposals than you think! Corporate buyers can't help themselves when it comes to prejudging a caterer in a "bad light" when they misspell a simple or complex word. Also, go to a book store and purchase a book on corporate business letters to be sure that you are doing it correctly.

4. The size of the paper. Why does your letterhead need to be only 8.5 by 11 inches? Why can't it be legal sized letterhead, 8.5 by 14 inches? Some caterers have found much success with this concept. It makes their proposal different.

5. The envelope. Color works well here, 9 x 12 envelopes are always suggested for impact.

6. How it's delivered. What do you put the envelope into? Or, what can take the place of the envelope itself? One caterer used a gym bag with a university's emblem on it to send a proposal for a sports award dinner. Another caterer used a miniature model aircraft to send to a client that was a pilot. I think you get the idea. Look for something unique that makes a statement about your creativity to the buyer. Also, mailing is not as good as sending it by FedEx which is not as good as personally delivering the proposal to the buyer.

7. How quick it's delivered. Most buyers will be suspicious if a major proposal got to them on the same day they called... so being too quick can work against you. Taking ten days will most likely make you look like you are not in control of your business. We suggest a time frame from two to five days for major proposals. We don't suggest faxing a major proposal.

8. To fold or not. No contest here! We don't mean to be catty, but folding a major proposal that is being sent to a buyer is a no no! Would you fold any work of art found in a museum? Neither should you fold your brilliant package of ideas! This means that you need to use 9 x 12 envelopes for all major proposals.

9. The stamp or postage. The case can be made that a stamp is more effective than a thin red outline of a postage indicia from a postage machine. Many caterers try to match the client's theme with a postage stamp to be found by the dozens at the post office. For example if you're making a bid for a party from a company that makes or sells automobiles, then it would be nice to get a stamp that shows the same.

10. Number of copies. If you only send one copy of your proposal to a buyer and three people at the company need to review it, the secretary needs to make two more "ugly" copies. Get our point? Also, if you are able to find out the names of the other buyers at the company, you can customize each copy with their names.

11. What else you include. Photos, testimonial letters, recipes, letter of reference from your bank, descriptions of your uniform, bios of your key serving staff, history of your business, customer lists, media articles, diagrams of the way you intend to set-up the event, equipment recommendations, lists of wine and liquor suggested amounts, sample dishes, sample linens, samples of your foods and anything else that will involve the five senses of the buyers... the senses of touch, smell, taste, sight, and hearing.

Power Additions to Bid / Proposals

1. **The objective of any sales proposal or bid is to:**

    A. Convince your buyer to select you over the competition.

    B. Create a value-added picture in the buyer's mind.

    C. Overcome any and all price sensitivity.

    D. Get a deposit check or other commitment.

    E. Create a long time buyer.

    F. Get referrals.

    G. Get cross-over sales from social to corporate or corporate to social.

2. **The single most important aspect of a proposal is to give the buyers the reasons and the words that permit them to constantly resell themselves and to sell others that need to be convinced!**

    The phrases that accomplish this are:

    A. "Unlike other caterers, we..."

    B. "At ABC Catering we..."

    C. "A great event depends on..."

    D. "It takes a special set of people to..."

    E. "Very few caterers have..."

    F. "One reason for our success is..."

    G. "Our clients tell us that..."

    H. "Remember, what we don't want to happen is..."

3. **Here's some of the factors that help and hurt your chances of getting the sale:**

    A. The weight and quality of paper.

    B. The length.

    C. The overall level of professionalism.

    D. The size of the paper.

    E. The envelop.

    F. How it's delivered.

    G. How quick it's delivered.

    H. The fold or non-fold.

    I. The stamp or postage.

    J. The number of copies.

    K. What else you include.

    L. The follow-up.

Super Phrases for Proposals

Here's some phrases that you might add to your proposals. They are random and unconnected from each other.

1. "Your price of $35.00 is guaranteed until September 3. After this date a review needs to be done to asses any increases in cost."

2. "When you call us, please use this special number 555-5555 which will place you with my associate Gregg Jones."

3. "Gratuities are not required, but are graciously accepted by the staff."

4. "Most importantly, we assume all responsibilities for planning and coordinating the total flow of your event."

5. "All of our ingredients are fresh, All of our portions are generous and you may be assured of ample quantities for your invited guests."

6. "We take pride in understanding and anticipating the special needs of our clients. We make them partners with us in creating memorable and treasured events!"

7. "The menu which is enclosed has been customized for you and reflects our earlier discussions. However, I will gladly make any adjustments you wish. The menu and services have been priced according to the number of guests you are presently estimating."

8. "All other charges for equipment rentals, flowers, music etc. will be on your final invoice or billed directly by our affiliate companies. Please note that we accept major credit cards for payments of deposits or invoices."

9. "The staff will leave your event at 1:00 AM and will cost $285.00 per hour for the 81/2 hours of service. In addition, a 12% Social Security and Unemployment Tax fee and a $20.00 gratuity will be charged."

10. "Enclosed please find a statement of insurance from our insurance carrier. We want you to know that all ABC Catering staff working at your event are legal employees and not casual labor. This means that, since they are covered by workmen's compensation, you are protected from possible claims by staff for any injuries that might happen while at your event."

11. "Once you have booked with us, you will receive unlimited phone assistance to confirm and reconfirm each and every detail."

12. "Over the phone yesterday, you mentioned the need for keeping costs down at this event. Bob, you're not alone in your wish. Most of our clients are voicing the same concern for value and lower cost impact ideas from us."

13. "Just in case you need me before, or after, regular business hours, my pager number is 555-5555 and my home number is 555-5551. My children are up at 6:00 AM each morning!"

14. "One reason for our company's success is because our planning department has the total support of our culinary team. This is not unique to our industry."

15. "Our clients tell us that after they reserved their date with us, they gained confidence in our team approach each and every time they called our office for assistance. This is because at ABC the entire team is aware of each event, so you can always get an answer, even when I'm not in!"

16. "Very few caterers have the commitment to service as ABC Caterers!"

What Every Salesperson Should Be Asking Themselves

1. Am I getting the sales volume I should?
2. How many sales does my company expect of me for this year?
3. Do I always talk to the right person when selling catering?
4. Do I have a consistent and proven sales script for qualifying the caller?
5. Do I spend too much time with clients who really can't buy?
6. Do I spend at least two days a week out of the office prospecting for customers?
7. Have I set my three year income goal?
8. Have I read at least three books on selling in the last 24 months?
9. Have I spent time analyzing my competitors?
10. Am I aware of your closing average?
11. Have I spent time during the last 30 days talking to the chef about the foods I sell?
12. When I'm going to an area to make a confirmed call, do I prospect for others?
13. Am I having some fun when I sell?

Proposal Template #1

PLATED DINNERS
All Dinner Selections include choice of Salad, Chef's Selection of Accompaniments,
Pastry Chef's Dessert Selection, Fresh Breads and Freshly Brewed Coffees & Teas

SAUTEED CHICKEN BREAST
with a Smoked Tomato Salsa
$29.00 Per Person

GRILLED CHICKEN BREAST
Topped with Tomato, Bacon and Mozzarella Cheese
Smothered in Sauce Bordelaise
$30.00 Per Person

GRILLED PACIFIC SALMON
on a Smoked Red Pepper Coulis
$34.00 Per Person

GRILLED MARINATED SWORDFISH
on a Citrus Beurre Blanc, Topped
with a la jardiniere of Julienne Vegetables.

ROASTED PRIME RIB OF BEEF, 12 OZ.
Served au Jus
$34.00 Per Person

LAMB CHOPS PERSILLADE
Rack of Lamb Rubbed with Dijon Mustard and Lightly Breaded
and Roasted in the Oven, Served with English Mint Sauce
$38.50 Per Person

MEDALLIONS OF ROASTED BEEF TENDERLOIN
Rubbed with an Ancho Chili Paste
and Served on a Yellow Pepper Coulis
$38.00 Per Person

May we suggest an Intermezzo or Appetizer to Compliment Your Selection

18% Service Charge and appropriate taxes
will be added to all food and beverage

Proposal Template #2

(DATE)

Mr. Jim Doe
2222 N. South Street
Somewhere, CA 44444

Dear Jim:

Dear Mr. Doe:

ABC Catering is pleased to propose the following menu for your sit-down dinner on Saturday, (DATE) for 150 guests.

HORS D'OEUVRES: Assorted hot and cold selections passed on silver trays @ $45 per hundred.
Imported cheese and fruit tray with crackers @ $29 each.
Fresh crudites' with several dips @ $31 per tray
Seafood Spread with cocktail sauce and thin sliced
crusty bread @ $65 per hundred

SIT-DOWN DINNER: Chateaubriand with Bernaise Sauce
Wild and White Rice
Honey Glazed Carrots
Broiled Tomato Halves with Parmesan Cheese
Caesar Salad
Rolls/Butter
Coffee, Tea
$13.50 per person plus tax

DESSERT: Strawberries with Sabayon
$2.00 per person plus tax

ABC Catering can also provide china, tables and chairs on a rental basis. Liquor, beer, wine and mixers can also be arranged.

There is an additional charge for servers of $10.00 per hour per server.

The above ideas are my suggestions based on our conversation. Obviously, I will be pleased to further customize a menu for your special evening.

If you have any questions, please don't hesitate to call. I look forward to working with you!

Sincerely:

Bob Smith
President

Proposal Template #3 / Page 1

(DATE)

Mr. Jim Doe
XYZ Corporation
2222 N. South Street
Somewhere, CA 44444

Dear Mr. Doe:

We appreciate the opportunity to present the enclosed menu and service suggestions for the Annual Achievement Dinner you are planning on Monday, (DATE) at the Bronson Mansion.

The menu which has been enclosed has been customized for you and reflects our earlier discussions. However, I will gladly make any adjustments you wish. The menu and services have been priced according to the number of guests you are presently estimating.

For your estimated guest count of 145, you will require a staff of fifteen to professionally attend to your guest's expectations. Your staff will arrive two hours prior to your guest's arrival. Each staff member is sixty-seven dollars for a seven hour period at the Bronson Mansion. Overtime, if needed, is twelve dollars per hour and will be billed after the event. Your staff will attend to all of the needs and expectations of your guests and will allow you, and the rest of your staff, to be a guest at your own event.

All other charges for equipment rentals, flowers, music etc. will be on your final invoice or billed directly by our affiliate companies. Please note that we accept major credit cards for payments of deposits or invoices.

Mr. Doe, as we have discussed I have placed a "red hold" on (Their DATE) for your exclusive use for a period of ten days from the date of this letter. To confirm your reservation and "green hold" please forward twenty-five hundred dollars to our office or call to use your credit card.

Please review all the enclosed information and feel free to call me if you have any questions or suggestions.

Sincerely,

Bob Smith
Sales Director

cc: Alice Perkins, President of ABC Catering

Proposal Template #3 / Page 2

DINNER MENU DESIGNED FOR XYZ CORPORATION
FOR Monday, (DATE)
CREATED BY BOB SMITH

**A Variety Of Hot And Cold Hors D'oeuvres Passed To Your Guests
On Floral Garnished Silver Trays By Formally Dressed Servers**

Notice that these words tell the buyer not just what the food is, but also what it is doing.

Fresh Ginger Shrimp
with Basil Horseradish Sauce

California Grown Fresh Snow Peas
filled with Fresh Pacific Salmon Pate
Salmon Supplied by North Shore Seafood

Chilled Italian Prosciutto and Melon Canape

An Elaborate 24 Foot Skirted Buffet Table with Chefs Serving Each Guest

Grilled Prime Tenderloin of Veal

Boneless Idaho Duck Breasts

Silver Terrine of Poached Red Snapper

Potato-Leek and Garlic Tart

Melange of Fresh "Organically Grown" Vegetables
To include: Broccoli, Green Beans, Cauliflower,
Carrots, Peppers and Turnips

**Dessert Selections To Be Displayed On Beautiful Serpentine Buffet
Using Silver Cake Stands and Country Baskets**

Cassis Mousse with Red Currant Sauce

Fresh Strawberries Specially Ordered With Stems On

**Our Baker Filling Miniature Cannoli Shells
As Guests Select Their Favorite Filling Flavors**

Freshly Ground Coffee To Include Decaffeinated

38.60 per person for 145 Guests
36.25 per person for 185 or more Guests
42.30 per person for under 135 guests

SUMMARY OF COSTS FOR XYZ CORPORATION'S DINNER
Monday, (DATE)
CREATED BY BOB SMITH

Customized Menu for 145 guests ... 5,604.25
Rental of all Event Equipment ... 2,834.65
Selection of Custom Linen ... 1,112.00
Valet Parking Service ... 467.00
ABC Catering Service Team ... 1,005.00
7% State Sales Tax ... 771.60
Total: 11,022.90

Services Provided At No Cost

Professional Event Planning by Bob Smith ... 250.00 n/c

Pre-Event Check of Bronson Mansion ... 125.00 n/c

Ice for bar and table use ... 135.00 n/c

Special Meeting with Service Team ... 125.00 n/c

Delivery of All Event Equipment to Bronson Mansion ... 340.00 n/c

Delivery of Food & Beverage to Bronson Mansion ... 155.00 n/c
Total No Charges: 1,130.00

NOTE:
We will be pleased to hold a tentative reservation for your event date, and
guarantee the above prices until (Deadline DATE). If not confirmed with
your deposit by this date, availability and prices will need to be renegotiated.

(DATE)

Mr. Jim Doe
2222 N. South Street
Somewhere, CA 44444

Dear Mr.& Mrs. Doe:

   We are delighted that you have asked ABC Catering to create an event plan to celebrate the wedding of Mary and Bill to be held at Temple Grace on Saturday, (DATE). The following proposal reflects your conversations with our sales manager Rick Jones on January 4 and will exhibit our interpretation of your expectations.

   Our planning team at ABC Catering believes that the menus and services presented perfectly suit your important occasion. Also, our plan is one that has been designed for a proper flow of your special event at Temple Grace. We have worked there many times and have built into this proposal all that we have learned that will guarantee the highest success and comfort for your guests.

   ABC Catering provides it's clients with a unique combination of culinary talent and logistical expertise. We will arrange, and take responsibility for all of the support services that you might need such as a photographer or florist.

   We are fully aware of the importance of this day in your life. We are excited about helping this day become one that all will remember with joy and happiness. The team at ABC Catering will bring to bear amazing concern for the success of this special event by paying meticulous attention to all of the details that insure success.

   Please do not consider anything in this proposal as final. However, please take quick action concerning your reservation for our services on (DATE) by signing the enclosed agreement.

Thank you again for allowing us to become involved in this special occasion!

Sincerely,

Bob Smith
Sales Manager

cc: Mary Gregg, Director of Planning, ABC Catering
    Bill Jinks, Executive Chef, ABC Catering
    Alice Franks, Owner, XYZ Rental Company

Proposal Template #4 / Page 2-5

**THE NEXT PAGE OR PAGES OF THE PROPOSAL WOULD BE
THE MENUS BEING OFFERED... AT LEAST THREE SHEETS!**

STAFF:

To insure a successful event, ABC Catering will provide our trained, professional staff of 22 wearing tuxedos to arrive at Temple Grace at 4:30 PM. This team will be headed by our Event Manager Jim Gregory who will supervise the team and work with you on all last minute detail changes or adjustments.

The staff will depart at 1:00 AM and will cost $285.00 per hour for the 81/2 hours of service. In addition, a 12% Social Security and Unemployment Tax fee and a $20.00 gratuity will be charged.

INSURANCE:

Enclosed please find a statement of insurance from our insurance carrier. It is important to note that all of ABC Catering's staff working at your event are legal employees on active payroll rather than casual labor. This protects you from possible claims by staff for any injuries that might happen while at your event.

RENTAL EVENT EQUIPMENT:

At your direction, we will arrange to rent everything necessary to correctly serve the selected menu in a style that befits the occasion The estimated cost of this equipment, such as china, stemware, flatware, tables, chairs etc. is between $12.00 to $15.00 per guest. The rental company will bill you directly.

Proposal Template #4 / Page 6-8

THIS PAGE OF THE PROPOSAL WOULD HAVE A SUMMARY OF COSTS.

SPECIAL SERVICES PROVIDED BY ABC CATERING

1. Assistance with any and all support services that you may need.

2. Pre-event visit to Temple Grace with you to explain the flow of the event.

3. Unlimited phone assistance to confirm and reconfirm each and every detail. We expect last minute changes and we'll be ready to respond.

4. Conference between yourself and our Executive Chef Mary James to explain in detail the menu and to get special requests from you such as the need for a salt-free plate for a guest.

AGREEMENT AND DATE RESERVATION CONFIRMATION

Enclosed please find our payment of $2,500 to confirm our wish for ABC Catering to provide food, staff, equipment and other services for our event on Monday, (DATE) at Grace Temple. This payment will be refunded in full, with no questions asked, if our plans change and if we wish to cancel our plans anytime preceding 30 days of (DATE).

The balance will be due in full at the conclusion of the event on (DATE).

Mr.Jim Doe

The "No Proposal" Proposal

The situation is simple: Are there times when a caterer might not wish to send a client a proposal packet or menu? Is it possible that some shoppers aren't really worth the cost of sending out a packet that cost $3.00 to print and .78 cents to mail? Is it possible that a "hot" shopper might be turned off, or slowed down, by getting our standard packets in the mail?

These are interesting questions. Each of them has a "pro" and a "con". The purpose of the education provided through the CaterSource Journal is to give our subscriber caterers an opportunity to have more than one way to handle a selling situation. So, with that in mind, let's look at the very interesting concept of the "no" proposal proposal.

This technique should be used with caution. What's interesting about the "no" proposal proposal is that it may be used with two distinct selling situations.

The first situation deals with a caller who wants you to drop everything and mail them your menus. Or, you get the feeling that they might not be a "real" buyer. They don't have a date for the event, or they aren't asking the type of questions most buyers ask.

In this case, the goal of the "no" proposal proposal is to get you off the phone as quickly as possible and to save you the costs associated with sending your expensive menu packet with it's postage, printing and office labor.

> *"Mrs. Smith, I think I can help you. Since you're not exactly sure of what you really want, I suggest that I send you some examples of some catering events that we've already sold. I'll look through my files and pull a few of the events that sound like what you're thinking of doing and I'll mail them to you."*

> **or**

> *"Mrs. Smith, we really don't have pre-printed menus and brochures at our company. What I can do is send you some examples of some recent menus we've sold. Is this acceptable to you?*

Do you see how this is another way to handle this type of situation? Do you also see that it's not for each and every selling situation?

You can actually select a variety of menus and have them waiting for you to send out as "no" proposal proposals. You can select, or create, a variety of menus that demonstrate your flexibility as a caterer and that shows your various price points.

By using the "no" proposal proposal you tend to take the pressure off your office and yourself. You can also give your caller quick response by mailing these sheets on the same day as they call. Think of the incredible amount of time you will save.

Remember, the "no" proposal proposal is a series of one, or more, 8.5 x 11 sheets of paper that are not connected to each other. They are examples of what you've done. Do you agree that, from a buyers point of view, it's exciting to get examples of what other people have already bought instead of just menu pages.

Let's look at the second situation where the "no" proposal proposal concept will actually make a sale quicker and easier. Suppose you are speaking with a caller who sounds really "hot", or is an experienced catering buyer. Perhaps they are a past client of yours.

If you want to take a short cut to the sale, or wish to enhance their belief that you are the caterer who is really different, than the no" proposal proposal is your next move.

> *"Mrs. Smith, I'm really excited by your thoughts on your party. I'd like to suggest that we move quicker. As you know, after this phone conversation, I really should make an appointment to meet with you and discuss the elements of your event, but you've already done such a great job of making me aware of what you're looking for, I'd like to suggest something first. Let me look through our records to find a few examples of catered events we've already done this year that are similar to what you're looking to do. I'll then make photo copies of these events that other customers have already done ... I'll take a black marker and cross out these past customer's names and addresses ... then, I'll send them right to you. In this way, you'll be able to see how other customers have handled similar types of parties and you'll be able to see what we charged for their catering. Does this sound like a great idea to you?"*

We can assure you that caterers from around the nation have reported to us that this concept has really worked well for them. It gives the client a feeling of importance. It also offers them "inside" information about what price others have paid for their catering.

Try this concept and see how it works for you. Just be careful how you do it, and who you do it with. It is a proactive selling technique that will permit a caterer to have another way to handle certain situations.

Checklist for Proposals

Before a proposal leaves a catering office it should be reviewed by at least one person other than the one who wrote it. In this manner, most of the "silly" and "profit losing" errors may be caught.

Here are some of the points that should be on your proposal check list:

1. Are all the parts enclosed?

• Your checklist should list everything that you might send i.e cover letter, menus, summary sheet, biography of chef, photo, linen sample etc.

2. Are the buyers names spelled correctly?

• Don't hesitate to look in the phone book or make a telephone call to verify the spelling. There is nothing more damaging than typos!

3. Is the date correct on all company records?

• You need to check the hand written info sheet, computer records and any kitchen listings. Don't forget your reservation book and wall calender.

4. Is the day of the week included with the date?

• In other words, never show a date without the day of the week. Monday, July 4, 2002.

5. Has the menu been approved by the chef?

• Can and will the kitchen be able to produce what is being promised. Is the seasonality of the foods correct.

6. Has the price been figured correctly?

• You're about to present a contract to a buyer. You will need to live with the price!

7. Is the buyer aware of what they are paying for menu, staff, rentals?

• Obviously important!

8. Is the buyer aware of all additional and potentially additional costs?

• Overtime, delivery, etc.

9. Has the salesperson used words that will be understood and/or liked by the buyer?

• Corporate buyers like certain types of words, while social buyers like others.

10. Has the deposit been requested?

• Obviously important!

11. Has the buyer been told how to pay their deposit?

• Including a pre-addressed envelope with postage already applied is helpful.

12. Have alternative prices been given in case of higher or lower final guest counts?

• Show up front what happens if they add or drop guests.

13. Is the proposal "user-friendly"?

• Obviously important!

14. Have the extra support materials been added? (references, photo, etc)

• Obviously important!

15. Is the envelope addressed correctly?

• Once again, don't take anything for granted.

16. Is the postage correct?

• Use a scale when there is any doubt!

17. Is the cover letter signed?

• Obviously important!

18. Should extra copies be sent?

• A sales advantage can be attained by sending extra original copies to those who need them.

19. Is the office copy filed?

• Obviously important!

Realistic Menu Development

What is consulting? To me, consulting is evaluation and comparison. First you evaluate what conditions exist, then you compare these conditions with those that exist elsewhere.

This is why the world has consultants. Not for their expertise, but for their exposure to diverse conditions. Most caterers have never been to other catering operations to see what is happening. I've been fortunate to have personally visited more than 900 catering companies over the last 20 years.

That's what this series of articles is about. I hope to give our readers some guidelines for "self-consulting."

It is important that each catering business receive ongoing evaluation in order to continually reach for higher levels of success.

Menus that work

I've verbally taught the following information for many years, but this is the first time I'm attempting to put it in writing.

When I refer to a menu that will work in a catering situation, I mean one that will be able to be put in front of the guest with the least amount of problems.

In other words, hot foods will be hot, cold foods will be cold and everything will go along with the pre-determined schedule.

You really can't have menus that work, if all you do is wish to please the client by promising them all that they want... even if the location will not support it.

Menus that work, start with the location that the event will be done in. If it's being done in your own banquet kitchens, you have a decided advantage, but if it's being done at an off-premise location you have potential problems.

It's Like Olympic diving

When Olympic divers gets ready to dive they must inform the judges as to what dive they intend to make.

This is done because some dives are more difficult than others. Because of this a diver who gets a medium score on a difficult dive may win over a diver who gets a higher score on an easy dive.

Catering menus are like dives. They have different levels of complexity. They have different levels of "worry." A cold

poached salmon filet is far easier to deal with than a hot grilled one. A pan of rice sent hot in a plastic thermal carrier is a lot easier to handle than rice being reheated on site.

What I've suggested to caterers for years now is to place a degree of difficulty onto each and every menu item with respect to its chances of success in normal catering.

So, with respect to this degree of difficulty, we choose a number from one to ten to represent good to bad. Let's make one the good and 10 the bad.

For example, since mashed potatoes in a 4 inch pan are very stable and stay hot for a long time they would tend to be a 1 or 2 on our degree of difficulty scale.

Sauteed veal scalloppine, on the other hand, because of its thinness and difficulty in cooking correctly and staying hot for very long would rank a 10 on the scale of difficulty.

Is this making any sense? Let's make a list of other foods and see if you might agree:

1. Beef tenderloin - 2,3, or 4 - rather easy to work with... cooks by length of time... takes only 30 to 40 minutes to cook on sight... high yield per piece.

2. Breaded Fried Chicken - 8,9, or 10 - difficult to do off-premise unless you have special equipment... cools off very quickly... loses its crunch factor...

3. Broccoli - 7,8, or 9 - can be a problem... needs constant attention... easy to make a mistake with and hard to serve at proper temperature.

4. Creamed Spinach - 2,3, or 4 - easy to handle, always looks great no matter how it hits the plate... stays hot forever once it gets hot!

5. California Roll - 1 or 2 - just put them out and they do their thing!

Are you getting my point? All of you have different types of menus but they all have the same types of worry... yield... staying hot... looking good in the chafer or on the plate... amount of space it takes up... etc.

The next step

Once you get your foods numbered by degree of difficulty you can now move onto the next step which is to create an awareness of the locations you do catering in.

> ... THINK OF THESE TIPS, TACTICS AND IDEAS AS A STARTING POINT FOR DOING SELF-CONSULTING FOR YOUR OWN BUSINESS.

Realistic Menu Development

You might do some events at a location that has a complete professional kitchen with six ovens and large walk-in coolers. On the other hand you might be doing events at a similar location where nothing exists... not even easily accessible water!

Both of these locations have their own joys and sorrows when it comes to catering. A menu that works well in one will not work at the other.

Why not take your locations and give them a point value also.... let's call this the operations value. The location with the full kitchen might have an operations value of 50 points while the poorly equipped location might only have a operations value of 18.

Do you see what's coming? We can now take our menus and add up the degree of difficulty of each item to see how many points we get.

If the menu degree of difficulty points totals 27 after adding them together, we now know that this menu can not be done at the location that doesn't have the full kitchen unless we decide to make some changes in the menu selections to use items with lower degrees of difficulty.

When the total difficulty points are higher than what we have established for operations value, than we can't do that particular menu.

A final thought

In addition to the two concepts above, I'd like to take a moment to get really basic because this is extremely important for catering success.

To make a total menu development strategy, a caterer needs to be able to visualize what the menu will do while being cooked or reheated at an event sight. Let's call this **LAUNCH CONTROL**.

Sound like fun? It really is. When planning a menu to be sold, you need to make sure that you can get it all done in time for serving.

This deals with the amount of food that goes into pans, the number of shelves you have to cook on and the time it takes to cook. For example, let's say that you need fifteen whole beef tenderloins for an event. You can put three into a pan for baking in an oven. That makes five pans. Now, the ovens you have to use have three shelves in them and you can get two pans on a shelf. That means that you have room in the one oven to place all the tenders at once.

But, the tenders take forty minutes to cook and you need them out of the oven by 7:45 pm, but you also have a starch to heat that also needs two shelves. And what about hors d'oeuvres that need to be cooked?

This type of thinking goes on endlessly in many catering companies each and every day that events are being planned. This is my point... it needs to be visualized and planned before the menu is sold!

In summary, a caterer needs to understand the importance of Degree of Difficulty, Operations Value and Launch Control in order to meet with the greatest success level they can when performing catered events.

Part of the fun of catering is solving these amazing problems, and potential problems, that arise when caterers sell the wrong menus for the wrong locations or cooking conditions.

Discuss these ideas with both your sales and culinary staff and see if they can make them better or custom tailored for your operation!

Great Words for Proposals

This page could be worth thousands of dollars to those who use it! Below is the list of 136 words that Mike Roman has at his side when writing brochures, advertising copy and menus. Get to know these words and see if you can use them to get some sizzle into your writing! We have a $100 coupon for the first five subscribers who can use 50 of these words in an 80 word paragraph about catering!

1. stunning	38. lively	75. vital	112. timeless
2. thrifty	39. vivid	76. important	113. exclusive
3. skilled	40. sizzling	77. plush	114. matchless
4. revered	41. stunning	78. real	115. useful
5. memorable	42. spicy	79. splendid	116. flexible
6. special	43. tempting	80. elegant	117. worthwhile
7. wonderful	44. staggering	81. classic	118. spectacular
8. proven	45. fascinating	82. invaluable	119. versatile
9. pure	46. heady	83. superior	120. natural
10. immense	47. breathtaking	84. posh	121. enlightening
11. substantial	48. explosive	85. intricate	122. crucial
12. unlimited	49. bold	86. masterpiece	123. irresistible
13. countless	50. talented	87. excellence	124. top-drawer
14. soothing	51. capable	88. profitable	125. stirring
15. roomy	52. ingenious	89. value	126. famous
16. relaxed	53. finesse	90. inexpensive	127. casual
17. unhurried	54. magnificent	91. affordable	128. essential
18. unassuming	55. sumptuous	92. revolutionary	129. outstanding
19. exhaustive	56. superb	93. futuristic	130. elegant
20. remarkable	57. unforgettable	94. modern	131. alluring
21. qualified	58. zesty	95. unprecedented	132. dynamic
22. weeping	59. festive	96. new	133. accomplished
23. extensive	60. carefree	97. legendary	134. extraordinary
24. comprehensive	61. revealing	98. celebrated	135. unforgettable
25. handy	62. genuine	99. favorite	
26. clarifies	63. integrity	100. dynamic	
27. prestigious	64. reputable	101. vitality	
28. respected	65. expanded	102. accomplishes	
29. major	66. refined	103. prevents	
30. prominent	67. perfected	104. magical	
31. acclaimed	68. changed	105. harmony	
32. fast	69. revived	106. glowing	
33. foolproof	70. reorganized	107. prestige	
34. quick	71. essential	108. elite	
35. clear	72. imperative	109. chic	
36. simplified	73. critical	110. sassy	
37. accessible	74. significant	111. current	

CHAPTER 7  QUESTIONS

1. What are the objectives of a written catering proposal?

2. What are four ideas that will make a proposal better?

3. Why shouldn't a proposal be folded when going into an envelope?

4. Should a caterer use a $ sign in front of prices?

5. In Proposal Template #2, what is the reason for breaking out the costs into three areas?

6. In Proposal Template #3 Page 1, what are the unique selling ideas?

7. Should a proposal have a time limit for acceptance by the shopper?

8. What are the advantages and disadvantages of the 'No Proposal Proposal"?

9. How many original copies of the proposal should be sent to the shopper?

10. When creating menus, what is "Launch Control"?

PRINTED MENUS

CHAPTER

8

TABLE OF CONTENTS

CHAPTER

8

*"A caterer is only as good
as their last performance!"*

Thoughts on Preprinted Menus

1. **Preprinted menus have the following advantages:**

   A. Give a quick response to the client.

   B. Less office staff needed for customized menus.

   C. Much easier on your kitchen staff due the familiarity of menu items.

   D. Helps to establish control and confidence of the client.

2. **Suggestions for creating preprinted menus:**

   A. Size of physical menu should be large enough to meet the other requirements listed below.

   B. Print should be easy to read with crisp contrast between paper & ink.

   C. Telephone number with area code needs to be easy to find.

   D. In some cases the address of the caterer should not be shown.

   E. If using pictures show scenes of entertaining rather than just food.

3. **A well written preprinted menu can increase volume with the least amount of effort. It can help create an order taking situation.**

On-Premise Banquet Info

To Begin...

A sumptuous Continental Cocktail & International Smorgasbord
One full hour of unlimited food and beverages served from beautiful,
elaborately decorated tables, done in imported laces, ferns, flowers,
candelabra and thematic centerpieces.

This buffet gives your guests an opportunity to "browse" among
the foods and to select only those items that they are interested in.
The overall buffet presentation gives the effect of an "over abundance"
of "gourmet foods" presented creatively.

Buffet Au Froid
Elaborately decorated and displayed by our own Garde Manger
on seasonally decorated banquet tables

Crudité...
Miniaturized raw vegetables served in oversized "country market"
baskets and served with a savory dipping sauce.

Melon Carvings...
Farm fresh, sweet, melons artfully carved into interesting shapes
and filled with a medley of fresh fruits. Attractively displayed
on huge trays with an assortment of smaller melons and
other fresh fruits creatively arranged.

Breads of All Nations...
An assortment of unique and exotic breads from around
the world served on maple butcher blocks and wicker baskets.

Cheese and Wine...
Many large wedges of Imported Cheeses, to include Swiss,
Gouda, Jarlsburg, Fontina, and Provolone artfully displayed
on a Maple Butcher Block with Fresh Fruits,
French and Italian Breads and accented with a Portuguese Rosé Wine,
French Chablis, Italian Soave and French Burgundy.

Country French Charcuterie...
Old Country French style willow baskets with tureens of Cornichons,
Pommeroy Mustard, Assorted Patés, Dijon Mustard,
Assorted Sausages and Salamis, all served with
Special Garnishes and Seasonal Fruits.

Caviar Display...
Traditional Red Caviar and Black Caviar served with Chopped Eggs,
Chopped Red Onions, Capers and an assortment of Flavored Crackers.

Mexican Sombrero...
A ceremonial Mexican Sombrero filled with several types of Nacho Chips
and served with two types of Salsa and a Dipping Cheese.

For Dinner...
The Toast to the Bride and Groom...
Traditional Bubbling Champagne served Ice Cold

Appetizers...
Fresh Fruit Princess, adorned with Shaved Coconut
and Miniature Marshmallows served in Silver Supremes
or
Fresh Fruit, Hawaiian Pineapple Boats
or
Melon Crowns Garnished with Berries
Baskets of Oven Fresh Rolls and Bowls of Creamery Butter

Pasta...
An incredibly delicious presentation of Old World Pasta,
Homemade, and Prepared to Perfection

Salad...
Three Lettuce Salad with a wedge of Tomato
and served with our Famous House Dressing and Seasoned Croutons

Entrees...
Your Guest's Choice of Four Entrees
Roast Prime Ribs of Blue Ribbon Beef, Au Jus
or
Grilled Alaskan Salmon Steak with a Lemon Butter Sauce
or
Chicken Cordon Bleu, a Boneless Breast
stuffed with Gruyere Cheese and Ham, rolled and lightly breaded
or
Stuffed Filet of Sole Monte Cristo with Sauce Cardinale

Vegetables...
Fresh Seasonal Vegetables or Fresh Broccoli, lightly steamed

Potatoes...
Baked Idaho Potato served with Sour Cream and Chives

Dessert...
A special ceremony presenting Flaming Cherries Jubilee
and French Vanilla Ice Cream

Beverages...
Steaming Coffee, Tea, Brewed Decaffeinated Coffee

Your Antun's Wedding Timetable

Twelve months before
- ☐ Choose attendants
- ☐ Select music, flowers, photographer, and videographer
- ☐ Order wedding dress, attendants' and mothers' dresses
- ☐ Arrange for Limousine Service ☐ Plan new home

Six - 4 months
- ☐ Compile guest list
- ☐ Order invitations, thank you's, and personal stationery
- ☐ Plan honeymoon trip (don't forget passports if necessary)
- ☐ Shop for trousseau ☐ Order rings
- ☐ Select bridal registry

Three months
- ☐ Visit doctor for physical including blood test
- ☐ Confirm delivery date for wedding dress and bridal party
- ☐ Purchase gifts for bridal party
- ☐ Choose formal wear for men
- ☐ Make rehearsal dinner arrangements

Two months
- ☐ Address and mail wedding invitations
- ☐ Arrange to get marriage license
- ☐ Contact local newspaper for wedding announcement

One month
- ☐ Arrange for final fitting on all gowns
- ☐ Make appointments for hair, makeup & manicure
- ☐ Have wedding portrait taken
- ☐ Confirm arrangements with band or D.J.

One month (continued)
- ☐ Confirm arrangements with photographer, videographer
- ☐ Confirm honeymoon reservations
- ☐ Write thank you notes as gifts are received
- ☐ Change name on legal documents

Two weeks
- ☐ Call Antun's for final arrangements, floor plan, etc.
- ☐ Arrange seating plan for reception with place cards
- ☐ Pick up wedding rings ☐ Pick up all gowns
- ☐ Pick up honeymoon tickets

5 days before
- ☐ Call Antun's with final count
- ☐ Begin packing for honeymoon
- ☐ Purchase traveler's checks
- ☐ Call your photographer, videographer, band or D.J.

3 days before
- ☐ Final consultation with Antun's
  floor plan, final balance due

One day before
- ☐ Pick up men's formal wear
- ☐ Rehearsal
- ☐ Present gifts to attendants
- ☐ Check your luggage

Wedding day
- ☐ Relax this is your special day!

MENUS, ABOVE AND LEFT, ARE PLACED INTO A QUALITY MULTI-PAGE BOOKLET PRINTED IN FOUR COLOR. BRIDES LOVE THE WEDDING PLANNER BELOW.

Focused Food Marketing

Salad bars have always been popular in restaurants. Interestingly, you would be amazed how few caterers offer a full blown salad bar to social or corporate customers. Those caterers who do offer the salad bar tell CaterSource that it is one of the best, and most often sold, entrees.

One of the best features of a salad bar to the buyer is that it offers a healthy menu, customization of selections, and can be eaten day after day without concern for repetition! Below (A) is a sample template for how the menu might be formatted and (B) is a photo of how it might look.

The salad and the additional items are placed in inverted plastic dome lids. These are the same lids that are used to go on top of the various foil and plastic trays used by caterers. By using these dome lids as disposable bowls your salad bar takes on a great look and is "one-way" because it doesn't have to be picked up later by the caterer. In this picture both 16 inch and 12 inch dome lids are being used.

Some caterers use cardboard pizza circles (the kind you get under your pizza when it's delivered) to give the bowls more strength while being transported. Why not offer it as a spring special.

A

Chef's Salad Buffet

This is a real winner! Bring our amazing salad bar right to your office! Your guests will be grateful for the opportunity to make their own unique salad. Here's what you get:

- Bowl, or bowls, of leaf, romaine, and iceberg lettuce
  - Choice of three (3) salad dressings
  - Selection of special breads & butter
- <u>PLUS</u> ten (10) additional items from the list below!

Diced Ham	Pepperoni	Cucumber Wheels	Alfalfa Sprouts
Turkey Strips	Salami	Seasoned Croutons	Tofu
Sardines	Diced Eggs	Zucchini Spears	Broccoli Pieces
Sliced Radishes	Carrot Curls	Walnut Pieces	Bean Sprouts
Real Bacon Bits	Tortilla Chips	Fresh Mushrooms	Red or Green Onions
Black Olives	Green Olives	Kidney Beans	Cherry Tomatoes
Cottage Cheese	Roast Beef*	Chicken Fajita Meat*	Pineapple Chunks
Snow Pea Pods*	Garbanzo Beans	Hearts of Palm**	Cheddar Cheese
Baby Shrimp**	Swiss Cheese	Artichokes**	Hot Peppers

B

1-Color 4-Page Picnic Menu

This is a 8.5 x 11 inch brochure folded down in half to 8.5 x 5.5 inches. Below are the two panels that make-up the front and back cover. On page 7 you have the two panels that make-up the inside of this easy to read and straight forward picnic brochure from Jenny's Caterers (Pawtucket, RI)

JENNY'S CATERERS
GUARANTEES AND OTHER COMPANY POLICIES

When your catering order is dependant on a per person price, we need to know the final numbers ahead of time. This is our Guarantee Policy.

The Tuesday before your event, by noon, we need to know your final guest count. From that time up until 48 hours before you may add guests, but you can not decrease, as our preparation has begun.

DEPOSITS are required on all bookings, except last minute arrangements. The deposit is non-refundable as we have probably refused work on that day and cannot recoup those turned away. This deposit will be deducted from your balance due.

PAYMENT will be expected upon presentation of the buffet or if service is involved at the conclusion of the event. We accept Visa & MasterCard for payment of deposit and invoices. Please inform us as to your preferred payment method, so we may have the proper forms with us. Billed arrangements made through sales office.

DELIVERY will be charged to all parties without service. The charge is a one time charge, for delivery and set up, we also have to drive back to pick up the equipment. Our driver will make arrangements with you at the time of delivery as to when would be the best time to return for pick up. You are responsible for all equipment.

We will set up and prepare for 5% more than your guarantee. You will be billed for your guarantee, or if we serve more than your guarantee, we will bill you what we actually served.

LEFTOVER FOOD When we are on location to serve food, we usually carry more than we expect to serve (running out is a traumatic experience). We also have extended food temperatures and holding conditions to a point that, in cooperation with the health department, we will not release leftover food to you or your guests.

Client is responsible for all rental costs; china, silverware, glassware and tenting if needed. This charge will be reflected on your proposal and invoice.

Service will be billed at an hourly rate. We have received many compliments on our service personnel and we look forward to hearing your comments or suggestions.

Chefs	14.00 per hour
Waitpersons	12.00 per hour
Bartenders	15.00 per hour

You will be billed for a 4 hour minimum, including travel time to and from the event. If service is continued 1/2 hour over scheduled time we will bill you at these rates above. Remember good help is hard to find, excellent service is impossible to forget... Let us put our reputation on your table.

Thank You in Advance
Jenny's Caterers

1-Color 4-Page Picnic Menu

Jenny's Caterers
"Catering with a unique touch"

COOKOUTS   CLAMBOILS   BBQS

In the park, your backyard, or at the company on a day off. These cookouts are served on top of the line disposable paper products. We come in, set up, cook, serve and clean up. You will be a guest at your own event.

ECONOMY BUSTER – Grilled Hamburgers and Hot Dogs, Assorted Condiments, Potato Chips, Hamburger Pickles, Watermelon. $5.95 / person

ALL AMERICAN – Grilled Hamburgers and Hot Dogs, Assorted Condiments, Lettuce, Tomatoes, Cheese, Red Potato Salad, Shredded Cole Slaw, Potato Chips, Hamburger Pickles, Watermelon. $6.25 / person

SOUTHWESTERN BBQ – Garden Tossed Salad, Cornbread with Butter, Texas Style Ribs, BBQ Chicken, Baked Beans, Corn with Red Pepper, Watermelon. $9.95 / person
    without Texas Ribs $7.95 / person

TO BEEF OR NOT TO BEEF – Steakhouse Tossed Salad Bar, Rolls and Butter, Charcoal Grilled NY Sirloin Steak, Baked Potatoes with Sour Cream, Corn on the Cob, Watermelon. $13.95 / person

INTERNATIONAL FARE – Red Leaf Salad, Lamb Shish Kebob, Grilled Lemon Chicken Breasts, Sweet Italian Sausage Links, Grilled Polish Kielbasa, Boston Baked Beans, Native Sweet Corn. $13.95 / person

NEW ENGLAND CLAMBOIL – New England or Manhattan Clam Chowder, Sweet Potatoes, Red Potatoes, Onions, Bratwurst, Sangy's Miniature Hot Dogs, Steamed Fish, Steamers.   MARKET PRICE

Service and Rentals

- Cooks   12.00 / hour
- Buffet Servers   10.00 / hour
- Grills   50.00 / 3'X5'

You may add to your event

- Assorted Soda   .95 / each
- Coffee (5 gallons) serves 100 Guests   27.95 / 5 gallons
- Fruity Punch or Country Lemonade   19.95 / 5 gallons
- Hamburgers   1.50 / person
- Hot Dogs   .75 / person
- Texas Style Ribs   2.00 / person
- BBQ Chicken   1.75 / person

Give us a call TODAY! Let's turn your event in to a special event. We can arrange and take responsibility for any support services you may need such as: Tents, Tables, Chairs, Linens, Grills and Port a Johns. Let us put our reputation on your table.

70 Pawtucket Avenue • Pawtucket, R.I. 02860
Tel. (401) 724-7090 • (800) 924-7093 • Fax (401) 724-1946
(In R.I. Only)

4-Color Fun Menu

CaterSource got a real charge out of this catering menu from Pepper's Catering (South Burlington, VT). It has humor and great marketing power. You know that the food is fun and good when you get a menu like this in the mail!

NOTICE HOW EFFECTIVE THE MESSAGE COMES THROUGH THAT PEPPER'S WILL BE HAPPY TO DELIVER THEIR BBQ RIGHT TO YOUR DOOR!

4-Color Corporate Brochure

Peter Graben tells us that this brochure is a proven winner! The buyer gets to see what they are buying and how much they are getting.

The brochure is 4-color printing on an 8.5 x 11 glossy sheet. Then it's folded down to fit into a 6 x 9 envelope. Prices will vary for the printing.

Self Serve: Great Box & Bag Menu

This is a CaterSource template. It is designed for a self-service corporate division. This is a page from a multi-page menu format used by some of CaterSource's consulting clients. It is a simple approach, but also has some intriguing marketing concepts. Don't be concerned with the prices listed below, they're just place holders.

1. Some people like to use a bag instead of a box, especially if it is recyclable.

2. The word "individual" is a clear buying preference for those who don't want a buffet.

3. The use of the (+) permits you to have single unit pricing but still adjust up for more costly foods.

4. In this menu format, the salads (sides) and desserts are placed on a special page. This allows less repetition in menu design.

5. A must to keep costs in line.

6. Sometimes this helps get earlier bookings.

7. This is a marketing ploy that has worked well. It also saves a lot of labor.

NOTE: Self-Service Catering ideas will be found in every issue of the Journal.

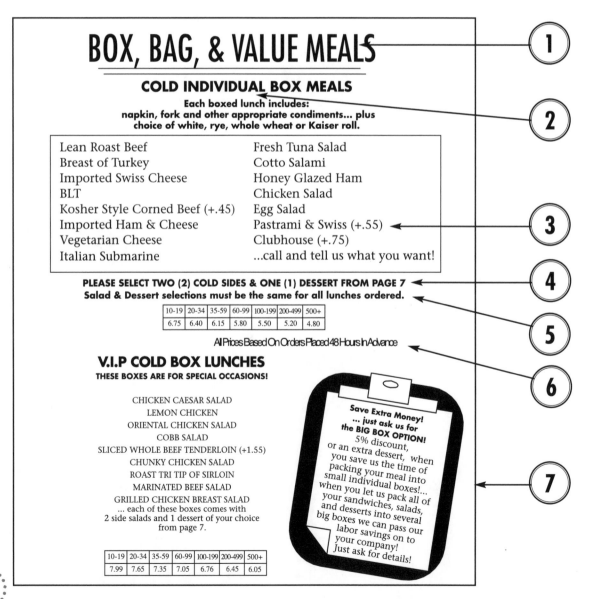

BOX, BAG, & VALUE MEALS ①

COLD INDIVIDUAL BOX MEALS

Each boxed lunch includes:
napkin, fork and other appropriate condiments... plus
choice of white, rye, whole wheat or Kaiser roll. ②

Lean Roast Beef	Fresh Tuna Salad
Breast of Turkey	Cotto Salami
Imported Swiss Cheese	Honey Glazed Ham
BLT	Chicken Salad
Kosher Style Corned Beef (+.45)	Egg Salad
Imported Ham & Cheese	Pastrami & Swiss (+.55) ③
Vegetarian Cheese	Clubhouse (+.75)
Italian Submarine	...call and tell us what you want!

PLEASE SELECT TWO (2) COLD SIDES & ONE (1) DESSERT FROM PAGE 7 ④
Salad & Dessert selections must be the same for all lunches ordered. ⑤

10-19	20-34	35-59	60-99	100-199	200-499	500+
6.75	6.40	6.15	5.80	5.50	5.20	4.80

All Prices Based On Orders Placed 48 Hours In Advance ⑥

V.I.P COLD BOX LUNCHES
THESE BOXES ARE FOR SPECIAL OCCASIONS!

CHICKEN CAESAR SALAD
LEMON CHICKEN
ORIENTAL CHICKEN SALAD
COBB SALAD
SLICED WHOLE BEEF TENDERLOIN (+1.55)
CHUNKY CHICKEN SALAD
ROAST TRI TIP OF SIRLOIN
MARINATED BEEF SALAD
GRILLED CHICKEN BREAST SALAD
... each of these boxes comes with
2 side salads and 1 dessert of your choice
from page 7.

Save Extra Money!
... just ask us for
the BIG BOX OPTION!
5% discount,
or an extra dessert, when
you save us the time of
packing your meal into
small individual boxes!...
when you let us pack all of
your sandwiches, salads,
and desserts into several
big boxes we can pass our
labor savings on to
your company!
Just ask for details! ⑦

10-19	20-34	35-59	60-99	100-199	200-499	500+
7.99	7.65	7.35	7.05	6.76	6.45	6.05

Self-Serve: Special Menus

This is a CaterSource, Inc. template which subscribers may use within their own businesses. It is page five from a 32 page self-service menu geared for corporate daily catering. It's interesting to note that on this single page the buyer can be health "nice" or health "naughty"!

1. This disposable salad bar has proven a big winner with many corporate buyers. It is fun and easy to put out and manage. Use the clear plastic dome lids for trays to hold the ingredients of the salad bar.

2. This is the single most important word in marketing. What have you done lately that is perceived as new by your buyers?

3. This permits you to place higher priced elective items on the "choice list". If they want it they will pay for it.

4. These are your thermalized plastic carriers. You should market your safer delivery methods.

5. Make the phone number easy to find and infer that they can ask questions.

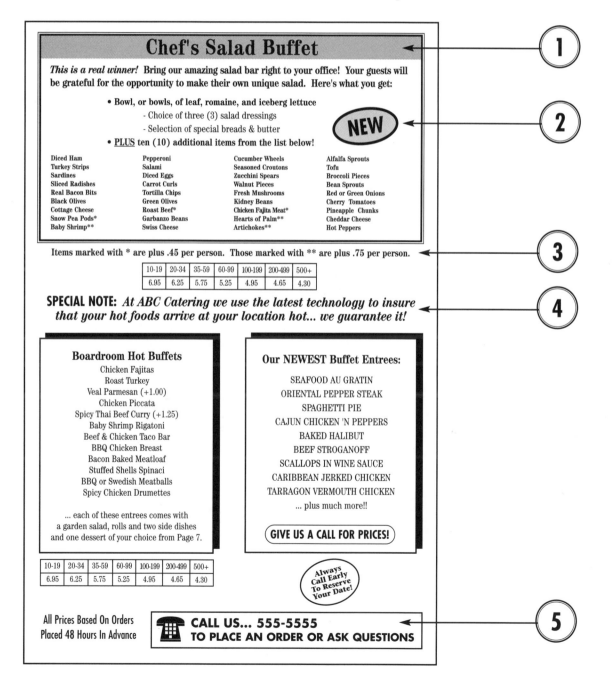

Chef's Salad Buffet

This is a real winner! Bring our amazing salad bar right to your office! Your guests will be grateful for the opportunity to make their own unique salad. Here's what you get:

- Bowl, or bowls, of leaf, romaine, and iceberg lettuce
  - Choice of three (3) salad dressings
  - Selection of special breads & butter
- **PLUS** ten (10) additional items from the list below!

NEW

Diced Ham	Pepperoni	Cucumber Wheels	Alfalfa Sprouts
Turkey Strips	Salami	Seasoned Croutons	Tofu
Sardines	Diced Eggs	Zucchini Spears	Broccoli Pieces
Sliced Radishes	Carrot Curls	Walnut Pieces	Bean Sprouts
Real Bacon Bits	Tortilla Chips	Fresh Mushrooms	Red or Green Onions
Black Olives	Green Olives	Kidney Beans	Cherry Tomatoes
Cottage Cheese	Roast Beef*	Chicken Fajita Meat*	Pineapple Chunks
Snow Pea Pods*	Garbanzo Beans	Hearts of Palm**	Cheddar Cheese
Baby Shrimp**	Swiss Cheese	Artichokes**	Hot Peppers

Items marked with * are plus .45 per person. Those marked with ** are plus .75 per person.

10-19	20-34	35-59	60-99	100-199	200-499	500+
6.95	6.25	5.75	5.25	4.95	4.65	4.30

SPECIAL NOTE: *At ABC Catering we use the latest technology to insure that your hot foods arrive at your location hot... we guarantee it!*

Boardroom Hot Buffets

Chicken Fajitas
Roast Turkey
Veal Parmesan (+1.00)
Chicken Piccata
Spicy Thai Beef Curry (+1.25)
Baby Shrimp Rigatoni
Beef & Chicken Taco Bar
BBQ Chicken Breast
Bacon Baked Meatloaf
Stuffed Shells Spinaci
BBQ or Swedish Meatballs
Spicy Chicken Drumettes

... each of these entrees comes with a garden salad, rolls and two side dishes and one dessert of your choice from Page 7.

10-19	20-34	35-59	60-99	100-199	200-499	500+
6.95	6.25	5.75	5.25	4.95	4.65	4.30

Our NEWEST Buffet Entrees:

SEAFOOD AU GRATIN
ORIENTAL PEPPER STEAK
SPAGHETTI PIE
CAJUN CHICKEN 'N PEPPERS
BAKED HALIBUT
BEEF STROGANOFF
SCALLOPS IN WINE SAUCE
CARIBBEAN JERKED CHICKEN
TARRAGON VERMOUTH CHICKEN
... plus much more!!

GIVE US A CALL FOR PRICES!

Always Call Early To Reserve Your Date!

All Prices Based On Orders Placed 48 Hours In Advance

CALL US... 555-5555
TO PLACE AN ORDER OR ASK QUESTIONS

Self-Serve: Fax Info Sheet

This is a CaterSource, Inc. template which you can use as a subscriber. It has been used by many caterers to add something special to a multipage menu format. It will work best in menus that are eight pages, or more, in length.

1. The headlines grab the reader with words that they've never read before in other catering menus. Everyone wants to collect more menu ideas, recipes and checklists to do a better job!

2. Use of simple check boxes, hopefully, make the reader take the step to fax the form.

3. What do you think? Will readers call for additional menus? The answer, based on actual use of this page, is yes!.

4. Why not? Let your reader know that your goal is to give them service and to sell them something! You will be surprised how many of these come back with lead information on them!

5. This whole section is interesting because it gives the reader some things to think about that they've never considered before. If you're lucky, this section will help create urgency for your readers.

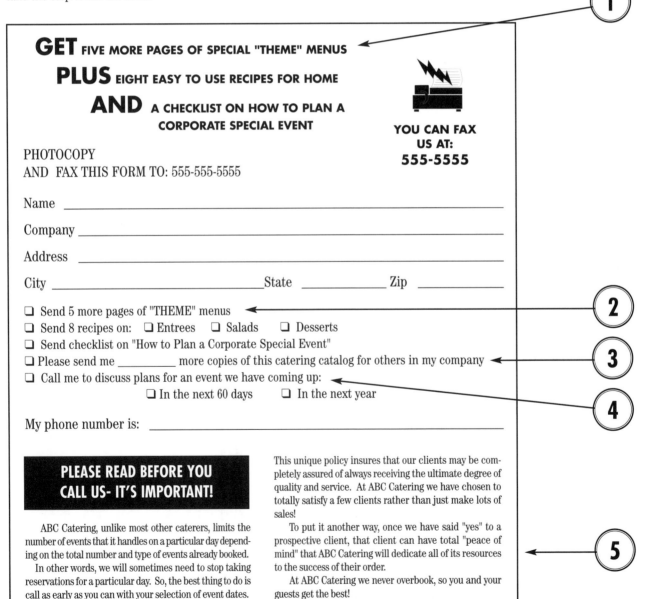

GET FIVE MORE PAGES OF SPECIAL "THEME" MENUS

PLUS EIGHT EASY TO USE RECIPES FOR HOME

AND A CHECKLIST ON HOW TO PLAN A CORPORATE SPECIAL EVENT

YOU CAN FAX US AT:
555-5555

PHOTOCOPY
AND FAX THIS FORM TO: 555-555-5555

Name _____

Company _____

Address _____

City _____ State _____ Zip _____

❑ Send 5 more pages of "THEME" menus
❑ Send 8 recipes on: ❑ Entrees ❑ Salads ❑ Desserts
❑ Send checklist on "How to Plan a Corporate Special Event"
❑ Please send me _____ more copies of this catering catalog for others in my company
❑ Call me to discuss plans for an event we have coming up:
         ❑ In the next 60 days   ❑ In the next year

My phone number is: _____

PLEASE READ BEFORE YOU CALL US- IT'S IMPORTANT!

ABC Catering, unlike most other caterers, limits the number of events that it handles on a particular day depending on the total number and type of events already booked.

In other words, we will sometimes need to stop taking reservations for a particular day. So, the best thing to do is call as early as you can with your selection of event dates.

This unique policy insures that our clients may be completely assured of always receiving the ultimate degree of quality and service. At ABC Catering we have chosen to totally satisfy a few clients rather than just make lots of sales!

To put it another way, once we have said "yes" to a prospective client, that client can have total "peace of mind" that ABC Catering will dedicate all of its resources to the success of their order.

At ABC Catering we never overbook, so you and your guests get the best!

Self-Serve: Daily Special Menu

This is a CaterSource template. It is designed for a self-service corporate division. The goal of this promotion is to offer a client a different way to save money while, at the same time, making it easier on the kitchen. You'll either like this, or not! CaterSource's clients have had success with it! Don't be concerned with the prices listed below, they're just place holders.

1. A unique product line name for the client to ask for when they call.

2. It's always good when you can use copy that the reader has never read from other caterers.

3. This paragraph gives the reader the "proof" or reason why they can save money if they help the caterer.

4. Be sure to pick a menu for the first day of the week that is easy for your kitchen to make, or pull from the freezer.

5. Cold and easy because you might have less staff on Wednesday.

6. Once again, pick a menu that fits into your hectic weekend preparations.

NOTE: Self-Service Catering ideas will be found in every issue of the Journal.

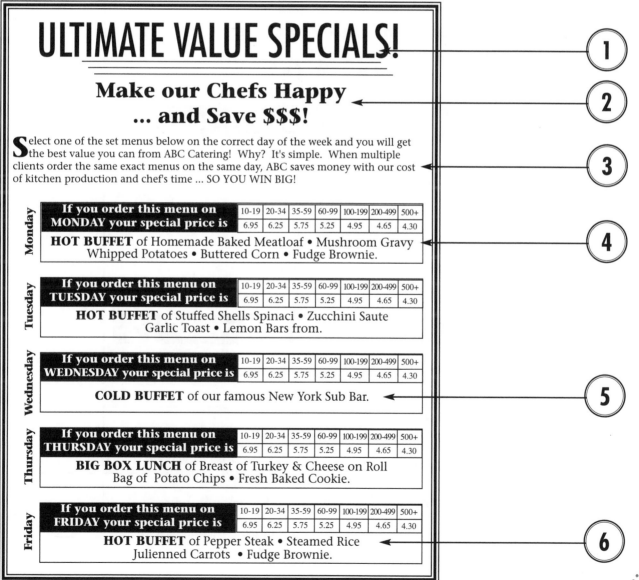

ULTIMATE VALUE SPECIALS!

Make our Chefs Happy ... and Save $$$!

Select one of the set menus below on the correct day of the week and you will get the best value you can from ABC Catering! Why? It's simple. When multiple clients order the same exact menus on the same day, ABC saves money with our cost of kitchen production and chef's time ... SO YOU WIN BIG!

Monday

If you order this menu on MONDAY your special price is	10-19	20-34	35-59	60-99	100-199	200-499	500+
	6.95	6.25	5.75	5.25	4.95	4.65	4.30

HOT BUFFET of Homemade Baked Meatloaf • Mushroom Gravy Whipped Potatoes • Buttered Corn • Fudge Brownie.

Tuesday

If you order this menu on TUESDAY your special price is	10-19	20-34	35-59	60-99	100-199	200-499	500+
	6.95	6.25	5.75	5.25	4.95	4.65	4.30

HOT BUFFET of Stuffed Shells Spinaci • Zucchini Saute Garlic Toast • Lemon Bars from.

Wednesday

If you order this menu on WEDNESDAY your special price is	10-19	20-34	35-59	60-99	100-199	200-499	500+
	6.95	6.25	5.75	5.25	4.95	4.65	4.30

COLD BUFFET of our famous New York Sub Bar.

Thursday

If you order this menu on THURSDAY your special price is	10-19	20-34	35-59	60-99	100-199	200-499	500+
	6.95	6.25	5.75	5.25	4.95	4.65	4.30

BIG BOX LUNCH of Breast of Turkey & Cheese on Roll Bag of Potato Chips • Fresh Baked Cookie.

Friday

If you order this menu on FRIDAY your special price is	10-19	20-34	35-59	60-99	100-199	200-499	500+
	6.95	6.25	5.75	5.25	4.95	4.65	4.30

HOT BUFFET of Pepper Steak • Steamed Rice Julienned Carrots • Fudge Brownie.

Self-Serve: Special Buffet Menu

This is a CaterSource template. It is designed for a self-service corporate division. This is a page from a multi-page menu format used by some of CaterSource's consulting clients. It is a simple approach, but also has some intriguing marketing concepts. Don't be concerned with the prices listed below, they're just place examples.

1. The unique concept is that the buyer gets both cold and hot food in the same order.

2. A typical cold buffet menu is used.

3. A typical hot buffet entree menu is offered. Again, the uniqueness is in the fact that they can purchase a normal cold buffet with an added hot entree.

4. This allows the caterer to charge more for more costly items.

5. Again, CaterSource is convinced that this style of pricing leads to bigger and more sales.

6. This allows the buyer to order more than one hot entree. It doesn't happen often, but it is good marketing.

NOTE: Self-Service Catering ideas will be found in every issue of the Journal.

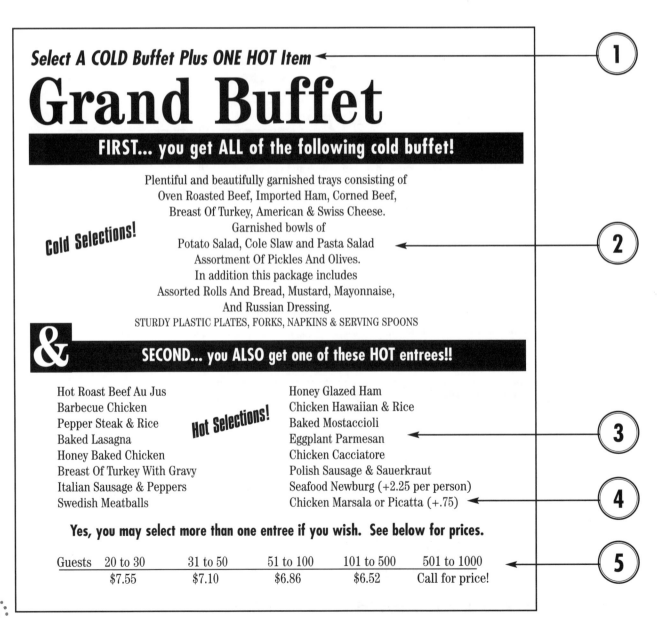

Select A COLD Buffet Plus ONE HOT Item ← ①

Grand Buffet

FIRST... you get ALL of the following cold buffet!

Cold Selections!

Plentiful and beautifully garnished trays consisting of
Oven Roasted Beef, Imported Ham, Corned Beef,
Breast Of Turkey, American & Swiss Cheese.
Garnished bowls of
Potato Salad, Cole Slaw and Pasta Salad
Assortment Of Pickles And Olives.
In addition this package includes
Assorted Rolls And Bread, Mustard, Mayonnaise,
And Russian Dressing.
STURDY PLASTIC PLATES, FORKS, NAPKINS & SERVING SPOONS

← ②

& SECOND... you ALSO get one of these HOT entrees!!

Hot Roast Beef Au Jus
Barbecue Chicken
Pepper Steak & Rice
Baked Lasagna
Honey Baked Chicken
Breast Of Turkey With Gravy
Italian Sausage & Peppers
Swedish Meatballs

Hot Selections!

Honey Glazed Ham
Chicken Hawaiian & Rice
Baked Mostaccioli
Eggplant Parmesan
Chicken Cacciatore
Polish Sausage & Sauerkraut
Seafood Newburg (+2.25 per person)
Chicken Marsala or Picatta (+.75)

← ③

← ④

Yes, you may select more than one entree if you wish. See below for prices.

Guests	20 to 30	31 to 50	51 to 100	101 to 500	501 to 1000
	$7.55	$7.10	$6.86	$6.52	Call for price!

← ⑤

Interesting Menu Selling Concept

This is a single page from a six paneled brochure from Plymouth Bay Catering (Kingston, MA). CaterSource likes its simplicity and suggestion that the buyer of a BBQ can participate in deciding how they spend their money. It also demonstrates that the larger your event is the smaller your price will become.

The bottom portion allows a buyer to add on significantly to the original menu they select. This allows for those who need special foods or for those companies who want to have even more variety than the regular menu provides.

Build a Texas BBQ!

Your Basic Texas BBQ Buffets Includes:

★ Pasta Salad ★ Potato Salad or Cole Slaw ★ Tossed Greens, Caesar Salad or Crudities ★
★ Steamed Hot Dog with Roll ★ Chile or Cowboy Beans ★ Nacho Chips with Salsa ★ Ice Tea or Lemonade ★

Disposables: Forks, Knifes, Spoons, Napkins, Wet Wipes, Plates, Bowls, etc.
Appropriate Condiments: Salt, Pepper, Relish, Mustard, Mayonnaise, Drawn Butter, Honey Whipped Butter, etc.

$6.00 Per Person — 251+ People

$6.50 Per Person — 125 - 250 People

$7.00 Per Person — 75 - 125 People

$8.00 Per Person — 25 - 75 People

Basic Build a BBQ Price

Count [   ] X [   ] Price = [   ]

Now... Start Building Your Own Texas BBQ!

Corn on the Cob with Butter	Count	[ ]	X	90¢	=	[ ]
Corn Bread with Honey Whipped Butter	Count	[ ]	X	1.10	=	[ ]
New England Clam Chowder w/Oyster Crackers	Count	[ ]	X	1.75	=	[ ]
Quarter Pound Hamburger (w/cheese add 25¢)	Count	[ ]	X	2.30	=	[ ]
Italian Sausage with Peppers & Onions	Count	[ ]	X	1.40	=	[ ]
1/4 BBQ Chicken Breast	Count	[ ]	X	2.35	=	[ ]
Split BBQ Chicken	Count	[ ]	X	1.80	=	[ ]
1/2 BBQ Chicken	Count	[ ]	X	2.85	=	[ ]
Grilled Marinated Boneless Chicken Breast	Count	[ ]	X	2.80	=	[ ]
Beef Ribs	Count	[ ]	X	2.90	=	[ ]
Baby Back Ribs	Count	[ ]	X	2.90	=	[ ]
Steamers with Drawn Butter	Count	[ ]	X	Market Price	=	[ ]
Boiled Lobster with Drawn Butter	Count	[ ]	X	Market Price	=	[ ]

Total [   ]

5% Massachusetts Meals Tax for the Governor X 5% = [   ]
15% Service Charge* X 15% = [   ]

Includes all necessary banquet tables for food stations, chafers, sternos, serving utensils, waitstaff with chef, rubbish containers & rubbish removal.

Your *BUILD A TEXAS BBQ* **Final Price** [   ]

Corporate Drop-Off: To-The-Point Menu

Here's a great example of what you can do with a single sheet of paper. ExecuChef Caterers (Citrus Heights, CA) simply purchased a design paper that was already printed with four-color excitement and just put it through their laser printer. Great work! They're using volume discount pricing.

ExecuChef Caterers

8144 Auburn Blvd., Citrus Heights, CA 95610
Phone (916) 726-2339 Fax (916) 726-7461

THE COMPLETE SANDWICH BUFFET
"Ready To Serve"

A Delicious Array of Assorted Sandwiches On A Variety Of Fresh Breads Attractively Arranged On A Large Platter. All Sandwiches Are Prepared With Fresh Leaf Lettuce And Tomato Slices. Condiments (Mayonnaise and Spicy Brown Mustard) Are Served On The Side. Your Buffet Comes Complete With A Bowl OF Our Fresh Home-Made Salad and A Relish Tray Filled With Pickles, Olives, Pepperoncini, Sliced Red Onion, Etc., **Plus** Your Choice Of Dessert. Includes Deluxe Disposable Plates, Flatware, Napkins, Salt & Pepper.
MINIMUM ORDER – 15 PEOPLE

"THE EXECUTIVE" BOX LUNCH
"QUICK AND EASY"

Each "Executive" Box Lunch Come Complete With A Freshly Made Deli-Style Sandwich, Home-Made Salad, Potato Chips & Dessert. You May Select A Variety Of Sandwiches however, Salad And Dessert Choices Will Be The Same For Each Box Lunch. All Sandwiches Are Prepared With Fresh Leaf Lettuce, And Tomato Slices. All Box Lunches Come In An Attractive Clear Plastic "Lunch Box" and Include A Dill Pickle Spear, Mayonnaise, Mustard, Salt & Pepper, Deluxe 3 Ply Dinner Napkin, Knife, Fork, and After Dinner Mints.
MINIMUM ORDER – 15 BOX LUNCHES

Sandwich Selection
Breast of Turkey   Roast Beef   Ham & Cheese   Tuna Salad   Salami
Egg Salad   Vegetarian

Salad Selection
Tossed Green, Choice of Dressings   Potato   Pasta   Fresh Fruit
Macaroni   Cole Slaw

Dessert Selection
Chocolate Chip, Oatmeal or Peanut Butter Cookies
Chocolate Mousse   Brownies   Bread Pudding

Beverages
Coca Cola, Pepsi, Dr. Pepper, 7-UP, Root Beer, Sprite, Spring Water
Regular or Diet - $1.25
Snapple (Regular or Diet) - $1.75   Mineral Waters—$1.50

Number of Guests	15-20	21-40	41-60	61-80	81-99	100+
Price Per Person	$7.95	$7.65	$7.50	$7.35	$7.05	$6.95

Special Sack Lunch
Perfect For Bus Trips, Plant Tours, Field Trips, Etc.
Each Sack Lunch Is Packed In A Crisp White Lunch Sack and Includes A Fresh Made Deli-Style Sandwich, Potato Chips, A Piece Of Whole Fruit (Your Choice Of Apple, Orange Or Banana), Condiments, **And** A Cold Soft Drink.
Minimum Order – 20 Sack Lunches
$5.95
Snapple Or Mineral Water - 50 Cents Extra

State Sales Tax & 18% Service Charge Will Be Added To All Orders

Tell Them How it Works

This CaterSource template can be used in many ways. When reviewing menus and brochures from caterers, we've often noticed that no information is given to tell the buyer "what they should do next" and "what the rules are".

This template is brief and to the point. It gives the buyer the directions they need to buy from you. Notice that the telephone number is easy to find. Notice too the American Express logo. Yes, one pays more percentage to Amex, but to offer corporate catering and not offer the American Express card is not logical. You won't fail, you just won't sell as much as you could because many corporations can only use the American Express card to make their purchases.

HOW TO ORDER

1. To place your order for delivery or pick-up please call: **1-800-555-5555.**

2. To ask any and all questions please feel free to call: **1-800-555-5555.**

3. Normal deadline for placing orders is 2:00 P.M. the day before you need it. However, orders placed after this deadline will be filled, whenever our kitchen production permits, subject to special conditions that will be discussed when you order.

4. The nature of our business often requires special charges during rush times or for deliveries going great distances. At ABC Catering our main concern is for on-time delivery with the highest degree of regard for the safe handling of your food.

5. Your order is usually delivered to your location within the one hour period prior to your serving time.

6. At ABC Catering there is really no official minimum. Your price goes up as you buy less. Your price usually drops as your order gets larger.

7. ABC Catering offers our clients as much extra assistance as they wish. Just ask us if you need staff, serving equipment, tables etc. As extra assistance is requested, additional costs will be billed accordingly.

 and other major credit cards

 To Place An Order! CALL: 800-555-5555

THE FINE PRINT

1. At ABC Catering we believe in providing our clients with ample portions of food. We will gladly discuss with you the amounts of food we're planning to send.

2. If for some reason you wish to have heavier portions for certain situations, just ask and we'll tell you how much the additional items will be.

3. Obviously, certain menu items need to be subject to seasonal availability and our Chef's concern for the proper level of quality, so we retain the right to offer substitutions after notifying you, so your guests and our management will always be proud of what we serve.

4. Changes and cancellations require concern on everyone's part. When a problem arises or a slight change is needed in your order, please call as early as possible. You will be responsible for all cancellations that happen after the 2:00 p.m. deadline on the day before your delivery.

5. Payment may be made by company check, or all major credit cards. If prior arrangements are established, you may request to be billed. On certain orders a deposit may be required to reserve your date.

6. Obviously, our prices will need to be raised or lowered from time to time due to the constantly changing costs charged by our purveyors and suppliers. However, you will always be informed of these changes before you order.

CHAPTER 8  QUESTIONS

1. What are the advantages of printed menus?

2. Where should the caterer's phone number be placed?

3. Why shouldn't the caterer's address be shown in some cases?

4. How should pricing be shown on printed menus?

5. What are your thoughts on offering the use of credit cards?

6. Can a caterer have more than one printed menu at a time?

7. What would be incorrect to place into a printed menu?

8. Do you think that prices should be placed into the printed menu?

9. What colors might work best for printed menus?

10. How important is the size of the menu both for number of selections and physical size?

CONTRACTS

CHAPTER

9

TABLE OF CONTENTS

CHAPTER

9

*"The goal of a successfull
catering contract is to
get the second sale!"*

Contracts / Agreements: Yes or No?

1. This is a matter of extreme controversy with just about every caterer. For most caterers the contract / agreement is viewed as a way of clubbing the buyer over the head when things get sticky!
Here's some questions to ask your lawyer on this topic:

    A. How much will it cost me as a caterer, to take a buyer to court?

    B. Is a verbal agreement legally binding in this State.

    C. Can a buyer be held responsible for loss or damage to the caterer's equipment?

    D. Can a caterer be removed by their liability for causing damage to the buyers

        stuff when a client signs a waiver removing the caterer from fixing the damage?

2. The point is, that in catering sales the contract/agreement, or paperwork, needs to be viewed as a "blueprint" or "road map" of what is expected from both the buyer and the caterer before, during and after the event.

3. Sales are lost because in catering, unlike just about everything else sold, the contract/agreement is sent to the buyer before they say "yes". This gives them the ability to examine all of the "ins and outs" of the paperwork in the privacy of their own home or office without a salesperson being there to interpret, explain and answer questions.

4. More sales would be made if the contract/agreements were written in a "user-friendly" manner.

5. Contract/agreements come in at least four ways:

    A. Written in a formal manner with signatures of both parties.

    B. Written in a casual manner with none or just one signature.

    C. Verbally explained.

    D. A combination of the above.

Contracts: Terms of Agreement

1. ABC Catering, Inc. requires a 50% deposit to confirm and reserve your event date on Saturday, (DATE). We need to receive your deposit of $3,600.00 no later than Friday, (DATE). Receipt of your deposit will guarantee ABC Catering's services for your important date.

2. Five days before your event , we will need to have your final number of guests to be served. This final number will be used to purchase fresh ingredients for our kitchen production, order equipment and arrange for the proper number of event staff. So, once you give us your final guarantee, you may only increase your count.

3. At present, you've told us that you expect 175 guests. The prices on the enclosed menu reflect this number of guests. If your final count increases or decreases more than ten guests, a price adjustment will be made according to the prices on your enclosed menu proposal.

4. Payment of the balance due ABC Catering will be to your event coordinator Ms. Sally Doe at the close of the event. Ms. Doe will contact you several days before the event, by phone, to review the invoice and confirm the amount for your check.

5. Cancellations sometimes occur. If your cancellation is 120 days before the event, 100% of the deposit will be returned. If it occurs 60 days before, 90% of the deposit will be returned. If it occurs 30 days before, 80% of the deposit will be returned. If it occurs less than 30 days, 70% will be returned. If you cancel and reschedule a new date at the same time, your deposit will be credited 100% to the new date.

6. We're looking forward to working with you on this important occasion. If you have any suggestions or questions don't hesitate to call us!

H ere's a CaterSource **template for part of your contract with a client. It is not for everybody, but does represent, in our opinion, the new move towards user friendly agreements that create win-win situations. The circled words above highlight the comments below.**

Paragraph 1 states the reason for the document, to get the deposit! Also, it includes the day and date of the event which is often overlooked by caterers.

Paragraph 2 gives a logical reason to the shopper why the caterer needs to get a final guarantee other than for billing purposes. CaterSource has had positive feedback from caterers who have used this educational sharing of an explanation for your guarantee. Instead of telling a client that they can't make any changes after the guarantee is given, they are told that they can always go up... but not down.

Paragraph 3 clarifies the guarantee at time of booking and makes them aware that if their number drops significantly, by a predetermined number, they will need to pay an increased per person charge. You may wish to review Example 1 in Pricing on page 8 of this Journal.

Paragraph 4 gives the client an answer to how and when they pay the balance owed. Even more significant, you have placed the name of the person who will be collecting the check into what they perceive to be a contract. This results in making the contract different than those from other caterers, and adds some feeling to the contract.

Paragraph 5 is probably causing some of our readers trouble! So, don't use it. CaterSource has learned, that most buyers are relieved when the caterer brings up the situation of cancellation. Also, we had good results when cancellation dollars were given in percentages instead of hard dollars. Also, the last sentence on rescheduling takes some of the heat off the situation.

Paragraph 6 has one key word that most buyers have never seen in contracts... "suggestions". This is a clear sign that the caterer is ready to discuss any concerns the buyer may have!

Example of a Firm Contract

Catersource always tries to bring you different examples of management ideas. The contract below is not for every company or for every customer. It should probably be used sparingly with those buyers who might be likely to cause some difficulty with proposed and final guarantees.

CHECK WITH YOUR ATTORNEY BEFORE USING THIS OR ANY CONTRACT!

TERMS & CREDIT POLICY

ABC Catering, Inc. requires a 50% deposit to reserve the date of your event. Receipt of the deposit is required to confirm ABC Catering's services for the specified event date below.

A confirmation of the guest count is to be made no later than seven (7)days prior to the event date. Thereafter, the number may be increased at the quoted per person cost, but not decreased.

The per person costs on the catering contract are based on the original guest count. If the confirmed guest count is less than the original proposed guest count, the per person costs may increase. The amount of the increase is calculated in proportion to the overall size of your event. If your final guest count decreases by more than 50%, ABC Catering reserves the right to withdraw from the event unless a satisfactory increase in price is reached.

The balance is due at the end of the event. Please provide your check to our Event Coordinator. If any additional billing is necessary, due to staff overtime or client's additional requests, ABC Catering will bill separately for these coverages. Payment on invoices for coverages are due within 10 days of receipt. Any unpaid balances will be subject to a 1.5% late charge.

Cancellations of confirmed events are subject to a cancellation fee. This fee is no less than 10% of the proposed cost of the event and no greater than the total of actual costs incurred in the preparation of the event.

Client's Name _____ Event Date _____

Amount of Deposit _____

_____ _____

ABC Catering, Inc. Client's Acceptance

Date _____ Date Signed _____

Sample Management Fee Agreement

What follows is a sample contract used by a caterer for a permanent management fee foodservice situation, like an employee cafeteria. It is being presented as a sample for educational purposes only. You must get an attorney's approval before using.

ABC CATERING, INC.
(Agreement for management fee foodservice contract)

This Agreement made as of the_____ day of_____, 20____ by and between ABC CATERING, INC., a Montana corporation, with its principle place of business at YOUR ADDRESS ("ABC'), and _____a_____ corporation, with principle place of business at_____("CLIENT").

WITNESSETH:

WHEREAS, Client desires to engage ABC and ABC desires to provide certain food and food related services upon Client's premises at:_____ ("Client's Facility");

NOW, THEREFORE, in consideration of the promises and of the covenants set forth herein, the parties agree as follows:

1.0 APPOINTMENT

(1.1)
Exclusive Right: Client hereby grants to ABC the exclusive right to operate all food
and food related services, at Client's Facility.

(1.2)
Term: This Agreement will commence as of _____,19____ and will continue until _____,19____ . Upon the expiration of such initial term, this Agreement will continue automatically from year to year, unless written notice of termination is given by either party at least ninety (90) days prior to the end of the initial term or any subsequent year.

2.0 FACILITIES AND EQUIPMENT

(2.1)
Client Facilities and Equipment: Client will furnish to ABC, without charge, facilities and equipment necessary to enable ABC to manage the food service operation hereunder. Such facilities and equipment will include, but will not be limited to, food preparation, service and dining areas and suitable furniture, fixtures, and equipment therein; storage space for inventory, equipment and supplies; restrooms and changing areas for employees; suitably furnished office space (not less than 400 sq. feet) ; and smallwares, such as china, flatware, glassware and other such items to do the job at hand.

(2.2)
Title: Title to any ABC property, including the machines, contents therein, and any smallwares, provided by ABC will remain in ABC, howsoever attached or fixed to Client's Facility, and Client will not encumber ABC's property with any liens or encumbrances of any kind.

(2.3)
Inventory: At the commencement of this Agreement, Client will purchase all necessary initial inventory.

3.0 OPERATIONAL RESPONSIBILITIES

(3.1)
ABC's Responsibilities: ABC will be responsible for the following as a charge or expense relating to the Food Service Operation:
(a) preparing, serving and selling wholesome food;
(b) establishing a price and portion list and corresponding menus;
(c) obtaining all necessary licenses and permits;
(d) routine cleaning of the food preparation, service and storage areas, including floors, counter tops;
(e) supplying and laundering kitchen linens, such as uniforms, aprons, cleaning cloths
(f) purchasing all inventory, and supplies required for the Food Service Operation;
(g) purchasing replacements of ABC supplied smallwares as necessary; and
(h) repairing any equipment that is provided for ABC's use under Section 2 above, which is not repaired by Client.

(3.2)
Client's Responsibilities: Client, at its expense, will be responsible for the following:
(a) cleaning the dining areas and the food preparation service and storage areas other than the routine cleaning performed by ABC and all related areas, including the washing and waxing of floors and cleaning of rugs, walls, ceilings, windows, draperies, light fixtures, tables and chairs, air ducts, hoods and flues;
(b) removing all trash and garbage;
(c) providing exterminator services on a regularly scheduled basis;
(d) maintaining, repairing and replacing all facilities and equipment that is provided pursuant to Section 2.0 as necessary to enable ABC to perform its responsibilities hereunder in an efficient manner and to ensure that the facilities and

Sample Management Fee Agreement

equipment comply with all applicable federal, state and local codes, regulations, policies and ordinances; and

(e) providing all utilities necessary for the Food Service Operation pursuant to

this Agreement.

4.0 CATERING

ABC will cater special functions at Client's request upon at least twenty-four (24) hours advance notice at prices and upon such other terms as are mutually acceptable to the parties. Client will be responsible for any charges made by third parties at Client's Facility for catering functions, and ABC will invoice Client for any such charges, payable in accordance with Section 5.5.

5.0 FINANCIAL ARRANGEMENTS

(5.1)

Estimated Charges: Prior to the commencement of the Food Service Operation, Client will deposit with ABC the estimated amount of one month's charges and expenses relating to the Food Service Operation, which will equal _____ (put amounts into words & numbers). Any portion of the foregoing not required to pay amounts owed to ABC upon termination of the Agreement will be repaid to Client within thirty (30) days after the termination.

(5.2)

Pre-Opening Expenses: Client will pay all charges and expenses relating to the opening for the Food Service operation, such as charges for the following: labor, including training crew labor, meals and lodging, forms and manuals, advertising, promotions and payment will be made within fifteen (15) days after receipt of an invoice.

(5.3)

Management Fee: In consideration of the services provided by ABC, Client will pay ABC an administrative fee of $00,000 for the first year with two and half percent, 3.5% annual increases for the second, 2nd and third, 3rd years of Net Sales and a management fee of four and six tenths 5.6% of Net Sales, which management fee and administrative charge will equal at least $$$$$$$$$$$, $00,000 per year. "Net Sales" means all cash and credit receipts from sales in the food service operation less any sales and use taxes. Client will pay all amounts due including all charges and expenses relating to the food service operation, to ABC in accordance with Section 5.5.

(5.4)

Reports: Within twenty-five (25) days after the end of each monthly period, ABC will submit reports of Net Sales during such period together with an itemization of all amounts due

ABC under this Agreement. ABC's accounting hereunder will be maintained in accordance with ABC's fiscal calendar, which is based on 4/4/5 weeks in each quarter.

(5.5)

Payment: Client will remit payment of the fees and other amounts due to ABC pursuant to this Agreement within fifteen (15) days after receipt of ABC's report showing the amounts due to ABC or receipt of an invoice for any amount due to ABC. If any amounts owed to ABC are not paid within thirty (30) days after the date due, ABC will be entitled to collect a late charge equal to one and one-half percent (1.5%) per month (or in the event local law prohibits the charge of such rate, at the maximum legal rate permitted) on the unpaid amounts from the due date until paid in full together with costs of collection, including reasonable legal fees. ABC will be entitled to withhold from any amounts which may be due to Client, including any cash or credit receipts from sales in the Food Service Operation, any sums owed by Client from ABC.

(5.6)

Record Keeping: ABC will maintain accurate records of Net Sales and will retain all such records for a period of at least two (2) years. Client will have the right, at its expense, to examine and audit such records at reasonable times during business hours.

(5.7)

Adjustment of Financial Arrangements: In the event of any increase in the charges or expenses relating to the Food Service Operation, such as increases in federal and state minimum wage laws, ABC may make commensurate adjustments in prices or, upon mutual agreements between the parties in the foregoing financial arrangements between the parties. In the event the population of Client's Facility falls below ___#_____, ABC may, at its option, terminate this Agreement upon ten (10) days prior written notice to Client if the parties do not mutually agree to adjust the financial arrangements within ten (10) days after written notice to Client.

6.0 EMPLOYEES

(6.1)

General Provisions: ABC will provide a staff of employees, including supervisory personnel, as required for the efficient operation of the Food Service Operation. All persons employed by ABC in connection with such operation will be on ABC's payroll and will be deemed employees of ABC for tax and insurance purposes. ABC's employees will comply with all rules stated by Client for the safe and orderly conduct of the activities carried out at Client's Facility. ABC's employees, agents and suppliers will have access to such parts of Client's

Sample Management Fee Agreement

Facility as necessary to enable ABC to carry out its responsibilities hereunder.

(6.2)

Agreement Not To Hire: Client will not hire or permit the employment in any Food Service Operation, any person who has been a ABC management employee within one (1) year after such employee terminates employment with ABC or within one (1) year after termination of the Agreement. Client agrees that ABC employees have acquired special knowledge, skills and contacts as a result of being trained by ABC. If Client hires or permits employment of any such employee in any food service operation within the restricted period, it is agreed by Client that ABC will suffer damages, and Client will pay ABC as liquidated damages an amount equal to fifty percent (50%) of the annual salary of any such employee hired by Client. This Section will survive the termination of the Agreement.

(6.3)

Employment Practices: ABC will not discriminate in any manner on the basis of gender, age, race, color, creed or national origin with respect to its employees, and it will conform in all respects to pertinent provisions of federal, state and local statutes, laws, regulations and ordinances governing employment practices.

(6.4)

Dismissal at Client's Request: If Client objects to the continued employment of any ABC employee, it will so notify ABC in writing, stating the reason for its objection. ABC will terminate such employment in Client's Facility as soon as possible in accordance with ABC's employment policies; provided, however, that ABC's obligation to terminate such employment at Client's request will be subject to restrictions imposed upon ABC by any federal, state or local statute, law, code, regulation, ordinance or policy or by any collective bargaining agreement or other contract affecting such employee.

7.0 INSURANCE INDEMNITIES AND WAIVERS

(7.1)

Insurance: ABC agrees to maintain insurance policies for comprehensive general liability for bodily injury and property damage at Client's Facility in all amount of not less than One Million Dollars ($1,000,000) combined single limits and will name Client as an additional insured to the extent Client is indemnified under Section 7.3 hereof.

(7.2)

Property Insurance: Client will maintain insurance on Client's Facility and all property contained therein for fire and other casualties. The parties agree to waive their respective rights or recovery, including subrogation, against one another for losses or damage to each party's property as a result of fire or other casualties normally covered under standard broad form insurance policies.

(7.3)

Indemnification: Each party will indemnify, defend and hold harmless the other party, its officers, employees and agents from any and all liability, loss, damages, claims, liens, costs and expenses, including attorney's fees, to the extent caused by the negligent acts or omissions of the indemnifying party, its officers, employees, and agents in the performance of its obligations under this Agreement. The indemnified party will give reasonable notice to the indemnifying party of any claim, action or proceeding in respect of which indemnity may be sought hereunder. An indemnifying party may participate, at its own expense, in the defense of any such action. This Section will survive the termination of this Agreement.

8.0 GENERAL TERMS AND CONDITIONS

(8.1)

Contingencies: Neither party will be liable to the other party for any nonperformance of its obligations under this Agreement caused by the occurrence of any contingencies beyond the control of the parties, including but not limited to, declared or undeclared war, sabotage, insurrection, riot or other acts of civil disobedience, acts of a public enemy, acts of governments or agencies affecting the terms of this Agreement, strikes, labor disputes, acts of third parties not within the control of the party whose performance is affected, shortages of fuel, failures of power, accidents, fires, explosions, floods or other acts of God. In the event any such contingencies occur, the party whose performance is affected will have a reasonable time in which to resume performance and such party's nonperformance will not constitute a default hereunder.

(8.2)

Confidential Information: Certain proprietary materials including menus, recipes, signage, surveys and studies, management procedures, operating manuals, software programs and similar information regularly used in ABC's operations ("Confidential Information") will be provided to Client by ABC for use in the food service operation. Client will not disclose any Confidential Information, directly or indirectly, during or after the term of the Agreement. Client will not photocopy or otherwise duplicate any such material without ABC's prior written consent. All Confidential Information will remain ABC's exclusive property and will be returned to ABC immediately upon termination of the Agreement. In the

Sample Management Fee Agreement

event of any breach of this provision, ABC will be entitled to equitable relief, including an injunction or specific performance, in addition to all other remedies otherwise available. This Section will survive termination of the Agreement.

(8.3)

Notices: All notices required by this Agreement will be in writing and will be delivered personally, or by overnight courier or registered or certified mail, return receipt requested, addressed as follows: Address)_____
To ABC: (Your Address)

(8.4)

Termination: Notwithstanding the provisions of Section 1.2 above, either party may terminate this Agreement without cause upon sixty (60) days prior written notice. Either party may terminate this Agreement upon the occurrence of material default in the performance of an obligation under the Agreement and in such event, the nondefaulting party will deliver written notice describing the breach in reasonable detail. If the default is remedied within thirty (30) days, the notice will be null and void, and if the default is continued after thirty (30) days, the nondefaulting party will have the right to terminate this Agreement upon the expiration of an additional thirty (30) days. The foregoing rights of termination are in addition to any and all other rights available under law or in equity.

(8.5)

Rights and Duties Upon Termination: Upon termination of this Agreement for any reason, the following provisions will apply:
(a) Client's Facility: ABC will return Client's Facility and all equipment therein in the same condition as existed at the time of delivery to ABC, excepting ordinary wear and tear, loss or damage occurring without the fault of ABC, and damage occurring as a result of fire or other like unavoidable casualties.
(b) Inventory and Supplies: ABC will submit to Client, within fifteen (15) days after the date of termination, a schedule of all usable inventory and supplies purchased by ABC for the food service operation, including any equipment purchased by ABC on Client's behalf, and Client or ABC's successor will reimburse ABC an amount equal to ABC's invoice cost for such inventory, supplies and equipment within five (5) days after receipt of such schedule.
(c) Final Accounting: ABC will deliver to Client, within thirty (30) days after the date of termination, a final accounting of the results of the food service operation and will remit to Client all amounts due, if any, after deducting any amounts which may be owed by Client to ABC.

(8.6)

Binding effect: This Agreement will be binding upon and will inure to the benefit

of the parties hereto and their respective successors, assigns and representatives.

(8.7)

Entire Agreement: This Agreement constitutes the final, complete and exclusive written agreement of the parties with respect to the food service operation at Client's Facility and will supersede all previous communication, representations, agreements or statements, whether oral or written, by any party or between the parties.

(8.8)

Modification: No modification of any of the terms and conditions of this Agreement will be effective unless such modification is expressed in writing and signed by the party against whom enforcement is sought.

(8.9)

Waiver: The failure of either party to enforce any of the terms of this Agreement on one or more occasions will not constitute a waiver of the right to enforce such term or each and every term of this Agreement on any other occasion.

(8.10)

Relationship of Parties: The parties agree that ABC will be an independent contractor to Client. Nothing herein will construed to create a partnership, joint venture or agency relationship between the parties and neither will have the authority to bind the other in any respect.

In WITNESS WHEREOF, the parties hereto have caused this Agreement to be
executed as of the date above.

ABC CATERING, INC.

By_____

Title_____
Printed Name

By_____

Title_____
Printed Name

REMEMBER:
GET AN ATTORNEY'S APPROVAL
BEFORE USING!

Salesperson Employment Contract

What follows is an example of a contract between a caterer and their salesperson. It is provided only as education and must not be used without first getting the approval of an attorney.

Example of a sales contract

(Company) Catering, ("(Company)") is pleased to offer (your salesperson) (hereinafter "(your salesperson)" or "Employee") a position with our company as an event specialist. In consideration of the terms and conditions set forth in the letter, (Company) and (your salesperson) agree as follows:

1. Employee at Will. Your employment with (Company) is at-will, which means that the employment relationship may be terminated by you or (Company) at any time, for any reason, with or without cause. No term of the agreement shall alter the employment at-will relationship.

2. Job Responsibilities. Your job responsibilities shall be described to you by (Company) from time to time, and shall include, but not be limited to, the job description attached as Exhibit A hereto and incorporated herein.

3. Work Hours. Your normal work hours shall be approximately from 8:30 am to 5:30 pm Monday through Friday, and/or such other or additional hours shall be scheduled in connection with your performance of scheduled events during evenings and on weekends. You will be required to use (Company)'s time clock.

4. Salary and commissions, and sales bonus.

(a) **Base salary.** As of July 1, 1999, you will no longer receive a salary. You will be paid on a commission basis only.

(b) **Event Specialist Sales Commissions.** You will receive event specialist sales commissions, as follows, for events that you personally solicit.

(c) **On New Accounts.** Each new B&I account will be evaluated on an individual commission basis and will not be part of your running total of annual sales or bonus structure. The B&I account can be re-evaluated once the account is established.

(d) **On Regularly Published Prices.** All sales are calculated for the (Company) calendar year of January to December.

On all of your sales, (Company) will pay you a 7% commission.

On events billed in excess of regularly published prices you will earn a split commission. You will be paid 50% of the upsell on food, disposable, decorations, beverage, and miscellaneous charges (with equipment and labor to be determined by you and Management on an event-by-event basis) with 50% of the upsell to be retained by (Company). Of your 50% upsell commission, you will retain 45%, with the remaining 5% to be paid into a pool for other purposes to be determined by you on a semi-annual basis. You will be paid your split upsell commission on the same schedule as your regular commission.

No commission is earned or payable to you until after the event has been sold and orchestrated to completion by you. All client invoicing must be completed within 72 business hours of the completion of the event. (Company) shall pay your commission monthly, but only after (Company) has received full payment for the catering function to which your commission relates. If (Company) does not collect the full amount of its invoice within 45 days of the event, your commission will be reduced to 75%. If (Company) does not collect the full amount of its invoice within 90 days of the event, your commission will be reduced to 50%. If (Company) does not collect the full amount of its invoice within 120 days of the event, you will receive no commission. Commission will be paid in the mid-month check no sooner than the second month following (Company)'s receipt of full payment. In addition, your commission shall be calculated only on the total cost to the customer of the food, disposable, decorations, equipment and beverage portion and personnel of any catering function, and shall not be calculated on any additional charges, such as tax, gratuity, delivery, etc. Furthermore, (Company) shall have the right to assign sales leads to its sales personnel at its sole discretion, and also at its sole discretion, to designate which catering functions shall be priced at a mark-up that is lower than the standard (Company) mark-up.

(e) **On Any Discount or Job Done At Less Than Regularly Published Prices.**

In the event that (Company) does designate a price mark-up for a catering function that is less than the standard mark-up, the commission percentages set forth above shall not apply to such catering function; instead, you and (Company) shall agree on a reduced amount of commission that you shall receive for such catering function, if any commissions are paid on that type of event. (Company) reserves the right in its sole discretion to exclude commissions altogether on some events.

(f) **Event Specialist Sales Bonus.** Your sales goal for personally solicited events in 1999 is $1,700,000. To encourage you to reach your goal, (Company) will give you the following bonuses when you reach each interim goal:

Salesperson Employment Contract

Reach $200,000 sales	=	$200 gift certificate
Reach $425,000 sales	=	$250 gift certificate
Reach $575,000 sales	=	$600 in industry-related education
Reach $650,000 sales	=	$1000 bonus on check
Reach 1.3 million sales	=	2 round-trip tickets on Airline miles certificate good for travel in the continental United States.
Reach 1.8 million sales	=	$1500 bonus on check

(g) Party Pay. You will be paid event pay in accordance with (Company)'s policy manual. Event work performed before 5:00pm on business days will not result in additional pay. To be paid for an event, you must work a billed slot. When working a waitstaff slot, you will be paid $11.50 an hour. When working a supervisor slot, you will be paid $16.00 an hour.

5. Confidential Information.
You understand that in the course of your employment, you are likely to become familiar with secret or confidential information of (Company) such as, but not limited to, lists of customers, specific information regarding successful customers, types and kinds of catering arrangement, lists of suppliers of food beverages and equipment and the costs thereof, and other information of a confidential nature which is required to be maintained as such for the continued success of (Company) and its business. Accordingly, you agree:

(a) While employed by (Company), to cooperate with and advise and acquaint (Company) of all confidential knowledge and information possessed by or entrusted to you so that (Company) may know at all times the extent to which knowledge of secret or confidential information is possessed and being utilized by you.

(b) If and when your employment with (Company) is terminated, whether voluntary or involuntarily, to surrender to (Company) all books, recipes, training manuals, computer discs, Rolodexes, records, notes, customer lists, documents, and any other secret or confidential information.

6. Employee benefits.
(Company) shall provide major medical and dental insurance for you under the terms and condition available through (Company)'s current major medical plan. (Company) reserves the right to change all aspects of insurance coverage from time to time at its sole discretion. You will not be eligible for insurance until 90 days after your start date. (Company) will pay 50% of the cost of said insurance. At your expense, your family members may also be covered by (Company)'s insurance. Long and short term dis-

ability insurance are also available at your own expense. If you desire, prior to your signing the agreement (Company) will provide you with information on the major medical and dental insurance that it currently provides for its employees.

(Company) shall also provide you with the paid vacation time set forth below:

(1) A one-week vacation after one year of employment with (Company);

(2) A two-week vacation after two years of employment with (Company);

(3) A three-week vacation after five years of employment with (Company).

You must schedule your vacation with (Company) at least three weeks prior to the beginning date of the desired vacation. Although you may request any vacation time that you desire within the limits of the agreement, (Company) shall have sole discretion regarding final approval of any vacation date that you request. No vacation may be taken during the following periods:

- May 1st through June 30th
- September 1st through October 31st
- the Monday after Thanksgiving to December 22nd

The contract shall be reviewed annually but all terms shall remain in effect until specifically replaced by a revised contract signed by both parties.

After one year of employment, you will be eligible to enroll in (Company)'s 401 (k) plan. If you desire, prior to signing the agreement (Company) will provide you with information on company contributions to your 401(k) and the company contribution vesting schedule.

We are looking forward to having you continue your work with (Company) and hope that you find the terms of the agreement acceptable. If so, please indicate your acceptance by signing the agreement below and returning it to us.

(Company).

By:_____

Read and accepted:_____

Date signed:_____

REMEMBER:
GET AN ATTORNEY'S APPROVAL BEFORE USING!

Copy for Catering Contracts

CaterSource, Inc. is presenting the following as examples of copy that might be used in catering contracts or agreements.

NOTE: THESE EDUCATIONAL EXAMPLES ARE PRESENTED INDEPENDENT OF EACH OTHER. THESE ARE NOT EXAMPLES OF A CONTRACT... THEY ARE EXAMPLES OF PARTS OF A CONTRACT. YOU CAN PICK AND CHOOSE WHAT MIGHT WORK BEST FOR YOU.

1. Customer Count

A. The number of persons listed on this contract shall be guaranteed by the customer, even if the number of guests served is lower than the guarantee given.

B. All costs are based on the guarantee given. However, a customer may reduce the given guarantee by up to 10%, as long as the customer notifies ABC Catering of the reduction more than 72 hours before the event.

C. Caterer has extensive experience in determining and preparing the correct amount for each menu item for the guaranteed group size. It is our custom to prepare enough extra to cover groups that eat above normal amounts of foods. However, in no case, are we required to have extra food for numbers higher than the guarantee given.

D. Customer agrees that they will pay additional, at the agreed per guest price, for any guests that increase the guarantee... even if the food is available.

E. If the final guest count is 10% greater than the guarantee, an additional 10% service charge will be paid by customer to cover the extra burden placed on the staff at the event by being shorthanded.

F. Customer agrees that the caterer will retain all foods and beverages, remaining at the conclusion of the event, that have been brought by the caterer.

G. The final count, or guarantee, is due 7 business days in advance of the event. Following the final count, the number may not be lowered, but may be raised. A 15% surcharge may be added to cover additional last minute expenses of getting the added food and beverages for the additional guests.

2. Cancellation

A. Customer understands that once a contract is signed, the caterer may decline other profit-making opportunities for that day. Accordingly, the client will be responsible for the entire contract cost even if the event is cancelled.

B. Customer understands that as the event date comes closer, the caterer has hired event staff, purchased foods and beverages, and contracted for kitchen labor. Accordingly, the client will be responsible for the entire contract cost even if the event is cancelled.

C. If the client notifies the caterer in ample time, the caterer will make every effort to rebook the date or lower the amount of the loss. In this case, these savings will be passed along to the client.

D. If the client's guest count drops more than 50% from original guarantee, the caterer has the right to cancel the contract unless a higher price is negotiated to offset the loss of profit.

E. In the event that a client cancels the function with not less than 2 weeks prior to the date, 50% of the deposit will be retained by the caterer. If the event is cancelled with less than 1 week notice, the client will be responsible for the entire amount due.

3. Damage To Property

A. Customer understands that all property brought to the event location, including but not limited to all serving equipment, floral arrangements, skirting and linens, non-floral centerpieces, and all other property belonging to caterer, shall be removed by caterer at conclusion of the event.

B. In the event that any of the caterer's property delivered to the event location is broken, stolen, or missing, whether due to actions of customer, their staff, or guests, the customer will be responsible for replacement cost of any such property. In the event that such loss is due to the caterer, the client will not be liable for replacement.

C. Client understands that all of the caterer's property will be removed at the end of the event. If the customer requires, or asks, for any of this property to be left behind, the client shall be charged an appropriate fee for use of this property.

> # REMEMBER:
> ## GET AN ATTORNEY'S APPROVAL BEFORE USING!

CHAPTER 9  QUESTIONS

1. What are some of the questions you should ask your lawyer before using a contract?

2. What are the goals of a catering contract?

3. When should a contract be given to the potential buyer?

4. What are four ways that a contract may be created?

5. What are the contractual concerns a caterer has about customer count?

6. What are the contractual concerns a caterer has about cancellations?

7. What are the contractual concerns a caterer has about damage to property?

8. Why should you always let an attorney check over your contract before you use it?

9. What did you think of the salesperson contract?

10. Is it alright to have clients not put their signature on the contract?

MANAGING

CHAPTER

10

TABLE OF CONTENTS

CHAPTER

10

*"An experienced caterer always
knows where the nearest
24 hour grocery store is located!"*

What is the Driving Force in Your Company

Caterers are in business to serve people. Caterers are also in the business of making money for themselves and their staff. What follows is a rather personal checklist for a caterer to refer to from time to time.

This checklist concerns itself with a particular caterer's basis for being in business. None of these are bad, but one or more of them can lead to certain problems in a catering business. Which of these "drives" do you have?

1. Get any, and all, orders booked because of the need for cash flow.

This "driving force" stems from the need to work with as many customers as possible. Caterers who have this drive, don't understand the meaning of "the straw that broke the camel's back".

These caterers are driven by volume and the number of events they do on a particular day. "Last year we did six events on July 4th, but this year we're doing eight", is the rallying cry of this type of caterer.

This type of caterer is obsessed with the need for more. More volume, more trucks, more staff, more cellular phones, more, more, more, and more. While this is not bad, special attention needs to be taken to insure that the "more" isn't leading to serious financial problems.

2. Get the job out

This "driving force" is usually found in the kitchen. You can recognize it easily if you listen because kitchen managers, and chefs, tend to usually yell to their staff to hurry! "Where's the salad for the Smith party", they exclaim to their staff.

Often, the need to "get the job out" is a result of too few staff, or bad time management in the kitchen. Also, it needs to be pointed out that some caterers need to constantly create crisis so they can rise to the occasion and solve the problems or save the day.

Caterers who have the "get the job out" drive, often have incredible kitchen turnover and greater accidents in production and delivery.

3. Keep everyone happy

What's wrong with having a "driving force" based on happiness? Perhaps nothing. However, if this happiness gets in the way of discipline and quality, then a problem exists.

When asked why one of their staff was smoking at an event the caterer answered, "Well, it's hard to find great workers, so I need to overlook some things". This is an example of how this "drive" can lead to a decay in the fabric of a company.

In companies with this type of "drive" we also find staff taking home leftovers, helping themselves to excessive meals while at work (using costly items), arriving late for events, etc.;

In a well run business, happiness should be created from the professional perfection and pride in creating beautiful catering.

4. Earning money

The caterer with this "driving force" watches the bottom line and everything else in their company for its impact on profitability. While this is not bad in itself, it can cause an unrealistic belief in the value of saving costs.

Costs are present in all businesses. The most important aspect of costs is its relationship to the selling price of the product. Often the caterers who are most concerned about making money, try to do it through cost savings only, instead of a possible rise in price. So, this "drive" can be good, but, at the same time, misleading.

5. Helping people

This "driving force" comes from the heart of many caterers. The need to "help" clients is the basis for successful selling. When a buyer understands that a caterer is concerned with helping them, the sale usually comes to be.

When hiring staff, this driving force is a must. Frankly, one has it or not. It usually can't be taught. It comes from past experiences and teachings from ones parents. This is an important "driving force" that crates great riches and peace of mind!

6. Treat it like a hobby

What can we say about this "driving force" that most caterers don't already know? It's deadly. Business is business ... play is play! The business of catering is not, and shouldn't, be an experiment, or causal attempt at an idea. This "driving force" often leads to bankruptcy if not corrected.

So, now you have some more "food for thought" from CaterSource. If you agree with these, or disagree, no matter. The important thing is that you come to realize that there are reasons why you have certain views, or take certain actions during the normal course of your day.

Catering is not, and never will be, easy. Catering is, however, one of the most rewarding professions that anyone can be involved with.!

Dealing With Refunds

Not a happy subject! But it is a topic that needs to be thought about by each and every caterer.

It may never happen... but, if it does... one needs a plan. Here are some thoughts on this subject.

The first thing to remember is that refunds, and requests for refunds, are part of the business! As a business grows larger, so does the chance of being confronted with a refund situation.

Most caterers tend to view a request, or demand, for a refund as a personal lose or even as an insult towards the company.

There are at least two types of refund situations. First is the **cancellation refund**. The event is just not going to take place or is cancelled leaving the matter of already paid deposits.

Next there is the performance refund. The customer believes, even if it isn't true, that the caterer has placed them in a bad situation during the execution of the event.

Examples of **performance refunds** are running out of some food items, stale rolls, the wrong color frosting on the cake, an unprofessional staff member etc.

Here are some questions to ask yourself when a refund situation arises.

1. Why is this particular refund happening?

Cancellation Refund. Did the wedding couple break-up? Is there a snow storm? Is the cost of the event too high? Is there a rumor going around about my company?

Performance Refund. How many extra people did they invite that weren't in the guarantee? Is my customer being influenced by anything that I said or did before the event?

2. What are my real losses?

Cancellation Refund. Is the event cancelling with just two days to go... or is it coming six months out? Can I resell my space or date? Are they leaving me and moving to a competitor?

Performance Refund. Can I get a credit from my supplier for the money I need to give back? Can the stuff I bought be used at a later date for another catering?

3. What are the consequences to my business if I don't handle this properly?

Cancellation Refund. How will my image be affected if I say no to the refund? How will it be affected if I say yes? Is this a local group?

Performance Refund. What will future customers do if they find out what I did for someone else? Will it save my relationship with this buyer?

4. What is the potential refund?

Cancellation Refund. Do I need to give it all back? Does it have to be cash, or can I give a credit towards a future event?

Performance Refund. Can I just send some extra food after the party? Do I send cash or food?

5. How should the refund be paid?

Cancellation Refund. Should it be a credit towards a new event? Should it be paid back only if the date is resold?

Performance Refund. Can I give them a refund account to eat in my restaurant? Can I make a donation to a charity in their name? Can I give them more food? Worth?

Cancellation Refund. Should I deduct a professional fee from the refund amount for my planning time?

Performance Refund. Did I give them anything free during the planning and selling that I can now charge against?

6. What are the real costs associated with this refund?

Cancellation Refund. What are the chances that I won't be able to resell my date or space? Do I still have to pay for any staff because the cancellation came so close to the date?

Performance Refund. How much volume will I lose from the community once they find out about my problem?

Refunds are not a happy topic for any caterer. They are going to come up from time to time. How a caterer handles the initial request from a client is very important.

The first thing to remember is not to react too fast to a client's request for a refund. Remember the words, "Thank you Mrs. Smith, but let me get back to you later today with an answer."

This will allow you to cool down, talk with other staff members who might have vital information on this topic, and get a response plan in your head to offer to the customer .

Table of Contents for a Policy Manual

During a recent CaterSource survey of 32 catering companies doing over 1 million dollars in sales, it was discovered that only 11 of the 32 companies had a formal employee policy manual.

With the concerns for employee rights in the 90's, along with the number of law suits pertaining to employee employer problems, it would be wise for all caterers to have a policy manual.

The purpose of the manual is to bring professionalism to a business and to provide the blueprint of what the company's and employee's obligations are perceived to be.

A policy manual is not a guarantee that a caterer will not get into a difficult situation. It is, however, a notification to all that the caterer has attempted to bring rules and guidelines out into the open for everyone to know and understand.

A trip to your city's library will give you contact with many books on the subject of employee policy manuals. Sometimes the Chamber of Commerce has them available for you to review. Software exists for both IBM and MAC computers to help you create your manual.

Above all, you should absolutely have your manual checked, revised or written by your attorney before you place it in the hands of your staff.

1. Purpose of the policy manual
2. Welcome letter
3. History of the company
4. Organizational chart of the company
5. Statement of Equal Opportunity Employment
6. Proof of right to work (I-9 Form)
7. Hours of business operations
8. Training
9. Work Schedules
10. Change of address
11. Parking and entering the premise
12. Use of time cards
13. Pay day procedures
14. Breaks and lunches
15. Purchasing food from the company
16. Pay advances
17. Overtime
18. Telephone calls and visitors
19. Emergencies
20. Smoking
21. Jury duty

22. Family leave
23. Sick leave
24. Unpaid medical leave
25. Keys
26. Security concerns
27. Injury or accidents
28. Use of company vehicles
29. Firearms or weapons
30. Gambling
31. Intoxicants and illegal substances
32. Theft
33. Tardiness
34. Sexual, or other, harassment
35. Vacations
36. Uniforms
37. Insurance
38. Holidays
39. Absences
40. Termination, Suspension and Discipline
41. Resignation
42. Driver authorization
43. Sample job evaluation form
44. Sample time off request form

SAMPLE WELCOME LETTER FOR A POLICY MANUAL

Dear Employee:

Welcome to (CO. NAME) . There is no single resource more important to (CO. INITIALS) than its people. Service to the public, which is the primary goal of (CO. INITIALS), depends a great deal on the diligence, innovation and cooperation of all our employees.

As you review this employee policy manual, please make us aware of anything that you don't understand or need clarification on. This manual is the basis for our team's success and dedication to outstanding hospitality.

Remember, above all, that you are an important member of this Company, and everything that you do affects the other members. As a team, working together, we shall all strive for success. We look forward to working with you throughout your employment with (CO. INITIALS).

Strategies for Smaller Towns

1. Always remember your roots... but, always try to bring your clients up to your level of doing things. As long as they still think that caterer's should offer prices like McDonalds, you can't win.

2. At parties, put out some foods that the client didn't order. These extra items should continually remind the host and guests that there is more to offer than just what tradition calls for!

3. Form partnerships with caterers in larger cities. Offer your help to them... and get their help in return.

4. Form a customer advisory board, or committee, to help you operate your business. Meet with them from time to time to ask their opinions and to have them sample some of your new foods "before you sell it to the public". The result will be a more informed town about what you do and how you do it! This is the positive use of gossip!

5. Try to position yourself as the "Martha Stewart" or "Emeril" of your area. This means that you will want to write free articles for the newspaper, get on the radio as a party expert, and do anything else to teach the concepts of entertaining in your market.

Trends Facing Caterers

Like all businesses, catering is subject to new trends... while losing older trends. Below are some of the more unique trends that are facing the on and off-premise catering segments of the food-service industry. As you review them, please don't think of them as absolute necessities for your company. Trends are different in different parts of the nation, and often take longer to get to smaller markets.

1. BANQUET VS. OFF-PREMISE CATERING. On-premise catering, or banquet facilities, are the largest growth area for catering as we enter the 21st. Century. They tend to make more money and are easier to operate. Because of the economy's strength, investment dollars seem to be available for building growth.

2. MOVING AWAY FROM RETAIL SELLING. Many caterers who have operated gourmet shops, or other retail outlets, have come to realize that the labor cost factor in these operations is taking profits away from the more profitable and larger catering orders.

3. SLOW MOVE TO MEAL REPLACEMENT. Catering is based on profitability through feeding large numbers of guests in a single order. Meal replacement, or the selling of several individual meals for a single household, is just the opposite. Therefore, caterers are still very anxious about getting into this business. Besides, everyone else is doing it already ... Boston Chicken, Supermarkets, etc.

4. TWO COOKS FOR THE PRICE OF ONE. Because it's so hard to find and maintain Executive Chefs for catering, many are taking the larger salary of the Executive Chef and hiring two chefs instead. The kitchen moves from recipes in one person's head, to written down or in a computer. Then, consulting chefs are brought in twice a year to create new menu items, build the recipes files and train chefs.

5. GUEST PARTICIPATION AT EVENTS. Menus are being designed that allow guests to get involved in the finishing touches of foods at events. For example, at station parties, guests are asked to select all their ingredients for a stir fry entree or their salad before giving them to the Chef who then finishes it off while they wait. Another, would be guests who get a chance to fill cannoli shells with their own choice of fillings. They actually get a lesson on how to "pipe" in the fillings.

6. CLOSING ONE DAY A WEEK. This trend is a healthy one. Caterers close one day a week to increase the quality of their lives. It's usually Monday, because sometimes they get Sunday also. The advantage is that everyone gets the same day off during the week. Also, you will be able to hire better staff because they know that they will have some personal time.

7. BI-CITY CATERING. It's a small trend ... but some caterers are deciding to own two different companies.... in two different cities. Examples would be: Vail, CO & Phoenix AZ • Atlanta. GA & Grand Rapids, MI • Chicago, IL & West Palm Beach, FL. Sometimes the companies are exactly the same, and sometimes they are different. Examples: BBQ & Weddings • Corporate & Social.

8. ELIMINATION OF SMALLER ORDERS. Many caterers are realizing that smaller orders under twenty-five are just not profitable enough to keep booking. This is not true in all cases, but many caterers have found that when they stop the smaller orders, they have time to grow the business.

9. SELLING PARTY POSTPONEMENT GUARANTEE. Call it what you will... some caterers are simply saying when appropriate "Mrs. Smith, one last item, for an additional $1.35 per guest, we can offer you our Event Postponement Guarantee which permits you to reschedule the event if you inform us 72 hours before." Its got some kink... but it is great in certain circumstances!

10. BONUS FOR UPSELLING. Everyone loves this one. When a salesperson upsells a client, they get to share in the upsell volume... everyone wins.

Sales Driven vs. Culinary Driven

What is consulting? To me, consulting is evaluation and comparison. First you evaluate what conditions exist, then you compare these conditions with those that exist elsewhere.

That's what this series of articles is about. I hope to give our readers some guidelines for "self-consulting".

It is important that each catering business receive ongoing evaluation in order to continually reach for higher levels of success.

What do I mean by "driven"?

When I refer to the term "driven", I'm giving recognition to the main energy of your business... what part of the business is the most important to you... what department do you favor the most.

Think of it this way. If you were an off-premise caterer facing a decision of whether to send coffee already made from your kitchen in thermal containers, or making it fresh at your event site for 600 guests... which would you choose?

If you selected to make it fresh at the event site the case could be made that you were a culinary driven company and that the fresh coffee came ahead of the resulting extra staff and equipment costs of making it at the event.

If you were sales driven, you might have thought of the problems of making that much coffee on sight on time and decided that the risks were too high for making it at the event.

Maybe coffee is a poor example, but I think you're getting the idea. An on premise caterer with three banquet rooms going at once would be sales driven if they tried to sell each of these groups the same menu. The culinary driven company would be concerned about losing creativity and the chefs would be resistant to doing the same menu for each client because it might look bad and take away from the culinary image of the company.

In either case, positive actions can result. There isn't really a right or wrong answer and we all know that so many exceptions exist, (especially in my coffee example) that it is hard to have hard and firm rules about what a company should do in every case.

> ... THINK OF THESE TIPS, TACTICS AND IDEAS AS A STARTING POINT FOR DOING SELF-CONSULTING FOR YOUR OWN BUSINESS.

Why are so many catering companies food driven?

It's quite simply that most owners of catering businesses are chefs by profession or heart. This is not bad. In fact, it is good for any company that is starting out in business because as a new caterer you're only as good as your last performance.

For this reason your culinary or food side is extremely important for the successful growth of your business.

Is it wrong to be driven by the culinary leaders of the company?

Absolutely not. Some of the finest companies I've worked with are emphatically food driven to the letter. All caterers need to take pride in their foods. They must have a clear view of how significant great food is to both the hosts and their guests.

However, one of the problems with a food, menu, or culinary driven company is that the leader is usually the chef. Because of what a chef stands for, they are often only consumed by the creation of the food and not with its potential for success, or failure, in a real catering situation.

This situation is increasingly aggravated, in many cases, when the chef is not an owner of a business and begins to really believe that the quality of the food is all that matters in each and every situation.

To most of these culinary leaders, food cost is more important than company profits or growth.

The hard truth about being driven by the kitchen

The simple truth, in my consulting opinion, is that while the culinary aspects of a catering company are truly of immense importance, the growth and profit result most often in catering businesses that are sales driven.

Let me explain... but first, let me clarify that what follows is only important if your business needs to increase its profits and you wish to grow the financial worth of the company.

A simple story will begin my explanation. Across America and Canada there are caterers who are known for their top quality foods. They make a fair profit and enjoy great comments from their public.

Sales Driven vs. Culinary Driven

All of these caterers have one, or two, competitors whose food is not of the same high quality, but still make a fair profit and enjoy great comments from their public.

So, what gives? If food is so important, why do caterers who have less quality food also have thriving businesses. Because of the way they sell their products and the manner in which they present their foods at events.

Now, prepare yourself for some bold ideas. Many of our readers will not like what I have to say. Food will not grow a successful company after five years in business. Only sales will keep your company strong.

This deals with holding your price and creating a following based on buyer loyalty instead of great food.

I realize that some are saying to themselves..."Why can't we have high quality foods and a great sales driven business at the same time?" I've seen a few. But the two don't necessarily go hand in hand.

The main reason for this is that most buyers want the lowest prices they can get. Low price is an enemy of high quality food. Yes, some will pay the price. Most, however, will have the Boston Chicken idea of good tasting food at moderate prices.

You don't have to think as I do, but you do have to think about this concept of culinary vs. sales driven companies. Most importantly, don't just look for where you disagree with my thoughts. Try to look at the value of what I'm presenting... if any. Bold thinking makes companies better at what they do.

The reasons to be sales driven

When you begin to move your company towards a sales driven position you begin to challenge why you're in the catering business. Both on and off-premise caterers start placing volume minimums on certain types of sales. One example of this is to not book a party unless it has a certain amount of dollar minimum. Or, some caterers have a minimum for self-serve corporate orders from new and sometimes regular customers.

If you wish to grow a strong healthy business over the next five years, you will need, in my opinion, to be a sales driven company with "great" food when a client will pay for it and exciting "good" food when they won't!

Chefs, who still are extremely important to our success, will no longer call the shots about what can and can't be sold. They will have a voice, but will no longer be "gods" who will look upon only one side of the issue.

In fact, we have had great success when chefs receive the added incentive of a percentage bonus on the volume of orders that go through their kitchens.

When you become a sales driven business, you will see clearly your goals and future profits because your emphasis will turn to more attention to customer's service, food presentations, styles of service and overall enhanced "sizzle".

This is where, I believe, the future of successful, profitable catering lies... in client loyalty. This customer loyalty will be to the company itself, the salesperson, or the system of ordering... not to the food. Food will be assumed to be "great" or "good".

Remember, it's healthy and perhaps wise to disagree with me. However, lets not forget that I've seen a lot more catering businesses than you have. I've seen companies that have thrived and some that have failed. My thoughts above are based on what I've observed over the last fifteen years of consulting with big and small caterers. Call me if you wish to discuss these points further.

Thoughts on Smaller Orders

What is consulting? To me, consulting is evaluation and comparison. First you evaluate what conditions exist, then you compare these conditions with those that exist elsewhere.

This is why the world has consultants. Not for their expertise, but for their exposure to diverse conditions. Most caterers have never been to many other catering operations to see what is happening. I've been fortunate to have personally visited more than 900 catering companies over the last 20 years.

That's what this new series of articles is about. I hope to give our readers some guidelines for "self-consulting".

It is important that catering businesses receive ongoing evaluation in order to continually reach for higher levels of success.

The DANGER ZONE!

Let's lay it on the table right away ... small orders may kill a catering business! That's one thing I've learned since I've had a chance to evaluate more and more companies.

In my opinion, a catering order has over 35 guests. Anything under that is carry-out! If you are a caterer with a retail outlet i.e a deli, restaurant, or gourmet shop; each and every order you do under 35 is a waste of time!

The only reason to do orders for 8, 12, 21 or 32 is when they are coming from clients who also give you catering for 424, 179, 610 and 135!

All right, maybe an order of 32 is borderline, but, orders of 8 and 12 need to stop!

The numbers will lead you to the answer

On a quiet day, sit down and analyze a normal month's selling pattern. Just take the stack of orders you sold in a normal month. Now list them by number of guests and total volume per order. I suggest that you make some columns that will help you visually see the impact of smaller orders in your kitchen. If you make an attempt to track your sales in this manner many of our subscribers would find this type of result:

- from (5 to 9) guests: 12 sales
- from (10 to 19) guests: 26 sales
- from (20 to 29) guests: 41 sales
- from (30 to 39) guests: 22 sales

- from (40 to 69) guests: 14 sales
- from (70 to 99) guests: 9 sales
- from (100 to 149) guests: 11 sales
- from (150 to 199) guests: 13 sales
- from (200 to 399) guests: 8 sales
- from (400 to 699) guests: 3 sales
- from (700 to 999) guests: 1 sale
- over (1,000) guests: 1 sale

In the above example, the caterer made one hundred and one sales below 40 guests and fifty-eight orders over 40.

In round numbers, 50% of the orders were over 40 and 50% were under.

Now, lets talk about volume. Let's take an average check sale of $7.00 per guest for those orders under 40 which would more than likely be self-service drop off orders, i.e box lunches, trays, etc. For the over 40 guests lets take an average check of $18.00 because these orders will more than likely be your full-service parties, i.e. weddings, dinners, etc.

If we just use the bottom number of guests for each category above we would get:

$12,600 volume from under 40
$146,520 volume from over 40

What this means is that 50% of your orders resulted in only $12,600 volume while the other 50% hit the jackpot!

Other factors

It is fair to say that in the above example, 50% of the kitchen's energy (work load) resulted in less than 15% of the month's volume!

If you believe that it often takes a kitchen team just as long to complete an order for 20 as it does 200, then you can add another factor to the case against smaller orders. Often, these smaller orders lead to extra overtime and additional staff being added just to get the work done.

In addition, the smaller orders are usually done before you work on the bigger ones, which means that often the "big dollar" events are prepared by a culinary team that is somewhat worn down from the glut of smaller orders earlier in the day.

Thoughts on Smaller Orders

Roman's axioms

1. Smaller orders should only be taken when they can be justified in keeping clients who give you larger ones happy.

2. Smaller orders should never be taken on days when you need your culinary staff focused on important larger orders.

3. Just because you needed the smaller orders to launch and build up your first customers doesn't mean you need to keep taking them.

4. It's insulting to a caterer when a customer buys smaller orders continually and never gives that caterer a chance to bid on their larger events!

5. It is not catering when a client calls in the day before, or that day, and orders for 16 people ... that is carryout.

6. The thought of opening a kitchen for a few small orders is simply silly!

7. The words, "Small orders don't hurt us since we already have the kitchen staff here already" or "As long as I have a truck going that way, it's o.k. to take a smaller order"... will only lead to continued incorrect profit margins!

8. Caterers who believe that by selling smaller orders to corporations, they get "their foot in the door" for the bigger ones, only get more small orders!

Positive Actions

I realize that everyone reading this article will not agree with me. I also realize that what I'm writing is making some readers take heart and rethink their position on this subject.

Here's some scripts that might help:

In response to a first time caller seeking a small order... "Thanks for calling, but unfortunately we don't do orders that small unless we also have the opportunity to do some of your larger ones. Do you also need catering for larger groups?"

or .... *in response to a corporate caller who requests a small cold buffet for 10 guests ... "How often do you do these small meetings? (answer: Once a month) Well, our company minimum is 25 guests... but, I would be able to do this luncheon free for you, once a month, if you let us do some of the larger events like your holiday party, customer receptions or picnics. Can I make an appointment to meet with you to discuss this win-win opportunity?"*

or ... *the old standby... "I've checked with the chef and its just as I thought ... we've got so much business for that date already, we would be doing a disservice to our other clients if we booked more... please call us earlier next time."*

Well, what can I say? When I was a caterer from 1974 to 1986... I took anything that moved! If they wanted us, we booked it! We took orders of under ten guests often.

I now realize that if I had known some of the ideas that I've since learned, I would have had a better catering business.

My suggestion to you is to rethink your position on smaller orders and test some of the concepts I've just written about. It's only natural to want to get as many orders as one can, but in catering this often leads to trouble!

Product Lines & Minimums

What is consulting? To me consulting is evaluation and comparison. First you evaluate what conditions exist, then you compare these conditions with others that exist elsewhere.

This is why the world has consultants. Not for their expertise, but for their exposure to many different conditions. Most caterers have never been to many other catering operations to see what is happening. I've been fortunate to have personally visited more than 500 catering companies over the last 17 years.

That's what this new series of articles is about. I hope to give our readers some guidelines for "self-consulting".

It is important that salespeople receive ongoing evaluation in order for them to continually reach new goals of selling success.

Beginning Your Product Line Evaluation

First we need to define a product line. A product line is a separate category of what you sell from your catering business. For example, a caterer doesn't have a product line of "catering". Instead, they have product lines of box lunches, weddings, picnics etc. In other words, your product lines are what types of catering you sell.

To begin your evaluation of your product lines you need to identify them by name and amount. Do you sell funerals? How many do you sell each year? How much profit do you receive from your funeral product line?

Once you have them organized and identified on paper, you can then begin to decide which of the product lines to do more of and which to eliminate from your business.

Let's make sure you understand me ... a caterer doesn't sell catering ... they sell what the catering does for the buyer.

In developing a list of product lines, almost everyone reading this article will list "weddings" as one of them. This is correct, but how many of our readers will also have a product line of "second marriages"?

So now we have the next concern for what a company needs to do with product lines. We need to evaluate whether they are relevant to your marketplace and community.

For example, a picnic product line could be expanded to include Corporate Picnics , Social Picnics, Last Minute Picnics, Winter Picnics, Beach Picnics, Mega Picnics, etc. Each of these would mean something different to your buyers. When you enhance and extend your product lines, you offer your company more of the marketplace.

A banquet business could have a product line mix of weekend catering and weekday catering. Each would carry different prices and conditions.

The next concept for evaluation of your product lines is to determine your ratio of business. For example, you might make 30% of your sales in weddings, 20% in box lunches, 25% in corporate cocktail events, 15% in cold buffets, and 10% in picnics. This tells us something about the stability of your company.

In the above scenario, the caterer might not be able to withstand a time when corporations cut back. Their "eggs are in one basket" so to speak.

A product line needs to fill a niche in your marketplace.

Here's some of the energies that you can build new product lines around:

A. The increase in working spouses.

B. The increase of single parents.

C. The aging baby boomers.

D. Second marriages.

E. New tax laws.

F. The increased desire for learning to cook.

G. A shopper's need for last minute purchases.

H. The impact of the supermarket.

Can you see how each of these lead to new niche product lines? If you don't, please call me so I can better explain this concept.

> ... **THINK OF THESE TIPS, TACTICS AND IDEAS AS A STARTING POINT FOR DOING SELF-CONSULTING WITH YOUR OWN BUSINESS.**

Product Lines & Minimums

Here's a simple list of possible niches that a caterer could build product lines around:

1. Movie catering.

2. Selling food to other caterers.

3. Last minute catering.

4. Kosher catering.

5. Food styling.

6. Securing an on-premise exclusive.

7. Private labeling of your foods.

8. Award programs.

9. Charity fundraisers.

10. Picnics.

11. Government contracts.

12. Corporate gift programs.

13. Coffee & meeting breaks.

14. Budget catering for large groups.

Finally, you should consider creating some new divisions for your business. This will cause the marketplace to perceive you as a growing caterer focused on giving clients specialized services. Some of these new divisions would be:

A. Corporate/Social Catering Division - This is where you sell to corporate clients social catering in a quicker corporate selling style. Many "power" men and women can't take time to ponder how a social catered party should be done... they just want it done!

B. Customized Foodservice Planning Unit - This division helps your clients plan the building of their corporate or home kitchens to make them ready for event giving. Even if you don't sell anything in this division, it sure will give you a mega look!

C. Food As Marketing Division - This division allows you to sell catering to other peoples customers. In other words, one company buys you to give catering to one of their clients as a gift from them.

D. Corporate Event Planning Team - This allows you to design events for companies for a fee. It is not required for them to use your catering division. You plan their menu, event flow, and other logistics and then help them find a caterer to do the job!

Beginning Your Evaluation of Your Minimum Order Size

As I work closely with many caterers, I've come to learn that many caterers simply take each and every order that comes their way... no matter what the order size.

As a consultant to the catering industry, I can assure you that most problems caterers face with profit and loss are tied into their inability to say "no" to smaller orders.

What is small? While there is no hard and fast rule about what is small, I believe that a caterer should not sell catering for less than 20. In some cases, the minimum number should be 35 guests.

I know what you're thinking ... that if you eliminate the smaller orders, you will have less business... you will need to let your staff go home early... you won't get into the back door of giant corporations... etc.... etc.

I've heard them all! The only thing that counts to this consultant is your profitability! In most cases, the smaller orders (those under 30) account for 50% of your kitchen's energy and costs, while they produce less than 20% of your volume and under 5% of your profits.

Are there exceptions? Of course. My point is that if a client only gives you the smaller orders without letting you do some of their bigger catering, then you would probably be wise to eliminate them! Call me... we'll talk!

Sales Tracking by Order Size

One of the main goals of accounting for your business is to simply know what you are selling... not just how much volume you have!

A caterer sells an incredible number of different product lines. That's right, just like cars that need to be produced in a different manner, so too, do caterers have product lines that have different joys and problems associated with them.

For example, a simple box lunch has different "manufacturing" requirements than a cocktail party. For that matter, a simple box lunch has a different impact on the business when it is for a group of 200 instead of for 20.

Speak with your accountant, or a selected member of your team, and begin to keep track on what you are selling by product line and order size. You will be amazed by what you learn. It will bring you much closer to both your food and labor costs.

Examples of Product Lines:

- V.I.P. Box Lunches
- Regular Box Lunches
- V.I.P. Cold Buffets
- Regular Cold Buffets
- Self-Serve Breakfast
- Full-Serve Breakfast
- Cocktail Events
- Weddings
- Bar Mitzvahs
- Picnics
- Plated Dinners
- Dinner Buffets

Notice, that if your company sells more than one kind of box lunch, then these are different product lines and need to be tracked separately.

As to size of order, CaterSource suggests that, in the beginning, you break your tracking down into groups of ten till you get over 100 and then group by 50 guests. For example, track each product line sold to clients in ascending groups of ten i.e., 10 to 19, 20 to 29, 30 to 39, ... and so on up to 100. After 100 track by groups of 50.

After you've finished your tabulations, you will be able to see amazing ratios between what you are selling and your food and labor costs in the kitchen.

Be particularly aware of the following ratio:

Product line success = ratio of product line unit sales to monthly sales volume.

In other words, how much of the company's energies were used to create what percentage of the volume.

Next, you will wish to review each product line breakdown to see what size orders are making up the total number of unit sales.

CaterSource promises you that if you do these things, you will be happy, or unhappy, with the results! While we're not accountants, CaterSource will be happy to speak with your accountants about what other caterers are doing.

Break Even Bookkeeping System

While there are many different systems for monitoring bookings versus cost, the break-even method seems to be one of the more popular with caterers. It will take the assistance of your accountant and a firm desire for you to put in the time it takes to get yourself ready to handle this method.

Step 1. Determine what your basic fixed and incremental fixed costs are on a monthly basis taking into account high and low seasons. This is the start of a break-even budget. The total figure might be $30,000 per month.

Step 2. Next divide this figure by thirty days to give you each days break-even dollar amount. In other words, that is what it costs you to turn the key in your door each day.

Step 3. As you book events keep accurate records of what each event's "contribution to break-even" will be for a particular

day. That is your proposed net profit for each sale... This is after all your variable costs are deducted. An example would be 20% profit that would result in a $1,000 event providing $200 towards that day's contribution to break-even.

Step 4. Keep subtracting these contributions to your break-even until the amount you assigned for that day is reduced to zero. Some caterers don't give each day an equal amount of break-even dollars. For example, they allot more dollars for break-even on Friday and Saturday when they know they will have big production days and less on a Wednesday when it is lighter.

Step 5. Once you reach your break-even point(zero) on sales for a particular day... the next sale for that day takes on a whole new meaning. The next sale is yours and shouldn't be taken lightly. When you have reduced your break-even to zero for a given day, you should hold your prices firm and not give things away... but if the day needs more contribution to break-even, you might want to deal.

When Not to Book an Order

Most caterers book everything that comes their way. While this is not necessarily bad, it may lead to some unfortunate situations that may cause a caterer loss of image, money and sleep.

All caterers would be wise to develop a set of criteria for deciding when it might be better to "pass" on an event instead of booking it.

Also, a number of caterers are now withdrawing from some already booked events after certain unauthorized changes are made by the buyer or the circumstances no longer are the same as when booked.

Here are some thoughts on when a caterer should not book an event:

1. When you, or your company, can't perform the event successfully.

The menu that the buyer wishes to use is too difficult for the event location i.e too many hot food items for a sit-down dinner. Consider not booking it.

2. When the individual salesperson, or company, already has too many, or too few, events booked for this particular day.

The day already has several huge events, or many smaller ones, or a combination of the two. Consider not booking it.

When you have no parties booked, you will often lose profit by taking an event... especially if it is a smaller one. Consider not booking it.

3. When you, or the company, has lost control of the client.

The event is already booked. The client calls back and requests that she be permitted to bring some of her own foods to place on the buffet. If you can't overcome this problem, you've lost control. Consider withdrawing from the agreement based on a change in the agreement.

Buyer calls and instructs you to remove three of your event staff from the party because she is going to use some relatives to assist in the serving and clean-up. Consider removing your company from this agreement.

4. When financial obligations have not been met.

The client was supposed to pay a $1,000 deposit by the 15th and has not done so. Consider withdrawing from this agreement. The client had agreed to send their final payment to you seven days in advance. If they don't ... consider withdrawing from this event.

5. When no significant profit, or goodwill, can be attained.

During the selling of an event, the client continues to work real hard to get the price dramatically down on a menu. For Example, they wish to pay $9.00 for your $14.00 menu. If they won't let you substitute some menu items, consider not booking this event.

Are you confused? Does it seem like these suggestions are too strong or even crazy? Well, you may be right! Remember, though, you will never be able to negotiate your position until you are ready to hold your ground.

Sometimes when selling catering, the only way to hold your ground is to let the buyer realize that you are at an impasse; that you will not budge until your requests are met.

Professionals are not desperate people. They have beliefs and policies that determine their business directions. They believe in "customer service" and the axiom "the customer is always right", but they also know that this is a real business that they are in. A business needs to be run by a professional business person. A professional can't always say "yes" to each and every buyer!

CATERSOURCE RULE #443

SUCCESSFUL CATERING SALES

ARE A CONSTANT BATTLE BETWEEN

WHAT THE CUSTOMER WANTS TO DO

AND WHAT WILL REALLY WORK!

Dealing With Your Accountant

1. Accountants are very busy people. However, they need to be able to give a caterer more than just a little time. Shop for your accountant. If they are reluctant to come and make a sales call to you to "see" what you do before you hire them, think twice.

2. Unfortunately, most accountants don't really understand what caterers do. Most accountants only know accounting procedures for restaurants, which tends to get them into trouble with caterers.

3. The single biggest area of concern deals with the fact that, unlike restaurants, caterers have prices and menus that are always different from those sold yesterday. They are for different size groups with different amounts being sent. These variables often "throw" the accountant.

4. Caterers tend to get into trouble with taxes. Therefore, it would be wise to select an accountant that has some tax expertise.

5. Most accountants will want the caterer to use a computer program to manage their books. This is a good thing for both parties.

Paying Sales Tax

In most states in the U.S., state sales tax needs to be charged on everything on the caterer's invoice that is sold to buyers. This would include everything that makes up the total selling price... including staff and service charges. While this doesn't seem logical to many caterers, it is important to seek out a written decision on this matter from your state's Department of Revenue. Most Americans have been taught that one doesn't pay taxes on labor.

Here is how it is defined by the State of Colorado:

"Caterers and other persons similarly engaged are liable for sales tax on the total selling price or items sold and/or charges for service essential to providing meals and beverages."

The important thing is to check this concept out slowly and carefully with the "powers that be" in your state. It might be wise not to take the word of your accountant as gospel on this subject. In some states, the rules covering catering are not the same as those covering restaurants.

The key concept here is to check it out and get it in writing!

Downsizing Your Business

Why? Why not? Profit stems from a ratio of costs against selling price. Why do we have to remain bigger? For most caterers, the need to sell more is simply a case of paying the bills with cash flow created by the extra orders. However, profit is more important than volume. This is a sign of the times. The concept is not to think small, but to think profit. The concept is to create a proper balance between what you need and what you have.

Here are some ways to downsize to gain profitability:

1. Raise your minimum order size in some, or all, of your product lines.

2. Limit the number of events you do on a particular day.

3. Tighten up your payment policies. If they don't pay on time... maybe you don't need this type of client.

4. Close one day a week.

5. Close for the slow season.

6. Take less full-service business in favor of self-service.

7. Raise your prices on those product lines that create the most work.

8. Institute a concept of extra charges for tent events and events that are a long distance from your location.

9. Eliminate any breakfast orders or third shift business that causes you to come early or stay late.

The concept is not to beat-up on your clients or to get tough. Instead, you are only trying to make your business more manageable and more user-friendly. These are just suggestions, but they do lead to simple downsizing of your catering business.

Quality of Life

What is consulting? To me, consulting is evaluation and comparison. First you evaluate what conditions exist, then you compare these conditions with those that exist elsewhere.

This is why the world has consultants. Not for their expertise, but for their exposure to diverse conditions. Most caterers have never been to many other catering operations to see what is happening. I've been fortunate to have personally visited more than 900 catering companies over the last 20 years.

That's what this new series of articles is about. I hope to give our readers some guidelines for "self-consulting".

It is important that catering businesses receive ongoing evaluation in order to continually reach for higher levels of success.

What is "quality"?

I really don't know. After all, we are all different from one another and we all have different levels of understanding what is good and not so good.

Just look at the different levels of quality we find in cars, homes, food, etc. So, quality for one may not be quality for another.

With respect to management and a catering business, quality of life refers to many small and some larger issues. Once again, they will have different meanings to one caterer over another because each caterer will measure quality in their own manner.

Quality of life to some is what happens when they are having peace of mind and a wonderful results from their hard work. Others will say its the time they have to spend with their families, or the amount of money they make for the strange hours they keep.

Quality of life to others deals with their ability to be their own boss, while still others would consider the need to keep worrying about making a payroll poor quality of life.

As I travel the nation speaking with caterers, I have learned that a good place to start with "quality of life" is with the simple concept of happiness.

I've met caterers who are at work bright and early and raring to go because they love what they do. I've met others who certainly don't "dislike" what they do, but don't come to work each day with a "I can't wait to get there" feeling. To some it's a job, to others it's a way of life. The question is "What is it to you?"

What are your options?

Quality of life can't happen very easily unless you are in control of your life and business. This is much more than just being the boss. You need to have people around you that have a genuine concern for the welfare of each other and the business.

About half of the owners that I meet during consulting all have a lessened quality of life because they have one, or more, staff members that they really don't believe in... or worse.

The problem is that they can't make any changes by letting them go or sitting down with them to explain what they need to do better or differently.

Owners must remember: it is your business and your business alone. If, on the other hand, you are a member of a giant corporation you must remember that it is your job and your job alone.

Management is not easy. But quality of life can't even begin to take root as long as one, or more, staff members is taxing your energy and mind. The trick is to make it their problem not yours.

You might wish to review the "Performance Evaluation System" in Back Issue #19. You need to have an open dialog with your staff. They also need to have a total understanding of what it is they are expected to do for the company.

It is my opinion as a consultant that some problem staff members can be changed for the better, while others can't or won't. In short, as unhappy as it is, those who won't, need to be replaced.

Quality of life can increase once your mind is free to think about hospitality performance with a clear and fresh point of view.

Next we need to think a little about money, which is one of the measuring sticks for quality of life. In our society, money is often the measure of your success. This is not true in all cases. However, in catering, money is one of the correct measuring sticks to judge quality of life.

I will take a gamble here and simply tell you that I believe less than one-third of the caterers in the nation have any sort of retirement savings account in place. Most caterers simply believe they will work for many years to come and this will give them time to accumulate money for retirement.

Recently, I met a caterer who let me see her money market retirement account. She has been in catering for 12 years. Her account had a balance of $840,000. She explained to me that once she hits $1,000,000 she plans to sell the business and move onto retirement or something else.

So, I think we can agree that for most caterers financial security is part of quality of life issues.

Quality of Life

The value of time and personal goals

Just about everyone will agree that good health is important and sought after by all caterers. I guess this goes without saying. Unfortunately, I've seen many caterers who are taking various prescription drugs to get them through the day. My point is that quality of life is not as possible when the tension and stress of the workplace requires one to rely on medication to cope.

I'm not attempting to be an evangelist here, I have problems with my own quality of life. But as an observer of our industry, I need to make the point, that attempts need to be made by caterers to lessen tension and stress.

I'm reminded of the singer, Harry Chapin who used to say that his grandfather always told him that there is "good work"and "bad work." Stress is different than energy or problem solving. Stress can injure or kill. The anchor of all quality of life concepts is to lessen stressful situations.

So, what about personal goals? Do you have them? Are they realistic? These goals are what gets most caterers through their day. For some it is to spend more time with their families. For others it is to travel and learn more about food and entertaining.

Quality of life issues for caterers all revolve around one important concept: What is the reason you're in catering? If you can answer this, you should be able to create a timetable of actions that will lead to your increased quality of life.

Let's remember that for most caterers the act of catering is their life. This is not bad in itself. As long as you remind yourself, from time to time, that catering has a beginning and an end. Also, a catering job may not be as crucial as attending (not catering) a birthday party for a loved one.

It is so easy for the days to slip into years. I've met a lot of caterers who have told me how different it would be if they had a chance to start over again. What I tell them is "Why not start over right now?"

They, and I, realize that it would be a major upheaval to start over again because it means change and nobody likes change. In fact, most, including myself, are worried about the consequences of change. This is only natural.

To be even more simplistic, "If you always do what you always did, then you always get what you always got." If you wish to increase your quality of life, this is a wise and wonderful saying to have around you wherever you look.

In closing, let me simply explain that the winning caterers I meet during my travels are ones that have a grasp on what business they are in and they know why they are caterers. In short, they are "dogs who are wagging their tails, instead of tails that are wagging the dog."

Quality of life is personal and important for all caterers. They need to constantly measure their actions and energies with respect to their goals. Will the ends justify the years of hard work? Is there going to be life for them after catering?

Measuring Your Hospitality Quotient

Sometimes caterers, like many business people, get so close to the forest that we can't see the individual trees. As you already know, selling catering is based on doing the "small" things correctly... not just the big ones! Also, the first impression you make on your caller, or past buyer, is crucial.

What follows is the CaterSource checklist to measure a company's hospitality selling quotient. As you review them we suggest you think twice about each one as to how it might apply to your company.

1. Is your facility clean? Is your staff looking sharp from a buyer's point of view?

2. Are your best people answering the phones? Do you have valid qualification scripts or is your staff just winging it?

3. Are your proposals getting out in a timely manner?

4. Do you give helpful information over the phone instead of just taking it? Do you sound like you are going through the motions to a caller?

5. Are you talking "at" the clients or sharing your thoughts with them?

6. Are you just listening to the clients or hearing what they're really saying... especially between the lines?

7. Are you speaking proudly about your company and team?

8. Do you call clients back in a timely manner?

9. Do you send clients who had a second party the exact same thank you letter as the first?

10. Do you get really excited in front of the client when they tell you "yes?"

11. Are you giving everyone you talk with the same amount of your valuable time or do you understand that some clients are more important to your success than others?

12. Have you given your best clients a special telephone number, or way, to get in touch with you?

13. Are all your thank you letters typed or are some hand-written?

14. When is the last time you took any of your best clients out to lunch?

15. Have you ever had a disagreement with a client or are you a "yes" seller?

16. What does your company do when they receive a "bad" letter, or call, from a client... do you hide it or discuss it openly?

17. Have you ever turned a shopper over to another salesperson because you were not getting anywhere?

18. Do you personally get excited when you make a sale?

19. Are you promising less than you deliver?

20. How long does it take you to call a client after an event?

Equipment: Rent or Buy?

Based on current practices there is no magic or correct answer to the question of renting or buying your "front" and "back" of the house items such as china, chairs, glassware, tables, portable ovens, grills etc.

Many caterers simply own everything while others continue to rent on an event by event basis. It isn't as much a matter of money as it is a matter of business focus.

Some caterers believe that the equipment (rental) business is a natural fit, while others believe that it is another type of business than catering that takes different energies and skills.

Money can be made or lost when owning your own equipment. Some of the factors that will help you make the right decision are:

1. Do you have the extra warehousing space?

2. Do you have the extra staff to handle the equipment?

3. Are you willing to increase your insurance coverage to handle the new risks of handling rentals? Back injuries increase dramatically!

4. Will you have the larger trucks to carry the rentals in? A 60" round table, like those above, will not go into a normal van.

Speaking of tables, the photo above should give you some feel about the scope of storing and handling problems that exist with doing your own rentals.

And then there are the chairs! The photo below shows you what space is needed to store 300 white wood chairs! Now, if you purchase a white wood chair for about $30 each and rent them for $3 each, you've technically paid for the purchase of the chair in ten rentals. This is good.

But, you also need to factor in the transporting, cleaning and repairing of the chair to get the full business impact.

CaterSource suggests that you begin to build a small rental department, while at the same time still using your rental agencies. Remember, during the busy seasons nobody has enough equipment!

It also might be wise to build your rental division around unique specialized china and buffet items. Don't get involved in tables and chairs!

Above all, caterers need to be aware that owning your own equipment doesn't necessarily give you an advantage over your competitors, unless you are willing to lose money by discounting or throwing in your equipment for free! This practice is not the wisest for the short and long run.

Caterers need to speak with their rental dealers about their needs for being competitive and having unique "one of a kind" pieces of serving equipment. If your rental dealer is listening, they will offer you the opportunity of investing in some specialized equipment that only your company can use.

In this manner, you can get the best of two worlds. Remember, the concept of owning your own rentals can earn you a lot of extra income, but if you don't commit yourself properly, you will wish that you never got into the rental business!

Thoughts on Leftovers

The dreaded questions from customers: "What happens to the leftover food?" or "How much extra food do you send?" or "Since I'm paying for the food... can't I take all that's left?" How a caterer answers these questions is apt to win or lose a sale... and at the same time create a legal, or emotional, nightmare for the caterer and the buyer.

Here's some thoughts on this issue:

1. **What is a leftover?**
   Anything that has not left the safe temperature zone.

2. **Can they be sold again?**
   Yes, if the food has not left the safe temperature zone and has been handled correctly.

3. **Should leftover food been given to the buyer or their guests?**
   If you check with your health department, you will most likely be told that the answer is NO!

4. **Should food that has been out of the safe temperature zone, i.e. from chafing dishes, be given away?**
   NO... unless it is to a recognized "food bank" that has insurance to cover your liability.

5. **Will taking leftovers damage a caterer's reputation?**
   Probably. Competitors will let others know that you "reuse foods".

6. **Will leaving leftovers increase your liability?**
   YES... this is not to be taken lightly! Check with your lawyer and insurance company.

7. **How does a caterer handle the leftover issue?**
   Bring into the event only what you think you will need. Have extras somewhere else.
   Remove leftovers from the event long before they become an issue with the client.

Sample Mission Statement

SAMPLE MISSION STATEMENT

The mission of (Co Name) is to continue to sell, produce and present outstanding catering to the people of (your area), and to provide opportunities for personal and professional growth for its staff, while earning a profit for the company.

Which Order Of Importance Would You Choose When Making Your Business Decisions?

1. *Customer*		1. *Company*
2. *Staff*	**OR**	2. *Customer*
3. *Company*		3. *Staff*

CHAPTER 10  QUESTIONS

1. What are the differences between a Cancellation and a Performance Refund?

2. What are the latest trends facing caterers?

3. What is meant by Sales vs. Culinary driven?

4. Why are smaller orders for caterers not wise?

5. Why is it important to sell Product Lines instead of just food and beverage?

6. What is the significance of the Break Even Bookkeeping system?

7. Do caterers pay state sales tax on staff?

8. When shouldn't a caterer book a party?

9. Why is quality of life an important issue for professional caterers?

10. Should a caterer rent or buy their event equipment?

11. Should a caterer leave leftover food with the customers?

STAFFING

CHAPTER

11

TABLE OF CONTENTS

CHAPTER

11

"The most important qualification for a part-time staff member during the holiday rush season is that they will show up at the party site!"

Hiring & Keeping Staff

1. Hold "Opportunity Meetings" at hotels.
2. Offer staff bounties.
3. Offer frequency bounties.
4. Use answering machines to take incoming employment requests.
5. Use "peer" group incentives.
6. Offer "buddy" job guarantees.
7. Utilize a staff newsletter.
8. Recognize the spouses, or significant others.
9. Form a staffing committee.

Other Info on Staffing

1. **Finding good staff is often difficult because of the number of other caterers who are also searching.**

2. **Some of the places to look are:**
   - **A.** Other food service businesses
   - **B.** Food service colleges
   - **C.** Hotels
   - **D.** Homemakers
   - **E.** Students
   - **F.** Actor's guild
   - **G.** State employment services
   - **H.** Unions
   - **I.** Community organizations

3. **Some of the better methods of getting your message out for employment are:**
   - **A.** Newspaper ads
   - **B.** Radio ads
   - **C.** Word of mouth/Referrals

4. Suggested traits to consider when hiring catering staff are: initiative, enthusiasm, assertiveness, health, experience, leadership and appearance.

5. Party staff needs the additional traits of enjoying the hospitality-service work ethic, being a team player, being a self-starter and loving and being able to respond to crisis situations.

6. Most training of catering staff is on-the-job. However, a higher level of professionalism is reached when classroom training is provided. Video tape is being used by some caterers to show what is expected.

THE EMPHASIS IN TODAY'S SUCCESSFUL CATERING OPERATION IS TO HAVE AS MUCH PART-TIME STAFF AS POSSIBLE. ALSO, PREVENTING STAFF TURNOVER IS A MAIN GOAL.

Paying Staff 1

The purpose of this report is to provide you with some of the traditional and unique concepts pertaining to staff compensation. It is hoped that this information will permit you to better understand the motivation and authority associated with compensation.

> **SPECIAL NOTE:** CaterSource, Inc. is providing this information as education and not legal advise. The suggestions and information in the pages to follow should be reviewed with a licensed attorney or accountant before utilizing any for your company or yourself.

PART ONE
Compensation: from the company's point of view.

Compensation plans for your staff, especially your salespeople, should be created with several goals in mind. The first goal is to assist the company in meeting its sales and resulting profit goals. Second, is to reward each staff person on the basis of the entire groups, or each individual's performance or contribution.

If you are an owner... you must try to remember how it was (or still is!) to work for someone else. Remember how much you thought of your take-home pay, especially when you started a new job. Or, can you recall how much you wanted that new car.

These are realistic concerns on the minds of your new and older staff. A well defined and useable compensation plan can do wonders for the attitudes of the staff, but its real goal is to achieve sales goals through the hard work of your sales team!

An important additional goal of a wise compensation plan is to maintain the loyalty of outstanding staff and to provide them good reasons for not leaving to work for the competition.

In other words, sales staff will stay on the job if they feel that they are getting their fair share of the profits of the company.

You will notice that the thought is to share in the profits of the company and not necessarily the profits only from the sale. Often it is a problem for staff to understand that volume and profits don't always go hand in hand. It is the task of a great compensation plan to continually educate each staff member about the battle between profit and volume. It is important to reward fairly, but the company's economic life needs to also be guaranteed.

In other words, the company, and it's owners, need to be paid correctly for the energy and risk that they have assumed in the catering company.

Company and staff attitudes toward a compensation plan.

Your sales staff will probably judge your compensation plan along these lines:

1. Superior income for superior performance.

2. Incentives for special effort, extra hours and results.

3. Fixed income for security.

4. Pay is the yardstick to measure success.

5. A sense of security through the awareness that he or she is respected and/or loved for their efforts.

6. An easy to understand pay system.

Your company, on the other hand, will probably view the compensation plan along these lines:

1. Rewards are in direct relationship to the company's ability to pay.

2. The matter of fixed expenses is one of the main concerns and a concern for the seasonal nature of the catering industry.

3. Anything that keeps the sales force happy and reaches the sales goals is alright for the company.

4. Payment needs to increase staff loyalty.

Special concerns for the company.

1. Remember that just as you control your staff's success, you also control yours. The staff usually knows what's really happening in the company, so its important to treat them as adults.

2. The best compensation plans are the ones that most accurately measure your staffs performance and then rewards them correctly.

3. Be sensitive to the real expectations and aspirations of your salespeople.

4. Use the compensation plan as a tool to reach the valid goals of the company.

5. Always reward performance with real earnings. Don't pay earnings that are not a result of successful company profits.

6. Attempt to remove any battle lines between the sales staff and management!

When considering your compensation plan, its best to speak with key employees about what they consider to be important to them. Sometimes its also good to allow all staff to give written suggestions about what they would wish to have in a compensation plan.

You will really be amazed at the responses that you often get. Many staff suggestions are very fair and structured to create a win-win situation between management and themselves. Your compensation plan is important for your success!

Paying Staff 2

The purpose of this report is to provide you with some of the traditional and unique concepts pertaining to staff compensation. It is hoped that this information will permit you to better understand the motivation and authority associated with compensation.

PART TWO
What about salary?

Salary has many advantages for both the company and the salesperson. First, a straight salary is the easiest for the company to handle. Deductions, income taxes, health insurance and other benefits are fixed and steady.

The over-riding reason for using salary is when the staff wants it. However, this does not mean that a company needs to offer salary over commissions. When people need security they always opt for a salary. They are usually suspicious of commissions. Also, there is no rule that requires you to have everyone on salary. So, you could have some on commission and some of salary.

When a business is subject to high and low seasons, as catering is, the thought of salary is often highly desired by the sales staff. After all, they have the same rent twelve months a year.

Another concern for the company is whether, or not, a salary is really going to draw the type of person you are searching for to represent your products.

A salary usually means that the staff will be more stable and less likely to leave. A salary is also desirable when you have decided to use a team effort to sell. Using a salary compensation plan, fixed for everyone, sometimes there is less tension and more teamwork.

Perhaps a salary that is variable to match the high and low season might be advisable. In other words, when making a deal with a new salesperson, you would offer them a higher monthly pay during your busiest months and less during your slower times.

This may not seem logical, but other industries do it and it might be suitable for your own needs.

The biggest problem with offering a salary is that it tends to let weak, unproductive staff remain on the payrolls longer.

For this reason, it is best to consider an agreement for a trial period of employment for your new salesperson to see if they are a self starter, or not.

A salaried team of sales staff lead by weak management, or poor company goals, is usually headed for disaster.

While salaried employees are often easier to direct, more success might arise from salespeople who have the view that the sky is the limit.

Many sales managers have learned that new trainees are happier with a salary. The implication of this is also true when a company is in a launch stage or when new profit centers or sales territories are being opened.

If this is true in your case, consider starting your staff out with a salary followed by a bonus plan or commissions. This often is the answer that creates a win-win selling situation.

A major concern with salaries.

During the growth stage of a company a salary might be a wise situation. Simply put, the sales staff is happy to receive the security of the known salary. On the other hand, the company is experiencing additional profit due to the rapid sales profits and paying only the fixed benefits to those making the sales.

The problems, if any, rest with the fact that the sales staff soon realizes what is happening and begins to look elsewhere or slows down their pace. In other words, if there isn't any incentive to sell more, or to be rewarded more, why then should they stay excited?

As a result the company often raises the sales staff's fixed salary often out of guilt or fear of losing them. The problem is created by the fact that the additional fixed expenses are being paid twelve months of the year.

This type of action usually leads to out of control costs for the company.

Again, one conclusion to this would simply be to arrange for higher salaries during the known higher profit months and the regular salary during the slower months.

It can also be concluded that a new venture will be hurt if fixed dollars are continually going out during a period of growth and experimentation.

A new company, or one that is low on cash flow, must be concerned with its cash position at all times. When you use salary, problems could arise with your cash flow during certain months due to the fact that the company is locked into fixed payroll costs that will not be friendly to them.

Paying Staff 3

The purpose of this report is to provide you with some of the traditional and unique concepts pertaining to staff compensation. It is hoped that this information will permit you to better understand the motivation and authority associated with compensation.

PART THREE
What about straight commission?

Paying commission has one super advantage over salary... it is a variable expense rather than a fixed one. When sales are made... money is given. When sales aren't made...no money is given.

In this way we can assure ourselves that we will only be paying for success. With salary a salesperson could be taking our money without bringing in the sales volume to pay for their earnings.

However, let's not forget that we don't live in an ideal world and it is hard to find staff persons that will work for only commission.

The commission plan also is very desirable when cash is short. Commissions are often not paid until the sale is paid for.

If sales volume is important to your goals, then a commission is what you will need. Also, commissions are advisable when dealing with part-timers or others who will be hard to monitor during work.

Most experts seem to agree that a sales force will work harder and produce more when reward is in line with amount or frequency of selling success.

It will be wise to realize that if you hire a person who is not self-motivated the commission benefit will be wasted.

Some companies are giving commissions, in place of salary, to staff working as secretaries and drivers. They earn commissions based on a percentage of the volume that they type or load in their vehicles.

While this may seem silly, or unmanageable, for some, others have received great results. Secretaries become less concerned with clock-watching and drivers seem to find room for another order on their truck.

One of the problems that is faced by a commission situation is during the time taken for learning or training. Salary gives the company more strength to demand excellence and attention while learning. Often the newly commissioned staff persons will create many problems because of their need to make sales to survive. So, many of these first sales are not proper ones! Some companies obviously use a combination of salary and commission.

The strengths of commission.

It obviously is no secret that in the vast majority of cases, commission will increase the incentive to sell more or better. In other words, the sales staff knows that they are masters of their own ship.

Many persons enjoy knowing that they will be paid according to their efforts and abilities rather than on a fixed income basis. It is also a great feeling that one is not dependent on getting raises when the company decides to give them. Instead one just has to put more effort and skill into their own work to earn more.

More caterers should consider adopting the concept of asking the new potential hire what they would like to do with respect to earnings... salary, commission, or a combination of both.

Again from the company's point of view, commissions are paid on a variable basis and do not heavily occur in unfair degrees during the slower selling seasons. So, selling expenses are more in line when cash is short.

The weaknesses of commission.

As in many things in life, the same strengths often become the worst weaknesses. For example, some sales staff are unable to budget themselves properly which causes hardship for themselves during slack seasons.

Also, when a new staff person starts, it is harder for them to make ends meet since they haven't had any significant client base to work with.

Often caterers tell of the problems caused by providing commission to a two or more person sales team. How come she got that lead instead of me? I was out working a party for you and you gave that lead to him? These are only a few of the problems facing some commission programs.

Other weaknesses deal with the loss of control of the sales staff by the management of the company. Authority is often looked upon differently from the commissioned salesperson's point of view.

In short, salespersons are often going to put their own interests ahead of the ones of the company. But is that all bad?

In closing, lets remember that there is nothing wrong with having some people on commission and others on salary.

Paying Staff 4

The purpose of this report is to provide you with some of the traditional and unique concepts pertaining to staff compensation. It is hoped that this information will permit you to better understand the motivation and authority associated with compensation.

PART FOUR
Opening thoughts on a drawing account.

This method of paying sales staff is probably the most misunderstood form of compensation.

The information that you will receive below is meant as a strong suggestion to owners. In general, catering salespeople don't like this method of payment because it puts a lot of pressure on them to succeed!

At present, it would be hard to find even one out of ten caterers using draw. So, as you review the information below, please remember that the use of a draw, while extremely fair to the owner, will cause discomfort to the staff.

That being said, it is still a valid method to use in certain situations, especially with new salespersons.

What is a drawing account?

Think of a draw as a minimum salary. It is either guaranteed or non-guaranteed. When nonguaranteed, the money given as an advance of expected future sales is not taken back by the company.

When the draw is guaranteed, the money advanced is not taken back if the sales don't happen.

Most companies keep track of what the plus or minus condition of the drawing account is in order to keep the relationship between salesperson and management on a professional basis.

Some companies provide a non-guaranteed draw which simply means that money given to a salesperson during the off months is taken back from earnings during the peak months. This is not done by many caterers. It seems that many caterers consider this too heartless and balanced by the question "Why would anyone want to work for a company that took money back?"

On the other hand, when you start with a new salesperson and give them salary for three, or more, months and they leave, you're out a lot of money! This is also unfair!

So, more caterers should consider, at least, giving a new salesperson a drawing account for the initial period of employment to protect the company.

The problems of a drawing account.

However, in most cases the failure to sell more than what the staff person is drawing is overlooked. For example, when a staff person gets $200.00 per week draw it should be considered an advance. Let's assume that the salesperson is selling catering at 10% commission of gross.

The $200.00 that has been paid is 10% of $2,000.00 which is what the salesperson should have sold to earn it. So, a staff person who sells less than $2,000.00 per week is getting a perk from the company. If they sold $1600.00 during the week they would have earned all but $40.00 dollars of their draw.

In a non-guaranteed draw, the forty dollars is owed to the company by the salesperson and needs to be paid back. It usually is carried over to the next pay period and deducted at that time.

In most companies, the minus balance of the salesperson draw is too often overlooked. This creates an unprofessional atmosphere.

If you decide to offer a non-guaranteed draw, then you must keep true to the concept of owing back to the company what is not covered by sold commissions.

Some caterers put new salespeople on a combination of both types of drawing accounts. For a certain period, perhaps three months, the salesperson is guaranteed a draw. After the trial period the salesperson goes on a draw that is variable and not guaranteed.

Drawing accounts against commission often puts both the excitement and burden on the sales staff.

Final thoughts.

The use of a drawing account overcomes the lack of security felt by new salespeople paid on a straight commission basis. A nonguaranteed draw is really nothing but an advance against future earnings.

A nonguaranteed draw allows for shortages not covered in the slower months to be repaid during the better ones.

Drawing accounts are effective in highly seasonal businesses like catering. They are also excellent to use when starting a new salesperson.

Some caterers would be wise to place a new salesperson on a guaranteed draw for a beginning period and then move to a nonguaranteed draw. When using a draw, the old adage "The cream always rises to the top" is put to the test.

Paying Staff 5

The purpose of this report is to provide you with some of the traditional and unique concepts pertaining to staff compensation. It is hoped that this information will permit you to better understand the motivation and authority associated with compensation.

PART FIVE
Tips On Paying Bonuses.

It is no secret that everyone loves to get bonuses! So, some reward special contributions to the attainment of the company's goals. Most caterers, who pay bonuses, pay them annually. From a manager's point of view the bonus is the ultimate "carrot" dangling in front of the salesperson for the whole year.

When bonuses are paid out over shorter periods than a year, the catering salesperson often "fudges" his accounts to respond to the earning pressure.

Another form of bonus is called the discretionary bonus and is declared when company profits are extra special. However, like most things in life, once you give it or set a brief pattern, most of the sales force will believe it to be coming always, whether they maintain their success or not.

So, all things considered, the fixed bonus is probably the wisest and best method that creates a win-win situation. In this type of bonus the salesperson is given, or creates their own, goals or quotas to reach over a certain period of time. Then, if the salesperson reaches that goal, or gets extremely close to it, an annual bonus is paid.

Here is an example:

A. The bonus for reaching 80% of the year's goal is equal to 1/4 percent of their actual annual sales volume.

B. The bonus for reaching 90% of the year's goal is equal to 1/2 percent of their actual annual sales volume.

C. The bonus for reaching 100% of the year's goal is equal to 1 percent of their actual annual sales volume.

D. The bonus for reaching 110% of the year's goal is equal to 1 1/4 percent of their actual annual sales volume.

E. The bonus for reaching 125% of the year's goal is equal to 1 1/2 percent of their actual annual sales volume.

These bonuses mean that if a salesperson sells 100% of their $200,000 goal, he or she would get an additional $2,000.00 at year end.

Both management and salespersons often enjoy the fact that the year end in December is often one of the busiest and most rewarding times of our fiscal year. This makes the paying of bonuses more comfortable for the company.

Remember that in some cases these fixed bonuses based on sales gross can backfire if the company is not making the correct profit.

A catering company will find itself in a tough jam if they can't, or shouldn't, pay the earned bonuses to their salespeople.

Also, if you don't have a fixed schedule for these bonus payments, you will probably have some unhappy campers!

What About Profit Sharing?

Should the sales staff know the inner workings of a company? The answer from some experts is no. This is one of the major reasons that a traditional profit sharing program is not considered best for entrepreneurs in small to medium sized companies, especially if it is privately owned.

When sales go up, profits sometimes don't! But, try to explain that to a sales force who has been working very aggressively and hard! Who will be able to know if one salesperson is more profitable to the company than another?

Fringe benefits?

Fringe benefits are considered a way of life for most companies in a competitive workplace. They can be everything and anything from dental and hospitalization to helping to pay for a child's education.

Sometimes the fringe benefit costs can be shared by the staff person and sometimes it is totally free.

The most common system in use today by caterers is a 50% sharing of costs by the employee. In any case, the company needs to be totally aware of the costs involved with any and all fringes.

Fringes for clothes, gasoline, and educational seminars are treasured by most sales people. Any benefit that permits the staff person to get time off is deemed extra special. So, if a trip is part of the fringe, the enthusiasm is greater.

Bonuses and fringes for staff, often improve morale and build loyalty among staff.

Paying Staff 6

The purpose of this report is to provide you with some of the traditional and unique concepts pertaining to staff compensation. It is hoped that this information will permit you to better understand the motivation and authority associated with compensation.

PART SIX
Percentages On Commissions

At the present time, caterers are using many different and varied methods to offer commissions to their full or part-time sales force.

Here are some general thoughts:

A. Most companies pay salespersons a commission on the profitable parts of a sale like the menu and liquor.

B. Commissions run between 2% to 15% depending on how much guarantee the salesperson is getting. If, for example, a salesperson is earning $25,000 per year guaranteed, then the commission is between 2% to 6%. If they're getting a lower guarantee, the commissions go higher.

C. Some pay a percentage on the profit (gross margin or net) of a sale after it has been performed and reviewed. This sometimes allows for more concern about waste and careless expenses on the part of the salesperson.

D. Some pay different levels of commission depending on the type of sale. For example, a purchase from an already existing client (house sale) carries the lowest commission.

The sale caused by the company's marketing money, energy or performance carries the next highest commission while a sale that is brought in solely by the salesperson's cold calls carries the highest.

E. Some offer bonus commissions on any client that has multiple orders during a specific period of time.

F. You can offer bonus commission for any referral sales coming during a specific time period.

G. Others offer bounty commissions for especially difficult or "wanted" clients.

H. Why not offer a higher commission if the salesperson is able to up-sell an existing order. For example, a salesperson may be entitled to a standard percentage after selling an event for $12.00. But before the performance of the event, he or she is able to earn a higher rate of commission for any additional volume increase sold to the client.

I. Offer a higher percentage of commission when the actual amount of volume increases. For example: when volume from an order is $10,000 or more the commission is higher.

J. Pay higher or lower commissions for different days of the week or seasons of the year. If Wednesday events earned greater rewards, than some salespeople would work hard to sell that night.

K. Offer larger percentages when the deposit is larger or given earlier. Or for getting final payment before a certain date.

Bolder moves...

A. Give a salesperson the actual price that you expect to get for a particular event. Say its $9.50. Then permit the salesperson to go as high as they wish with the price. The salesperson gets 25% of the extra money while the company gets 75%.

B. When your company needs additional salespeople let your present salesperson be involved as you hire them. Say your present salesperson gets 10% on his or her sales... let them participate in the hiring of the new salesperson who will get 8% commission during a six month training period. The remaining 2% goes to the "old timer" who will probably encourage and assist the new "kid" to greatness!

C. Why shouldn't ownership, management and key people (chef) get a 1/4 percent on all sales?

D. Put the entire staff on just straight commissions from every sale. (secretaries, drivers, etc.)

E. Allow the sales force to pool their commissions during all or part of the year.

One of the more important aspects to a commission program is to remember that everyone doesn't have to get the same commission or be under the same program. Why not let them tell you what they wish to choose from the different programs you have to offer. There is also no reason why the staff can't change from one plan to another.

Also, why shouldn't the management provide the amount of commission based on the difficulty of the sale? For example:

F. When a sales plateau is reached either over a year, calendar month or any 30 day period the commission goes up until a new period starts.

G. Or, as sales plateaus are reached the bonus factor is added.

The above information demonstrates the many varieties of options for paying staff.

Paying Staff 7

The purpose of this report is to provide you with some of the traditional and unique concepts pertaining to staff compensation. It is hoped that this information will permit you to better understand the motivation and authority associated with compensation.

PART SEVEN
Important Concerns

When should commissions be paid? There are many views on this concept. Some caterers believe that commissions shouldn't be paid until the event is performed or until the client pays either a handsome deposit or for the entire event.

Other caterers pay their salespeople in the next pay period after the completion of the sale or the event.

Many pay partial payments based on the amount of the deposit. For example, a salesperson who gets a fifty percent deposit will get more of their earnings up front, while the one who only gets a twenty percent deposit will get much less advance of commissions earned.

The matter of how to account for commissioned sales is also troublesome. When a staff person sells a December event in October, when is it counted and paid for?

To solve this problem many companies keep two figures and reward them in different manners or use them as a guide post. The management wants to know what the company's sales volume is projected to be for December while the salesperson wants to pay October's car payment!

This also brings up the point of reversal of paid commissions if the sale is canceled. In many industries, a certain amount of the salesperson's earning is held back to cover charge-backs from cancelled sales. Check with your attorney on this one for sure!

What Are The Numbers?

There is no question that 10% is the most widely used commission figure followed closely by 8%. Yet some of the most successful companies offer 2% to 6% commissions.

Obviously, the more fixed salary or guaranteed draw that is offered, the lower the commission rate.

Also, the general success and maturity of the company often sets the commission rate. For example, a higher volume company where a salesperson can make sales more easily usually offers lower commissions.

Some successful companies offer a salary of $18,000 to $25,000 in conjunction with a 2% commission on sales over a certain plateau. Sometimes an annual bonus is also paid.

Remember that much can be gained by giving partial commission points such as 2.25%, 4.5% or 3.75%!

Some caterers have different commission percentages for different times of the year. Pooling commissions is becoming more and more popular.

Some caterers pool tips during the busy seasons because it is a team effort that gets the job done. Plus, why should a salesperson make less money just because management tells them to take the Governor's dinner party, which consists of just 12 guests. The commissions are small, but the responsibility is high.

Staying Out Of Trouble...

Whatever methods you use it is mandatory to have a written agreement of understanding between the staff person and the company! You should seek the advice and counsel of your attorney in this matter.

We remind you that many caterers have decided to offer various options to each salesperson so, in fact, three different staff members may have three different payment plans.

Also, it is best if periodic job evaluations are given in order to assess the value of the commission program from the salesperson's point of view.

Your turnover will be less if you give adequate and exciting opportunities for staff to make money. The measure of a salespersons success is to be measured both in customer satisfaction and financial rewards.

Remember to always be open and fair with your compensation plans. Your compensation plan is your message to your staff on how you feel about them, your clients and the company.

You can be sure that most of your staff will talk secretly to each other about how much they earn, even though they pledge secrecy to you when they are hired. So, in most cases, you'll damage morale when certain aspects are discovered by staff about each other's pay.

Faulty compensation plans can be held responsible for low morale of a sales force along with increased complaints from clients. On the other hand, just rewards seem to keep the service ethic alive and well between the client and the salesperson. Good pay makes a job good... great pay makes a job better!! **Money speaks!**

Paying Staff 8

The purpose of this report is to provide you with some of the traditional and unique concepts pertaining to staff compensation. It is hoped that this information will permit you to better understand the motivation and authority associated with compensation.

PART EIGHT
The Future of Paying Staff

Over the last seven months we've brought you a variety of different and unique thoughts on paying your staff.

As we've pointed out, more than once, the topic of how and what to pay staff is complicated and confounding at the same time!

For example, the emphasis of the past series of articles has been on the paying of commission to sales staff based on volume. Rusty Morin, Morin's Catering (Attleboro, MA),on the other hand, wrote to us explaining that he has had outstanding success with the opposite concept.

At his company, he has done away with the traditional commission program. Instead, he has developed an "open book" policy where the salespersons can actually read the monthly profit and loss statements from the accountants.

In this way, they are able to see, first hand, how much success their selling has done for the company. Bonuses are paid, or not paid, to the staff on the basis of these accounting reports.

Rusty is convinced that his staff has never had as much "team" spirit. He credits great success to his "open book" methods and considers them more realistic for the future than competitive commissions.

The Decision is Yours

What should you do? Perhaps the best method of pay is the one that your staff likes the most. So, why not just ask them in a meeting, or private situation what type of payment method they would like the most.

While this may not work for everyone, it will bring you closer to your staff and to the solution of which methods your might use.

Again, we point out, that your staff are all unique individuals who may like to have a payment plan that differs from others in your company.

Often, when asked, the staff will respond in ways that we would never guess. For example, they might wish to have a company car, or child care instead of commissions.

So, don't assume that your staff always wishes a raise. They might actually wish something else. Besides, there are certain tax advantages for both the staff and company when paying them in other ways than payroll dollars.

CaterSource believes that the future of business will be based, more than ever, on the necessity for honesty and frankness between management and staff. So, any methods you use that contribute to this healthy, and professional, concept will provide your business with more success.

What About You...

That's right ... what about the owners right to a share of the rewards? CaterSource is aware of many catering companies, where the members of the staff individually get more money than the owners or leaders.

While this has a basis in the business world, it seems a shame that the person who has kept the dream alive and growing, can't achieve the rewards they deserve.

Do what the realtors do. The owner of a real estate business takes a very small override on all the sales of the company. It may be a little as .25 %, but they take it and it adds up into a handsome amount of money.

It's sometimes hard for a manager of a baseball team to know that they are getting paid far less money than the rookie ball players!

So, for your own "peace of mind", consider taking steps that will capture a greater part of your just rewards for starting and building your catering company.

In closing, we wish to remind our subscribers that an important step in developing and doing a proper payment system for your company is to have yearly evaluations with your staff.

During these meetings, it is the manager's job to make the staff person understand how they are, or aren't, living up to their end of the bargain with respect to staff pay.

Failure to hold these meetings tends to give your company a false sense of security and creates a great deal of "rumors" about who gets what.

So, now you have it... our opinions on different ways to pay your staff. We really don't have a favorite, except our belief that each worker should have the method of pay that they enjoy the most.

Feel free to give us a call to discuss any aspect of these eight articles on paying staff. Remember, at CaterSource you always will have someone to talk with about any and all of your management concerns.

IRS: Independent Contractor?

Caterers have strong opinions about whether their event and kitchen staff, especially those working only part-time, need to be paid as employees, which does require W-2 reporting and withholding, along with matching payroll taxes, or as independent contractors, that only requires the 1099 reporting.

The IRS has a series of rules that help determine whether a worker is an employee or independent contractor.

CaterSource has reviewed these rules and has presented them here for you to view. We've also provided some additional thoughts on how they might effect caterers.

CaterSource understands that the determination of whether a worker is classified as an employee or independent contractor is based on the IRS interpretation of a mix of these 19 concerns. It could take just one or two or many to determine the outcome. Check with your CPA or lawyer.

REMEMBER: we're not accountants, CPAs or lawyers. It's just being presented as information that should lead you to further discussion with your lawyer and/or CPA.

1. Instructions. The requirement that a worker is to follow the caterer's instructions regarding when, where, and how he or she is to dress suggests employee status. It is important to note that merely the right of the employer to give instructions, even when none are given, is reason enough to make a worker an employee.

2. Training. Caterers who train a worker formally or on the job, how the work is to be done, again indicates control and employee status.

3. Integration. If the worker is provided as a service of the caterer, usually from a list of names, the worker is probably not an independent contractor. Also, if a type of employee is necessary for the service to become successful, the worker is usually an employee.

4. Services rendered personally. If a worker, who is assigned a party to work, is not allowed to replace him or herself, without permission of the caterer, then that worker is an employee.

5. Hiring, supervising and paying assistants. If the worker hires, supervises and pays assistants for the caterer, this suggests control and, therefore, employee status.

6. Continuing relationship. A one-shot arrangement probably suggests independent contractor status. However, a continuing relationship, which makes a worker an employee, can exist where work is performed at frequently recurring, although irregular intervals, such as high and low seasons.

7. Set hours of work. If the caterer can, or does, set work hours and the amount of work, this indicates control and employee status.

8. Full time required. If the worker is required to work only for one caterer, than an employee relationship usually exists.

9. Doing work on employer's premises. If a worker is working at the caterer's location, such as in the kitchen, this usually means employee status because of the control factor. However, merely performing the work away from the employers site, does not necessarily break the employee relationship.

10. Order or sequence set. If a worker is required to follow a schedule for setting up, serving, or taking down an event, then this suggests an employee relationship.

11. Oral or written reports. If a worker is required to report back to the caterer about a job, then control has been shown, therefore an employee status.

12. Payment by the hour, week, or month. A fixed payment shows employee status. Payment by the job, or on a commission basis, usually indicates independent contractor status.

13. Payment of business and/or traveling expenses. A catering worker who is being paid for travelling to and from a job, would probably be deemed an employee.

14. Furnishing of tools and materials. If an event worker is supplied tools of their trade such as trays, chafers, towels, etc., then these workers are under the control of the company and therefore they are employees.

15. Significant investment. If a worker invests in the facilities used in performing the services, this shows independent contractor status.

16. Realization of profit or loss. If a catering worker is subject to an economic risk of loss beyond the mere nonpayment for their work, this shows independent contractor status.

17. Making services available to general public. When a catering worker advertises their services on a regular and consistent basis, and works for multiple companies an independent status is usually the result.

18. Right to discharge. When an employer can discharge a worker it is clear that the worker is an employee.

19. Right to terminate. When a worker can quit without incurring liability, this suggests employee status.

IRS: More on the Independent Contractor

A s a reminder to our subscribers... you will not win the argument with the I.R.S. that any of your catering workers are independent contractors and not subject to withholding taxes or matching funds! Others may be doing it... but you will be the one who gets caught!

Please review Journal # 1 from June, 1994. On page nine you'll see the I.R.S. qualifiers used to determine whether a worker is an independent contractor or a waged employee.

Now let us get to the point:

1. Having the customer pay the staff directly will not keep you out of a business threatening situation with the government.

2. It will certainly not work if you pay your staff cash "under the table".

3. Just because others might be doing it... doesn't make you innocent while doing the same.

4. Paying your staff 1099's will not release you from paying major penalties when you are caught.

Here's how to think of your workers. If you give them direction, tell them what to wear, tell them where to go, when to start, when to stop, and enforce smoking rules... then these staff persons are not independent contractors.

Because of what we do at CaterSource, we hear from caterers each month that get themselves in serious trouble with the I.R.S. owing $30,000, $75,000 and, even, $340,000 in uncollected taxes, fines, interest, and added penalties! Please be careful.

Many accountants don't really understand the difference between workers in a restaurant situation and those in catering. We'll be happy to speak with your accountant about what we've learned from the problems of other subscribers.

Don't make the mistake that some caterers do by thinking that you'll never get caught. You might not get caught, but the chances of a competitor, or staff member, turning you in is higher than you think.

Non-Disclosure & Non-Compete

CaterSource, Inc. received this "Non-Disclosure and Non-Compete Agreement from a mid-west caterer. This caterer used this agreement on advice from their company lawyer. It was used, according to the caterer, successfully in court to block the harmful actions of an employee who had left the caterer, taking unauthorized names of past clients of the company.

> **PLEASE REMEMBER** that CaterSource, Inc. is not trying to give legal advice, or suggest that the information below can, or should, be used by your company. You need to get approval from your lawyer as to the advisability or legality of this information as it pertains to State and Federal laws before you use it. CaterSource, Inc. is providing this information as education only.

NON-DISCLOSURE AND NON-COMPETITION AGREEMENT

In consideration of employment with ABC CATERING, (the "Employer"), the undersigned employee, (the "Employee") further agree to the following:

1. Confidential information. Employee acknowledges and agrees that the customers and customer lists of ABC Catering, and its procedures and methods of operation are confidential, and the employee shall not, during or after employment with ABC Catering, divulge, utilize or otherwise disclose for the benefit of any person, including the employee, or directly or indirectly assist, whether as an employee or otherwise, any other person or entity in the business of food catering.

2. Non-competition. Employee further agrees, as part of the consideration of employment, that the employee shall not, during employment and for a period of twelve (12) months thereafter, be employed by or assist, directly or indirectly, with or without compensation, any person or entity conducting a similar catering business in the Metropolitan (anytown) area.

3. Training. Employer, as compensation of this agreement, agrees to use its best efforts to train and educate employee in the business of the employer and provide such materials and procedures as deemed necessary by the employer in furtherance of the employee's employment.

Dated this _____ day of _____, 19__.

Employer: _____   Employee:_____

By_____   By_____

90 Day Trial Employment Agreement

S ometimes you wish to hire someone, but you're not sure if they will work out. The form below, is used by some caterers to offer a 90-day probationary period to all new employees. It's important that you check this out with your attorney before using it.

We at (ABC) are pleased to offer you employment with our company as a _____. Your job responsibilities shall be described to you by ABC from time to time, and your employment shall be on the terms and conditions listed below:

Term of this agreement. It is agreed, by both parties, that a trial period will be undertaken in order that both parties may better understand the nature and scope of the responsibilities and opportunities that may exist. It is agreed that ABC shall hire you for an initial period of 30 days, beginning on _____ and subsequently shall employ you for two (2) additional successive 30-day periods. Either you or ABC may terminate your employment for any reason and at any time during the initial 30-day period upon giving the other party 15 days notice of such termination. Furthermore, your employment may be terminated by ABC at any time after the 30 day period upon 15 days notice of such termination. Furthermore, your employment may be terminated without notice by ABC upon the occurrence of any of the following events:

1. You shall completely neglect your job responsibilities for a period of five days or more.

2. Fail to show-up for work for more than two days without reasonable cause.

3. You shall be guilty of fraud, dishonesty, or other acts of misconduct in the performance of your job responsibilities.

At each of the 30 day anniversaries of this trial period, both parties shall meet to discuss and answer questions pertaining to the job. At the end of the ninety days, or sooner, a final decision will be made as to full time employment.

Work hours. Your normal work hours will be from _____ to _____ on _____
thru _____. Your day off will be _____. You will receive _____
dollars per hour in full accord with state laws.

If you wish to enter this agreement for the trial period at ABC Catering please sign below:

Employee_____

ABC Catering By:_____

CHECK WITH YOUR ATTORNEY FIRST!

Sales Manager Job Description

Successful catering companies are sales driven! Driving the sales force is the sales manager. They are extremely important to the growth of a company. They are as important, if not more important, than the chef! If the salespeople can't sell it, the chef can't cook it!

Hiring

The first job of any successful manager of sales is to make the hire. They are the coach and need to have direct participation in the hiring of all salespeople.

Each salesperson needs to be convinced that they are working for the sales manager... not the company. The salespeople need to please the sales manager by meeting the goals that are established.

During the employment interview the sales manager needs to get certain commitments from the salesperson. It is during this interview that the sales manager decides if the salesperson has the correct mix of talent and energy to meet the company's selling goals.

Training

A great sales manager makes every selling situation a lesson! Training must be ongoing and never ending. A combination of both scheduled and impromptu training needs to be the focus of the sales manager.

The biggest mistake made by sales managers is trusting that their team will bring them their mistakes and weaknesses for correction. Sales managers need to sit-in during live sales presentations given by their team members and they need to let the salespeople sit-in while they themselves are selling someone. Sales training is a show and tell process!

Another way to accomplish this observation process is by audio or video tape. Have a salesperson run a tape recorder so the sales manager can evaluate the experience later. Some capture video tape and watch the tapes together after the fact!

Leadership

This is a combination of stroking and nipping! The great coaches learn one thing and one thing only ... it's important not to become predictable!

Leadership needs passion and enthusiasm and energy! Each day needs to begin with goals and reminders about what is needed to make successful sales. The sales manager needs to be two, or three, steps ahead of the team at all times.

A constant balance between short term and long term goals are required for success in selling. The sales manager needs to keep everyone running a "movie" in their heads about what the end result will be of successful selling.

The sales manager leads by making things seem possible and within reach. Leadership is the springboard for successful selling. The sales manager makes most of the sales even though they aren't with the salespeople when they meet with their clients. Sales leadership is a state of mind! The sales manager needs to be in the mind of the salesperson!

Morale

In a sales atmosphere, the foundation of great team morale is truth! Truth is the greatest of motivators. The sales manager needs to call them as they see them. Never protect a salesperson from the truth.

When a sales team knows that they are always going to be treated truthfully, they have higher morale.

Numbers

The big one for any sales manager. We live and die by the numbers. I suggest that most sales managers that I've met have put too much credence in the numbers. Training, leadership, and morale are more important to the sales success of a company than numbers.

Numbers should only be used to judge the success and value of the sales manager ... not the salespeople! When numbers are not being made, the sales manager has done something incorrectly.

Peace in the kitchen

This is an important, but minor, role for the sales manager. They should be the voice of reason in all spats between the culinary and selling team. Enough said about this!

Evaluation

The sales managers need for evaluation of the team is ongoing and subject to constant review. They must know where a particular sales talents mind is at all times. They need to know the past, future and present attitudes of each and every member of the sales team. This is usually done through written evaluations that are also shown to the salesperson.

The Sales Manager is important for catering success!

Staff Coordinator Job Description

In an effort to provide subscribers with as much assistance as possible in building their businesses professionally, we offer another example of a job description. You will find other examples of job descriptions in Journal 2/Page 2 and Journal 4/Page 4.

Job Description for Staff Coordinator

Duties to Include:

1. Schedule service staff for events. Work with Executive Chef to schedule kitchen staff for events.

2. Reconfirm service staff within one week of events for which they are scheduled.

3. Hire service staff to include: writing and placing of ads, phone screening, personal interview and reference check.

4. Approval of uniforms and the maintaining of the employment file.

5. Orientation and continual training of servers and other event staff.

6. Attend to any disciplinary actions needed with regard to service staff.

7. Supervise events.

8. Attend meetings, and site inspections, with clients if salespeople request.

9. Review details of events with sales person and relate these details to the event supervisor.

10. Write a monthly newsletter to the staff.

11. Provide payroll information for the event staff and approve monthly payroll sheets.

12. Answer phones and office support as needed.

Executive Chef Contract

EXECUTIVE CHEF AGREEMENT

ABC Catering ("ABC) is pleased to offer _____ (hereinafter know as "John" or "Doe" or Employee) a position with our company as an executive chef. In consideration of the terms and conditions set forth in this letter, ABC and John Doe agree as follows:

1. Employee at Will. Nothing in this agreement will change the employer/employee relationship between ABC and John Doe as that of an "employee at will," that is, either ABC or John may terminate John's employment for any reason at any time.

2. Job Responsibilities. Your job responsibilities shall be described to you by ABC from time to time, and shall include, but not be limited to, the job description attached as exhibit A hereto and incorporated herein.

3. Non-Compete. Doe agrees that during his employment with ABC and for a period of one year after he leaves ABC's employment, in any geographic area within twenty-five (25) miles of ABC's facility at 222. West Green Street, Chicago, IL, Doe will not directly or indirectly, individually or on behalf of or in concert with any other person or entity, solicit or perform catering services for, any person or entity which placed catering with ABC at any time during his employment with ABC. Notwithstanding the foregoing, if Doe's employment is terminated for ABC's business reasons or for any reason other than Doe's job performance, this clause shall not be binding on Doe's choice of replacement employment.

4. Salary, commission and sales bonus.

    A. Base Salary. Your base salary shall be _____ per year, which shall be payable semi-monthly.

    B. Incentive Bonus. In addition to your salary, ABC will pay you an incentive bonus on all quality work produced by you as follows:

Dollar Value of Work (Monthly / Company wide)			(BONUS)
$0	to	$100,000	$0
$101,000	to	$175,000	$700.00
$176,000	to	$225,000	$1,000.00
Above		$226,000	$1,500.00

Continued...

Executive Chef Contract

C. Food Cost Bonus. In addition to your salary and other bonuses, ABC will pay you .0025 of the net savings for each .01 ABC's total food costs are reduced over the previous year's costs.

D. Quality Bonus. In addition to your salary and other bonuses, if, in ABC's sole discretion, your work during the year reflects the diligence, quality, and maximum effort in the execution of all the job responsibilities enumerated in the job description attached as Exhibit A, ABC will pay an additional bonus commensurate with its evaluation of your performance.

All of the above-described bonuses shall be considered annual bonuses and, if applicable, they shall be paid in the mid-month January check in the next year except for the Incentive Bonus which is a monthly bonus and if earned shall be paid on the 15th of the month following its accrual. To be eligible for any of the above-described bonuses, you must be an employee in good standing through the completion of the year. No bonuses will be earned or pro-rated if you cease your employment with ABC for any reason before the end of the year.

5. Loss Prevention Penalty. As part of your job responsibilities, you have agreed to vigilantly supervise the return of all of ABC's equipment and other property to ABC from outside job sites. Thus, where items whose value exceeds $25 are not returned to ABC, your commission will be reduced by the fair market value of the replacement costs of all items not recovered, said amount to be paid one-half (1/2) by Doe and one-half (1/2) by General Manager.

6. Confidential Information. You understand that in the course of your employment, you are likely to become familiar with secret or confidential information of ABC such as, but not limited to, lists of customers, specific information regarding such customers, types and kinds of catering arrangements, lists of suppliers of food, beverage and equipment and the costs thereof, and other information of a confidential nature which is required to be maintained as such for the continued success of ABC and its business. Accordingly, you agree:

A. While employed by ABC, to cooperate with and advise and acquaint ABC of all confidential knowledge and information possessed by or entrusted to you so that ABC may know at all times the extent to which knowledge of secret or confidential information is possessed and being utilized by you.

B. If and when your employment with ABC is terminated, whether voluntarily or involuntarily, to surrender to ABC all books, Rolodexes, records, computer disks, or notes containing lists of customers, documents and any secret or confidential information.

7. Employee Benefits. ABC shall provide major medical and dental insurance for you under the terms and conditions available through ABC's current major medical insurance program. ABC reserves the right to change all aspects of the insurance coverage from time to time. In its sole discretion ABC will pay 50% of the cost of said insurance. At your expense, your family members may also be covered by ABC's insurance. If you desire, prior to your signing this agreement ABC will provide you with information on the major medical and dental insurance that it currently provides for its employees.

Continued...

Executive Chef Contract

8. Vacations. ABC shall also provide you with the paid vacation time set forth below:

    A. A one-week paid vacation during the first year of employment with ABC.

    B. A two-week paid vacation after two years of employment with ABC.

    C. A three-week paid vacation after five years of employment with ABC.

You must schedule your vacation with ABC at least three weeks prior to the beginning date of the desired vacation time. Although you may request any vacation time that you desire with the limits of this agreement, ABC shall have sole discretion regarding final approval of any vacation date that you request. You may not schedule a vacation during the months of May, June, September, October, and December.

This contract shall be reviewed annually but all terms shall remain in effect until specifically replaced by a revised contract signed by both parties.

We are looking forward to having you continue your work with ABC and hope you find the terms of this agreement acceptable. If so, please indicate your acceptance by signing this agreement below and returning it to us.

ABC CATERING by _____

Read and accepted by _____

Date Signed: _____

Continued...

Employee Work Application

Wwe wish to thank Karen Smoots of Eli's Catering (Charlotte NC) for permitting us to reprint the application for employment that they have used.

Take time to read it closely... it has some very unique features that you might like to use.

NOTICE:
CATERSOURCE REMINDS YOU TO HAVE THIS APPLICATION CHECKED BY YOUR ATTORNEY BECAUSE OF THE MANY DIFFERENT STATE AND FEDERAL LAWS.

ELI'S Catering

Application for Part-Time Employment

Last Name	First	Middle	Date of Birth	Date of Application

Street Address			Position applying for:	Social Security Identification

City	State	ZIP code	Desired salary	Telephone no. Home: Work:

How were you referred to this company? (Circle only one)	A By your college	B Advertisement	C Employment Agency	D By an employee	If so, give name:	E Military service	F Walk-in	G Resume or letter	H Other

In case of emergency contact:

Last Name	First	Middle	Relation

Street Address			Phone no. ( )

City	State	ZIP code	

Employment Record
Starting with present or most recent, list all previous employers. Include self-employment and summer and part-time jobs. If more please continue on a seperate sheet. You may attach resume, but complete application as well.

Last or present company	Type of business	Title or job classification
Street address	Phone no.	Brief description of job duties
City	State	ZIP code	
Supervisor's name and title	Phone no.	
Base salary	Dates worked From	To
Reason for leaving		May we contact?

Last or present company	Type of business	Title or job classification
Street address	Phone no.	Brief description of job duties
City	State	ZIP code	
Supervisor's name and title	Phone no.	
Base salary	Dates worked From	To
Reason for leaving		May we contact?

TURN OVER TO CONTINUE APPLICATION

Professional/Work References
List two past supervisors and one person who is not related to you who have knowledge of your qualifications for the position for which you are applying.

Name	Title/relationship	Address (street, city, state, zip code)	Phone no. (include area code)	Occupation

Miscellaneous

Were you previously employed by this company?	☐ Yes ☐ No	If yes, when
Do you have any relative(s) currently employed by this company?	☐ Yes ☐ No	If yes, list below
Name	Realtionship	Name	Relationship

Have you been convicted of any crimes other than minor traffic violations during the past seven years?	☐ Yes ☐ No	If yes, list below
Will visa or immigration status prevent lawful employment?	☐ Yes ☐ No	

Shirt size:	S M L XL	List any other skills you have:
Neck size:	Sleeve size:	
Jacket size:		
Shoe size:	width:	

Provide all information requested.
Your complete application form will be maintained in our active files for six (6) months from the date of application. You may submit a new application at any time.

An Equal Opportunity Employer
We are an equal opportunity employer, and we do not and will not discriminate on the basis of race, religion, national origin, sex, age, handicap, marital status, or status as a disabled veteran or Vietnam-era veteran. Information provided on this application will not be used for any discriminatory purpose.

I hereby certify that the answers and other information on this application are true and correct and that I understand any misrepresentation or omission of facts on my part will be justification for separation from the company's service, if employed. I understand that my employment may be contingent upon my receipt of an alien registration number, verification of birth and any other pertinent information bearing upon my employ-

Sous Chef Job Description

The position of Sous Chef is an important one. What follows is an example of a job description for this crucial kitchen position. CaterSource reminds all our subscribers that staff will work more professionally when they have a clear understanding of what their job, or duties, are. In today's legalistic world, it is important to give staff their job descriptions in writing so they can be reminded of what they need to do.

Job description for a catering Sous Chef

1. Take primary responsibility for menu development.

- *Working with the salespeople on new ideas.*
- *Continually searching for new ideas in magazines, etc.*
- *Routinely practicing with new food ideas.*

2. Conceive, test and develop new recipes and menus.

3. Focus on culinary creativity and expanding the company's range of food styles.

4. Conduct ongoing training of kitchen staff to include:

- *Culinary training.*
- *Sanitation training.*
- *Safety training.*
- *Equipment training.*

5. Develop and maintain a recipe system.

6. Maintain responsibility for general cleaning, maintenance and sanitation of kitchen.

7. Assist head chef, and owner, with hiring and evaluation of kitchen staff.

- *Assisting with the actual interviews.*

8. Participate in special projects.

9. Take monthly inventory of all food and beverage items.

10. Assist head chef with item costing, price checking and price updating.

11. Run kitchen's daily production.

12. Write production schedules and daily prep lists.

13. Order food items.

14. Check in deliveries of foods coming from vendors.

- *Working with accounting department to insure that bills are paid correctly.*
- *Checking all weights and counts to insure that all has been received.*

15. Take responsibility for checking all food leaving the kitchen for events.

16. Monitor taste and quality control of all food production and presentation.

17. Take responsibility for matching the right event equipment with each menu item.

Ads for Chefs

Advertising for a new chef is often an ongoing process for many caterers. Too often, the caterer places an ad that doesn't give the reader important information, or clues, about what type of chef the caterer is searching for.

Here's three template ads that CaterSource has used to find chefs for our customers. You will notice that these ads "walk to the beat of a different drummer." Pay particular attention to the Chef/Partner ad (#1) since it might be the answer to the question "How can I ever get a day off?" Ad #2 eliminates the "non-working" chef that wants a desk job. Finally, #3 makes the reader aware that working for a caterer is not the same as working for most restaurants and hotels.

1

Chef/Partner

One of Denver's finest caterers is searching for a chef, with a full range of culinary abilities, who wishes to invest for part-ownership. Besides fulfilling the tasks of an executive chef, you will need to create new menu items and train other staff. $30,000 investment required. Send resume and brief paragraph about yourself to Mike Roman, CaterSource, Inc., PO Box 14776, Chicago IL 60614.

2

Catering Chef

One of Birmingham's finest caterers is searching for a chef, with a full range of culinary abilities. Besides fulfilling the tasks of an executive chef, you will need to create new menu items and train other staff. 70% of time will be spent cooking with 30% management. Send resume and brief paragraph about yourself to Mike Roman, CaterSource, Inc., PO Box 14776, Chicago IL 60614.

3

Food Glorious Food!

Ready for a change! We're looking for secretaries who wish to learn a new profession. Start by using your present secretarial skills to become an associate party planner. Work right along with our Event Planners as you learn the ins and outs of this business. Send resume and/or letter to: Jim Sheedy, CaterSource, Inc., PO Box 14776, Chicago IL 60614.

Salesperson Job Description

NEW BUSINESS ACCOUNT EXECUTIVE

Job Description

• The New Business Account Executive will report to Bob Smith.

• The Account Executive position is multifaceted.

• Generating new business is the primary responsibility. Duties include; researching for leads, cold calling, correspondence, consulting with various ABC Catering departments, follow-up and limited attendance at some events.

• Researching is the first step to generating new business. Newspapers, magazines, yellow pages and trades are just a few sources to pursue. Contacts met through social/formal organizations are also an excellent source.

• Cold calling is the activation of leads. It's important that data is kept, such as contact names, etc. Use of ABC Catering "account cards" is mandatory. At this point, there is a set goal of 15 calls per day or 75 calls per week. This includes follow-up calls to prospects.

• Correspondence through letters is an excellent way to follow-up with a prospect, and a great way to initiate contact. Sending an introductory letter with a menu allows the prospect to see ABC Catering's professionalism. We prefer to send out letters and menus during the same week of contact. For quality prospects that have been contacted but have not ordered, it's a good idea to keep in touch. Holidays are a good excuse to send cards and it doesn't look too pushy.

• Appointments give the New Business Account Executive a captive contact. Pictures are worth a thousand words and our portfolio portrays a quality company. Seeing our work in pictures or tasting a sample of food either hooks a prospect or helps to relax a nervous client. It's important for the New Business Account Executive to project the feeling that ABC Catering will listen to the client's wishes and work with the customer! The number of appointments per week directly correlates to cold calls and follow-ups. Remember, for every no you get, you are closer to a yes.

• Consultations with prospects are extremely important because this demonstrates that ABC Catering has the potential to bid on their parties. Use the sheet of questions and listen to the client. Be very careful when discussing cost. Always emphasize that at this stage you can only give a ball-park figure. This is also a good opportunity to ask those questions that appear on the materials we've given you.

• It's the Account Executive's responsibility to confer with the ABC Catering staff regarding menu, customer wishes and ABC Catering policies. When doing this, keep in mind the optimum time of availability for each department, i.e. the kitchen is busier in the morning; therefore, it's best to speak with the Chef in the afternoon. Proposal development is the actual hammering out of costs and eventually typing the outlines of the event for client review. The Account Executive should show Bob Smith the proposal before it's sent to the client.

• Follow-up consists of confirmation that the contact has received the proposal and making yourself available for client questions or comments. Find out at what stage the bidding process is; has the client already weeded down the list of potential caterers; what's the next step on the client's agenda?

• Attending the event is good public relations and helps put the Account Executive's mind to rest. Turn this first time customer into a repeat by showing him that ABC Catering not only has delicious food but also understands the importance of customer relations.

Checklist for Hiring a Salesperson

The ideal salesperson probably doesn't exist, but here are some of the areas of awareness a salesperson needs for maximum success. When considering a person for hire in your sales department use some of these topics in making your decision.

1. Food Preparation. There is no guarantee, but chefs often make the best salespeople. They understand the food and have a clear understanding of what will, and won't, work well. The more your prospective hire has worked in a catering kitchen the better their chances of being a star! Many companies let prospective hires work in the kitchen (they pay them for this) for a couple of days to see what their knowledge of food really is.

2. Etiquette. Be sure to have certain questions ready to ask your potential hire about the etiquette of serving and of being a guest.

3. Local Traditions. Each locale has certain traditions that need to be adhered to. For example, in some locales a Sunday wedding starts at 3:00 pm and consists of a set of very special rules.

4. Food Presentations. This is important. Some caterers actually give their whittled down list of candidates a "hands-on" test. They are asked to set-up a buffet and display their skills with design and style. Or, you might wish to show them some pictures of your catering and ask them to critique what you've done... ask them "What would you have done?"

5. National Foodservice Trends. Focus on what type of vacations they've taken over the years. What are their favorite restaurants in Boston? What foodservice magazines do they subscribe to? How do they feel about Southwestern cooking? These should give you some vital insight into their knowledge of foodservice on the national scene.

6. Friends & Business Contacts. The first thing they ask insurance salespeople is "Who do you know?" So, you need to find out what their grasp of your market is. If you hire them, will it get you into any new markets?

Here are some of the skills that a salesperson might need to reach maximum success.

1. Staff Relations. Getting along with the staff seems like an obvious characteristic for a new hire. But... how do you measure for this? It's difficult at best, but you need to try. Let your final candidates get a chance to work with, or at least meet, your other key staff. This could be during work or after work over dinner. Then give your staff a chance to tell you what they feel... and what their observations were.

2. Client Relations. The ability of your new salesperson to understand that they are going to be looked upon as "servants" to most of their clients is a foundation for super success. "Nothing is more important than a happy client", is the only motto that you want on the mind of a salesperson. Ask them hypothetical questions on "How they would handle..." Listen carefully to their answers!

3. Organizational Abilities. One caterer told CaterSource that if a prospective hire for a sales position couldn't produce a list, on the spot, of things they needed to get done, they wouldn't hire them! This is probably too strong, but your salesperson needs to understand the general concepts of time management and follow through.

4. Sense of Humor. What can we say? We don't mean they need to tell jokes successfully. They need the ability to see humor in things and, above all, they need to be able to laugh at themselves! Ask them about some situations in their life that were difficult but now are funny.

5. Positive Mental Attitude. A great point to end on. Is the glass half empty or is it half full? Remember: A salesperson is either a blessing or a sea anchor! Think twice and think carefully before hiring anyone.

Ads for Secretaries that Become Salespeople

Here's an interesting idea. Build secretaries into quality salespeople! Think about it ... many secretaries handle incredible stress and know what it means to put out fires. Secretaries also have a desire to better themselves. Well, let's give them a chance to learn our business from the bottom up!

Below are some sample ads that CaterSource, Inc has run for some of it's clients. The feeling is that moving a secretary into a support situation in your office will allow you to develop them quicker, because they really don't have any "bad" habits, that another person might have if they have sold catering elsewhere.

1

Changing Careers?... Let's PARTY!

Corporate secretaries make great catering salespeople! You're prepared to handle stress and last minute changes. If you want to learn more about this great opportunity please send resume and brief paragraph about yourself to: Jim Sheedy, CaterSource, Inc., PO Box 14776, Chicago IL 60614.

2

Food Glorious Food!

Ready for a change! We're looking for secretaries who wish to learn a new profession. Start by using your present secretarial skills to become an associate party planner. Work right along with our Event Planners as you learn the ins and outs of this business. Send resume and/or letter to: Jim Sheedy, CaterSource, Inc., PO Box 14776, Chicago IL 60614.

3

Nothing to do on Weekends?

Our catering company needs to find a creative secretary to work with our event planners. You will work with menus, speak with clients, and handle last minute changes in events for thousands of guests. Sound interesting? Send resume to Jim Sheedy, CaterSource, Inc., PO Box 14776, Chicago IL 60614.

Income Survey

The following report is simply to provide some insight into what various types of high level owners, executives and highly placed managers are being paid. The information comes from an informal survey by Mike Roman over the last two years.

All incomes are annual and they are averages.

REMEMBER: Since these are averages, some are higher and some are lower.

Owners/Presidents / HIGHLY PLACED MANAGERS

Under $100,000 in volume $31,000

From $100,000 to $250,000 ....$39,000

From $250,000 to $500,000 ....$46,000

From $500,000 to $700,000 ....$55,000

From $700,000 to $1,000,000.............................$80,000

From $1,000,000 to $2,000,000 ....$88,000 to $110,000

From $2,000,000 to $3,000,000 ....$95,000 to $135,000

From $3,000,000 to $4,000,000 ....$110,000 to $160,000

From $4,000,000 to $5,000,000 ....$135,000 to $200,000

Executive Chefs

Under $100,000 in volume $22,000

From $100,000 to $250,000 ....$28,000

From $250,000 to $500,000 ....$34,000

From $500,000 to $1,000,000.............................$40,000

From $1,000,000 to $2,000,000 ....$55,000

From $2,000,000 to $3,000,000 ....$75,000

From $3,000,000 to $4,000,000 ....$90,000

From $4,000,000 to $5,000,000 ....$110,000

Peer Group Evaluations

One of the most "giving" contributors to the CaterSource Journal is James Barrack, owner of Cater Inn, Inc., a thriving on and off-premise catering business in Peoria, IL.

What follows is yet another example of Jim's incredible desire to share with other subscribers what has worked for his company. This Peer Evaluation has done much to give Jim a better handle of his staff's strengths and weaknesses and has led to his ability to help all his staff reach the pinnacle of their success. We thank Jim Barrack for his continued contributions to the Journal!

PEER EVALUATION

EMPLOYEE BEING EVALUATED: _____ RETURN BY:_____

Please answer the following questions to the best of your ability about the above named person. A 5 is the HIGHEST score you can give and a 1 is the LOWEST. Return this sheet to the Director of Personnel by the date indicated above.

1. How would you rate this person's willingness to share the work load?	1	2	3	4	5
2. How willing is this person to fill in for you?	1	2	3	4	5
3. How friendly and pleasant is this person to work with?	1	2	3	4	5
4. How much do you trust this person?	1	2	3	4	5
5. How professional is this person?	1	2	3	4	5
6. Does this person take pride in their work?	1	2	3	4	5
7. How would you rate the quality of their work?	1	2	3	4	5
8. Does this person follow through with work assignments?	1	2	3	4	5
9. Does this person aspire to advance?	1	2	3	4	5
10. Does this person accept constructive criticism?	1	2	3	4	5
11. Does this person follow a "clean as you go" routine?	1	2	3	4	5
12. How would you rate this person's organizational skills?	1	2	3	4	5
13. How would you rate this person's productivity?	1	2	3	4	5
14. Does this person refrain from engaging in horseplay?	1	2	3	4	5
15. Does this person adhere to company rules?	1	2	3	4	5
16. How much do you like working with this person?	1	2	3	4	5

In what single area should this person improve to increase his/her overall performance?

_____

If you were to describe this person with one word, what would it be? _____

Comments: _____

(Use other side of paper for additional comments)

Tips for Managers

The list below was sent to us by subscriber James Barrack of The Cater Inn (Peoria, IL), a frequent contributor to the Journal. It's a good list to keep around when things get crazy or you need to get some ideas for a training session.

1. Stand behind your staff in times of stress and crisis.

2. Treat others the way you want to be treated.

3. Be especially considerate to front-line staff.

4. Dress for success. Look professional.

5. Improve your oral communication skills.

6. Praise in public. Criticize in private.

7. Carefully manage your time. Its your scarcest and least renewable resource.

8. Remember: Success is getting up just one more time than you fall down.

9. Don't ask someone to do something you wouldn't do yourself.

10. Remember, friends come and go, but enemies accumulate.

11. Maintain an optimistic outlook.

12. Be curious and open-minded.

13. Be an active listener.

14. Be a mentor to someone on the way up.

15. Celebrate the personal and professional accomplishments of your staff.

16. Use "we" rather than "I" when talking about the firm.

17. Keep all promises. Don't promise more than you can deliver.

18. Strive for total quality/continuous improvement at all times.

19. Look at problems as opportunities.

20. Bring more humor into your company.

21. Use the K.I.S.S. principle (keep it simple… stupid) whenever possible.

22. Say "I don't know" when you don't.

23. Lead a healthy lifestyle focused on weight control and exercise.

24. Be a positive roll model for others.

25. Never underestimate the competition.

26. Never tolerate discrimination or harassment of any kind.

27. Remember that you never get a second chance to make a first impression.

28. When in doubt, trust your intuition.

29. Be confident and comfortable, but not complacent.

30. Keep your ear to the company grapevine.

31. Recognize that no one is indispensable.

32. Take your job very seriously but don't take yourself too seriously.

33. Don't do it because it feels good; do it because it's right!

Evaluating Your Sales Staff

What is consulting? To me, consulting is evaluation and comparison. First you evaluate what conditions exist, then you compare these conditions with those that exist elsewhere.

This is why the world has consultants. Not for their expertise, but for their exposure to diverse conditions. Most caterers have never been to many other catering operations to see what is happening. I've been fortunate to have personally visited more than 900 catering companies over the last 20 years.

That's what this new series of articles is about. I hope to give our readers some guidelines for "self-consulting".

It is important that catering businesses receive ongoing evaluation in order to continually reach for higher levels of success.

Elements that the best salespeople have!

You really can't be sure of what characteristics determine who will be the better salesperson. Nothing takes the place of talent, timing and luck when it comes to making sales.

However, here is our list of some of the elements that seem to be possessed and practiced by many of the better catering salespersons:

1. Uses time properly. Isn't afraid to stop a selling situation to move on to someone else.

This is a rather advanced concept. Very few catering salespeople decide to stop their sales presentation because they have decided the buyers in front of them do not hold any promise for a successful sale. The ability to take this action will result in increased sales volume and prevents "burnout" in the salesperson.

2. Is always honest and user-friendly to the buyer and those influencing the purchase.

When a salesperson truly realizes that buyers are looking for an honest style from their salesperson, magical things happen. This is especially true when the honesty is in direct response to a question from the buyers.

User-friendly means much more than just being happy or getting coffee for them. It means that the salesperson, after deciding what are the "hot buttons" for the buyer, makes it clear that the client's "wants" and "fears" will be met.

> **... THINK OF THESE TIPS, TACTICS AND IDEAS AS A STARTING POINT FOR DOING SELF-CONSULTING FOR YOUR OWN BUSINESS.**

3. Speaks clearly and precisely at all times, particularly during a selling interview.

This may seem obvious to you, but I've often watched salespeople who really don't understand how they sound to the buyers.

The best technique for understanding how you sound is to audio tape some presentations. Do it while speaking over the phone or during actual selling situation with buyers present, and then critique how you sounded while replaying the tape.

4. Understands why the sale was missed.

The best salespeople never think they "lost" a sale. Instead, they believe that they "missed" something that permitted the buyer to select the competition over them!

They think about what they said to the buyer and what the buyers said to them during the missed sale. In many ways its like football players watching the tapes of last weeks game.

5. Plans sales calls in advance... and really makes a plan for each day!

This is one that I also watch for when determining if a particular salesperson is "great." Anyone can react to callers who come to them, but great talents are proactive and go after sales before they come into the company's system.

These great talents know who they are going to call and who they are going to see long before they begin to do it.

6. Asks good, probing questions.

Questions maintain control in any sales situation. The best salespeople learn to ask a variety of important, and not-so-important, questions that give them information about the event and an understanding of the "buying attitude" of the clients.

7. Uses sales aids while selling. Involves all of the buyers senses, i.e. smell, hearing, seeing, touching and tasting.

Don't just talk about a special chair... show it! Demonstration will sell more than explanation. Try to let the buyer involve each of their five senses. For example, let the client feel a china plate instead of just looking at it. You either get this concept... or not!

Evaluating Your Sales Staff

8. Sells the concept of "not embarrassing" the buyer in front of others.

The best salespeople have learned that buyers are buying them (the salesperson) not the menu! When giving a party for friends or strangers, all hosts want to be free from embarrassment.

9. Takes the risk out of buying when possible.

No buyer wants to be a "fool." The great salespeople assure the buyer that nothing will go wrong and that if it does this is what our company is ready to do. Telling a client that they must pay for the guarantee number of guests is not the same as saying that if a few don't make it to the event, we will make some sort of an adjustment.

10. Listens to the meaning of what the buyer is saying... not just the words.

A great salesperson is not always in a hurry to speak. The ears of their ears are always listening and carefully analyzing what the buyer has just told them.

11. Decides ahead of time what they are going to sell to the buyer.

Ordinary salespeople let the buyer buy what they think they want. Great salespeople sell the client what they "really" wish!

12. Acts professionally at all times.

This deals with such things as dress, speech, courtesy, and manners. It also deals with a need to stay in control of what is happening.

13. Never apologizes for price... only explains what the price does.

The only answer to a buyers remark about your prices being higher than others is... "Yes, we do have higher prices ... let me explain why."

14. Is in constant search of competitor data.

A great salesperson knows their competition. They understand their advantages and disadvantages over their own company. They know their prices and procedures. They've seen marketing and selling materials used by the competitors.

15. Answers typical buyer objections before they arise.

I know you've heard this before. Great talents always anticipate the objections that might be coming from a buyer and they do answer them before they are asked. Often it is placed in the context of "Last week a client pointed out to us that (give the objection), but after a little thought they decided that (give your answer).

16. Is always honest in their approach to selling.

This is the second time we've mentioned honesty. It is the cornerstone of all sales. Don't confuse honesty with telling sales stories like "that date is really busy" that build urgency. We mean that honesty in the "deal-making" is extremely important.

17. In theory, is ready to sell twenty-four hours a day!

You never know when a buyer is going to be around... so always have a card and a smile ready to go!

18. Isn't afraid of making mistakes.

Mistakes result either because of lack of preparation or because of taking a chance. Great sales talents always are ready to "risk it all" if they think that's what's needed to dislodge the buyer into action! In other words, these talents are not afraid to get out on a ledge and take some risk to make a sale happen today instead of waiting for tomorrow!

In closing, let me stress that it is difficult to predict who will be a "great" sales talent and who will be "not-so great." Also, it is very possible for a particular person to change and get better with practice and desire being channeled towards learning new ways of selling catering.

The eighteen factors above will help you determine what type of salespeople you now have and more about those you wish to hire!

CHAPTER 11  QUESTIONS

1. Where can a caterer look for new staff?

2. What are ways a caterer can motivate staff to work for them?

3. What are some unique ways to recruit new staff?

4. What are six different methods for paying staff?

5. Is it legal for a caterer to pay a worker in cash without taking out State and Federal taxes?

6. What other methods of paying staff are considered illegal?

7. What should a caterer be looking for when hiring a salesperson?

8. How can a caterer help motivate staff?

9. What are the main ideas in the contract for an Executive Chef?

10. What is your feeling about the nondisclosure agreement?

LETTERS

CHAPTER **12**

TABLE OF CONTENTS

CHAPTER

12

*"Catering has always been
and will always be a
make-do situation!"*

The Powerful Receipt Letter

(Date)

Mr. & Mrs. James Saddlestich
1550 W. Gump Street
Anytown, US 333333

Dear Mr. & Mrs. Saddlestich:

We are pleased to acknowledge receipt of the agreement that you have signed and returned to our offices confirming the catering we will be performing in your home on Thursday, (DATE).

Our entire team of catering professionals in enthused by the confidence that you have showed by selecting us to handle this important event. Please be assured that we intend to more than justify this confidence in all respects. This will result in a memorable occasion for you and your guests!

Enclosed please find a list of twelve "Catering Reminders" that you may wish to review. We have found that this list has helped many of our first time customers better understand all that goes into a successful catered event.

 Also, in the future, when you call our office, please advise our receptionist that you have a definite party booked for (Date) and you wish to be transferred to your account representative Bob Smith.

Once again, thank you for selecting us as your caterer!

Most cordially yours,
ABC CATERING COMPANY

Bob Smith
Account Representative

Enclosure: Catering Reminders

cc: Sally Sands, President ABC Catering

2 Page Customer Evaluation Letter

(Date)

Mr. Jim Doe
2222 N. South Street
Somewhere, CA 44444

Dear Jim:

This sheet will help us learn why you're not ordering from us anymore. Please review these statements and check-off all that apply. (You may check off as many as you wish)

[ ] No problem... just not using catering anymore.
[ ] Please call and we'll talk about it.
[ ] Call I'm ready to order again.
[ ] Dissatisfied with quality of food.
[ ] Dissatisfied with promptness of delivery.
[ ] Dissatisfied with payment terms.
[ ] Experienced customer service problems with your office.
[ ] Prices are too high.
[ ] Not enough variety in menus.
[ ] Other (Please explain.)

_____
_____

What will it take to get your business back?
_____
_____

Please mail or FAX this to 555-5555.

Thank you!

NOTE:

STAY IN TOUCH

WITH YOUR CLIENT'S

JOYS AND CONCERNS

WITH YOUR CATERING!

NOTE:

TRY TO USE A STAMP

FOR THE RETURN ENVELOPE

THAT IS SIGNIFICANT

FOR YOUR CLIENT'S INDUSTRY

OR JUST ONE THAT IS NEAT!

(Date)

Mr. Jim Doe
2222 N. South Street
Somewhere, CA 44444

Dear Jim:

In reviewing our accounts we noticed that we have not received any orders from your company for our self-service lunches during the last 60 days. In the preceding year, you had ordered an average of 6 times per month. Naturally, we're concerned.

It's important to us that we keep informed of our customers' degree of satisfaction with our products and service so we can continue to serve them well. It's particularly important that we learn why past customers no longer order from us.

Won't you please help us by completing the following evaluation and returning it to us in the enclosed stamped envelope? It will only take a minute and your answers will help us provide better services in the future.

Thank you for your time, and we hope you'll be placing an order with us soon.

Sincerely,

Bob Smith
President

Examples of Collection Letters

THESE LETTERS ARE USED FOR THE UNHAPPY TIMES WHEN A PARTICULAR CLIENT HAS NOT RESPONDED TO YOUR NORMAL INVOICING METHODS.

(Date)

Mr. Jim Doe
XYZ Widget, Inc.
2222 N. South Street
Somewhere, CA 44444

Dear Jim:

Time is money. Unfortunately, we have been wasting much of both trying to collect XYZ Widget, Inc.'s debt to ABC Catering for the work we did at your facility on (DATE). In every management meeting, we discuss with disbelief the fact that XYZ Widget, Inc. continues to shrink from its obligations. The outstanding balance of $3,544.42 is overdue by an excessive 160 days.

I am responsible for our company's accounting, and your lack of action has forced me to cancel all future extension of credit. Because ABC Catering is a fair company, management has developed two options that will allow XYZ Widget, Inc. to fulfill its obligations:

1. Remit the full balance owed of $3,544.44.
2. Remit a partial payment of $1,000.00 with the under standing that the balance will be paid by (DATE).

Your immediate response is imperative. ABC Catering is not going away, and I would like our business affiliation to continue. However, only your actions can allow this to happen, and time is running out.

Sincerely Yours,

Bob Smith

(Date)

Mr. Jim Doe
XYZ Widget, Inc,
2222 N. South Street
Somewhere, CA 44444

Dear Jim:

Life can be so hectic at times that even good habits fall by the wayside. We neglect the simple things like eating lunch or reading the paper. Many times, people call with requests for our catering, and we need to drop everything to meet their expectations.

XYZ Widget, Inc. has an obligation to ABC Catering too. Your good credit history suggests that simple oversight is the reason for your lack of promptness in remitting payment to ABC Catering. Our records indicate that the amount of $3,544.12 is currently past due by 120 days.

It is never too late to make payment on your account with us. If this letter crossed paths with your check, please accept my apologies for this friendly reminder. We simply want to revive XYZ Widget, Inc.'s good habits before the situation has a chance to get out of control. Thank you for your assistance.

Sincerely,

Bob Smith
President

REMEMBER:

ONCE YOU BEGIN THE PROCESS OF TOUGHER COLLECTION METHODS, YOU CAN'T STOP UNTIL YOU GET WHAT'S DUE TO YOU FOR YOUR HARD WORK

Announcing Your Location Move

Gary Wisotzky of Contemporary Caterers (Boca Raton, FL) used this successful mailing to announce his move to a new business location in South Florida.

The marketing piece was printed on heavy weight glossy card stock. It measured 8.5 by 11 before it was folded in half to save postage.

The colors were blue ink and gold foil stamping. According to Gary, who's also this month's interview on page 13, clients received the mailing with great humor. They particularly enjoyed the caricature of Gary pushing the cart.

CATERING/SPECIAL EVENTS

HERE WE GROW AGAIN !!!

Thanks to your continuing support, we've out-grown our previous location.

Our new address is:
1101 Holland Drive, Suite 23
Boca Raton, Florida 33487

Phone (407) 989-8730
Fax (407) 989-8715

In a world where special event catering offers endless possibilities, **Contemporary Caterers** is synonymous with outstanding and innovative events. We offer all types of catering for all types of budgets. Whatever you need think of **Contemporary Caterers!**

In the corporate realm where time is money, save valuable time by having breakfast or lunch delivered to your office for an important meeting or to treat your special clients. Or let your "imagination" be your guide and **Contemporary Caterers** will be your "hands" in planning your next social or fund raising event. Allow us to assist you in all phases of planning and catering your unique and fun party!

WE ARE READY TO SERVE YOU...FROM JUPITER TO THE FLORIDA KEYS AT OUR NEW AND CENTRALLY LOCATED CATERING FACILITY!

1101 Holland Drive #23 Boca Raton, Florida 33487
Phone (407) 989-8730 FAX (407) 989-8715

1101 Holland Drive #23 Boca Raton, Florida 33487
Phone (407) 989-8730 FAX (407) 989-8715

Wholesale Catering Template Letter

Let's think "out of the box" for a moment. Why shouldn't you think about offering your food to other caterers, restaurants, etc.? Below is a letter that you could use that would start the process. Addresses of caterers in your town can be obtained by looking in the yellow pages under "mailing lists"

CaterSource® knows of several caterers who have had success with this type of promotion.

WHOLESALE Catering Foods!

Let us worry about making the party food you sell!

Date:

To: The person who sells catered meals for events to the public.

From: ABC Catering

Subject: Party food purchased at wholesale from our kitchens to use for you clients!

Dear Fellow Foodservice Professional:

Would you like to make more money... with less work and worry? We can do the catering for you at wholesale prices that will allow you to expand your menu offerings for your customers while saving you time, work, and mess.

Our food is made from scratch and can be sent hot and ready to serve. It tastes great and can run from simple to gourmet. We will be happy to drop your food off and let your own staff serve it.

Our prices to you will be wholesale... which means you will get an advantage when pricing parties for your customers. Also, you can tell your customers that you did the food, not us... we don't need the praise... just your business.

Sound interesting? For a no obligation discussion on how we can provide your kitchen team our support, at wholesale prices, that will leave you plenty of room to still make a profit, call 555-555-5555... ask for more information on our wholesale parties.

P.S. The food we sell is produced in our licensed, insured commissary, sent in bulk pans and is ready for your staff to serve. Our food is not the typical mass produced fast food stuff... we love our food!

2 Page Letter When Sending a Brochure

(Date)

Mr. James Doe
Vice-President
Bob's Widget Company
2222 W. North Street
Anytown, USA 99999

Dear Mr. Doe,

Thank you very much for your interest in our new Corporate Catering Menu. Please read and review your copy of our menu that we have enclosed. You will quickly realize that our chefs at ABC Catering have a wide range of creativity and skills!

WE CAN DO JUST ABOUT ANYTHING THAT YOU WANT
AT ANY LOCATION THAT YOU WISH!

The menu represents over five years of testing new recipes. Even more important, over 1,000 hours have been spent by our entire team to create brand new display and garnishing ideas in order to bring you the highest quality food in the most appealing presentation!

You also may be just a little curious about who we are at ABC Catering, and why we have chosen to put so much effort and time into the creation of our new menu. In fact, Mr. Robert Nelson, of the Bank of Lincoln put it this way in a letter we just received "We were all amazed at how perfect everything was! Your food and staff made our management team look great in front of our customers!"

We believe that catering is much more than just food and beverage delivered on time to a client's location. We realize that you are ordering from a caterer to assist you in your own business.

Perhaps you've got a special client coming to your offices to close a deal or, perhaps, you need to start your work day off with a 7:00 AM meeting with your staff. In either case... ABC is ready to help you!

That's what we're all about. Helping others has allowed us to build our own company into one of the strongest catering businesses in your area. We are one of the few that offer 100% guaranteed satisfaction on all of our products and services.

2 Page Letter When Sending a Brochure

When we started our business, we decided to always offer the best quality and presentation at a fair price. Fair price, however, doesn't mean lowest prices. Let me explain.

In catering, as it is with most products and services, you tend to get what you pay for. At ABC Catering our price insures many things such as fresh foods, sanitary preparation, on-time delivery, generous portions and many small extras that are not easy to see.

For example, all caterers are offered chicken from their suppliers in at least three different quality grades. We at ABC Catering only buy the best. We realize that what people put into their mouths needs to be of highest quality and best taste!

SOMETIMES WE FORGET THAT GUESTS EATING THE FOODS
ORDERED BY A COMPANY WILL JUDGE THAT COMPANY BY
WHAT THE LUNCH LOOKS AND TASTES LIKE!

There really is nothing else quite like the catering at ABC Catering! We care about everything we do and while we're not the most expensive caterer in town, we're not the cheapest either! Please see the enclosed coupon which will give you a 25% discount off your first order with us. Also, please feel free to call us at 555-5555 to discuss your catering needs and expectations.

Many thanks again for your interest. We hope to hear from you very soon, and we're going to do everything we possibly can to make sure you are 110% satisfied with any catering from us!

Sincerely,

Bob Smith
Director of Sales
ABC Catering

P.S. If you need extra copies of our new Corporate Catering Menu just call Alice at 555-5555, extension 22 and she will get them off to you immediately.

Letter to Get Contract Business

Why not consider running an employee cafeteria? Yes, that's a big job, and for most of our readers, its an area that needs new expertise. What you need to know is that many caterers who have never done this type of foodservice before are now entering this high-volume, modest profit segment of the industry.

If you wish to "test the waters" you might wish to use the template below. You would send this letter to some of your present catering clients who have a cafeteria already. You might be surprised what will happen!

(Date)

Mr. James Doe
Purchasing Director
World Communications
22334 W. Des Plaines Street
Denver, Colorado 99334

Dear Mr. Doe:

ABC Catering is pleased to offer our proposal for the total food service and catering at World Communications.

The opportunity to provide you with the enclosed information, is in itself a recognition of our reputation in the community. The information enclosed was easier than expected to put together because of your willingness to provide us with sincere and honest information about your expectations towards our possible services.

You are probably already aware of the importance of putting your food service needs into the hands of professionals that are going to look upon your business as an important addition to our business growth.

As you know, we are approaching this from a quality and service point of view. Because we are not a "billion" dollar company with thousands of accounts, we will provide your employees with tasteful foods presented with the same flair that we have offered to our catering clients.

By selecting Roman Catering, with it's team of professionals, you will be enhancing the morale of your workers. Gone will be the jokes about "cardboard" tasting foods!

Mr. Doe, you will also be able to call us for quick response to any and all situations that need handling since we are a member of your community. In short, we are going to give you the attention that the "giant" food service companies are unable to offer.

Thank you again for the opportunity to present the following business plan.

Sincerely,

Jim Smith
President

Letter: After Making an Appointment

One method to begin demonstrating to a potential buyer your professionalism, is to send the letter below. It establishes a rapport with the shopper, gives them a reconfirmation of their appointment time, and starts to establish your sales tactics.

Notice that this letter allows for the salesperson to send some examples of past sales for the shopper's review. This often proves worthwhile because it gives them the opportunity to see the level of catering you offer.

(Date)

Mr. Robert Roberts
Vice-President
XYZ Widget Company
2233 S. Everett Street
Toledo, OH 55555
712-555-8377

Dear Robert,

Thank you for calling ABC about your upcoming 10th Anniversary! We're honored that you are considering us as your caterer. I look forward to our meeting next week on Thursday, April 12 at your offices from 2:00 PM till 3:00 PM to discuss your important event.

During this time I'll be able to better understand all your wishes and requirements. In addition, I'll be able to see, first hand, the venue where we're going to hold the event.

Enclosed you will find an event proposal for DEF Corporation who recently became one of our clients. This will give you some idea of our depth and enthusiasm for creating events that exceed their expectation! I've also enclosed our company brochure and some additional information about ABC.

On the phone yesterday, you mentioned the need for keeping costs down at this event. Bob, you're not alone in your wish. Most of our bigger clients are requesting the same concern for value and lower cost impact ideas from us. We are happy to accept this challenge!

Thank you again for your call. I'm sure that our team will be able to work with your team to create the right event for XYZ Widget Company!

Respectfully,

Mike Mikey
Director of Catering

P.S. Just in case you need me before or after regular business hours, my pager number is 888-8888 and my home number is 555-5555. My children are up at 6:00 AM each
morning... so early calls are great!

Confirmation & Thank You Letter

(Date)

Mr. Robert Sample
American Widget Company
333 W. 33rd Street
Anytown, KS 33333

Dear Mr. Sample:

"ABC Catering" is pleased to confirm that we will be
assisting your company with their special event on (DATE). The event will
take place in your warehouse from 3:00 pm to 8:00 PM.

"ABC Catering" enjoys a reputation for providing unique and exciting ideas
that will combine your thoughts with ours to create an outstanding and memorable affair.

Mr. Sample, for your convenience, I have enclosed our deposit slip and self-
addressed stamped envelope to return your deposit of $750.00.

I will be in contact with you next week to finalize all aspects of your event.
Please call if you have any questions or
suggestions.

Sincerely,

Jim Maxwell
President

cc: E-mailed to entire staff.

**PLEASE NOTICE THE DATE
OF THE THANK YOU LETTER...
IT IS DONE THE NEXT DAY.
CAN CATERERS REALLY CONSIDER
THEMSELVES PROFESSIONAL,
WITHOUT SENDING A
THANK YOU LETTER?**

(Date)

Mr. Robert Sample
American Widget Company
333 W. 33rd Street
Anytown, KS 33333

Dear Mr. Sample:

On behalf of our entire staff I wish to extend our appreciation for the
opportunity to have served you on (DATE).

We trust that our ongoing tradition of maintaining the highest standards of food preparation and service has resulted in a successfully
catered event!

"ABC Catering's " continued success depends greatly upon the
renewed support of it's satisfied customers. We are hopeful that you
will allow us to assist with your future catering needs.

Once again, thank you for your business support.

Sincerely,

Jim Maxwell
President

Cooking Classes Letter

THE SIMPLE TRUTH IS... HAVING A PARTY IS A LOT OF BOTHER!
BUT, IT'S IMPORTANT TO OFFER ENTERTAINMENT TO YOUR FRIENDS!

(Date)

To Our Friends and Future Catering Customers,

People are just not going out to restaurants or clubs as much as they used to. While there are lots of reasons for this fact, it seems that one of the biggest factors is simply that people want to casually get together and talk!

Well, ABC Catering has created a whole new idea for home entertaining! We're ready to make you into a skilled home catering chef! That's right, we have created a new training program that will teach you a whole new set of cooking skills using a simple electric wok.

Here's how it works! You, and any others that you wish, will be invited into our kitchens to take two cooking classes on how to use the electric wok to thrill your friends with dazzling dishes that will make your next home party a real "special event". These classes cost just $10.00 for each person attending each class. During the class you will use our electric woks and recipes to create, under the direction of two of our chefs, new and exciting entrees for your parties. We will even supply you with the recipe ingredients at no additional charge!

As you learn and taste you will gain confidence on how easy and effortless giving a party can be! If you don't have a wok at home, we can offer you one for just $42.00 or you can buy one yourself at the appliance discount store in your neighborhood.

Now... for the real treat! While at our kitchens you will learn to prepare seven dazzling recipes. To make your next party even easier we will be happy to sell you all of the recipe ingredients, the same ones that you learned about in class, ready to use in your home. The cost for these ready to go "ingredient pouches" will run between $3.00 to $11.00 per person depending on what recipes you choose to serve. All we need is 24 hours advance notice to have your "ingredient pouches" ready to go!

I can see you now... standing in a chef's hat cooking for your friends! Only your caterer will really know how easy it was! You friends, however, will be convinced that you have worked for hours preparing everything!

Sound interesting? Please give me a call at 555-5555 so we can discuss our new program at length. Or, when you call simply ask for Alice and give her your name so we can send you some additional information!

Sincerely,

Bob Smith
Director of Catering Education

P.S. Advanced classes and recipes are also available.

The Famous "NO FREE LUNCH" Letter

WHOEVER SAID THERE'S NO SUCH THING AS A FREE LUNCH
DIDN'T KNOW ABOUT THIS OFFER FROM ABC CATERING!

Hello...

My name is Bob Smith. I own ABC Catering and I'd like to offer you a free sampler lunch from our kitchen to your office with no obligation!

I'd rather spend my advertising dollars on putting my beautiful product "into the mouths" of my potential clients rather than spend it on "tasteless" media like radio, television or newspapers.

It's really quite simple. Just look over the enclosed menu and give me a call at 555-5555. Or, you can talk with my assistant Mary Jones. One of us will be glad to answer your questions and/or your request for the FREE SAMPLER LUNCH.

Thanks for taking time,

Bob Smith
Owner

P.S. I forgot to tell you that your free lunch will serve ten guests.

cc: Mary Jones, Assistant Manager

2 Page Classic

Direct mail is a very important marketing strategy for caterers. This two-page letter is a suitable template letter for you to use in your marketplace.

Nothing in this letter is done by accident. For example, you will notice that the last line on page one is not complete. It continues onto page two.

The sentence itself is not an accident. It is a highly interesting one about a subject that most readers will wish to completely understand. Therefore, they will go on to page two!

CaterSource suggests that a caterer always makes an offer when sending direct mail marketing. In this case, the offer is an enclosed coupon worth 25% off the buyer's first order.

The P.S. is also planned to give the reader a name (Alice) and an extension (22) to call when the buyer responds.

As with all direct mail concepts, your goal is to keep the reader reading. This is accomplished with 20% skill and 80% luck! With trial and error as your guide, you will eventually learn what brings success when mailing out information about your catering.

This particular letter is sent in response to someone asking for information about your catering. So, it will probably be read more carefully since it contains information that was requested.

If you wish, you could add a real testimonial from a satisfied client right into the body of this letter. Testimonials bring more success to most direct mail because they provide some proof of your company's overall success record. Get permission to use the testimonial before using it.

Because of this, you might wish to type Information That You Requested onto the front of the envelop. In most cases this will add some importance to the letter.

Dear Friend,

Thank you very much for your interest in our new Corporate Catering Menu. Please read and review your copy of our menu that we have enclosed. You will quickly realize that our chefs at ABC Catering have a wide range of creativity and skills!

WE CAN DO JUST ABOUT ANYTHING THAT YOU
WANT AT ANY LOCATION THAT YOU WISH!

The menu represents over five years of testing new recipes. Even more important, over 1,000 hours have been spent by our entire team to create brand new display and garnishing ideas in order to bring you the highest quality food in the most appealing presentation!

You also may be just a little curious about who we are at ABC Catering, and why we have chosen to put so much effort and time into the creation of our new menu.

We believe that catering is much more than just food and beverage delivered on time to a client's location. We realize that you are ordering from a caterer to assist you in your own business.

Perhaps you've got a special client coming to your offices to close a deal or, perhaps, you need to start your work day off with a 7:00 AM meeting with your staff. In either case ... ABC is ready to help you!

That's what we're all about. Helping others has allowed us to build our own company into one of the strongest catering businesses in your area. We are one of the few that offer 100% guaranteed satisfaction on all of our products and services.

When we started our business, we decided to always offer the best quality and presentation at a fair price. Fair price, however, doesn't mean lowest prices. Let me explain.

In catering, as it is with most products and services, you tend to get what you pay for. At ABC Catering our price insures many things such as fresh foods, sanitary preparation, on-time delivery, generous portions and many small extras that are not easy to see.

For example, all caterers are offered chicken from their suppliers in at least

---

three different quality grades. We at ABC Catering we will only buy the best. We realize that what people put into their mouths needs to be of highest quality and best taste!

SOMETIMES WE FORGET THAT GUESTS EATING THE FOODS ORDERED
BY A COMPANY WILL JUDGE THAT COMPANY BY WHAT THE LUNCH
LOOKS AND TASTE LIKE!

There really is nothing else quite like the catering at ABC Catering! We care about everything we do and while we're not the most expensive caterer in town, we're not the cheapest either!

Please see the enclosed coupon which will earn you a 25% discount off your first order with us. Also, please feel free to call us at 555-5555 to discuss your catering needs and expectations.

Many thanks again for your interest. We hope to hear from you very soon, and we're going to do everything we possibly can to make sure you are 110% satisfied with any catering from us!

Sincerely,

Bob Smith
Director of Sales
ABC Catering

P.S. If you need extra copies of our new Corporate Catering Menu just call Alice at 555-5555, extension 22 and she will get them off to you quickly.

Examples of Letter Openings

1. Does your present caterer have liability insurance?

2. Is your caterer approved by the city to operate legally?

3. If you, like me, are one of those particular people who don't like to compromise on the quality of what they offer to their friends, then you will approve of what I'm about to offer you!

4. Here's how caterers decide how much to charge for their services.

5. What does your caterer do with leftover food at your party? Let me share with you what the law is on this important matter.

6. It happened recently at a company Christmas party. One of the company's key employees stated for all to hear... "If this were really a Christmas Party to thank us for our hard work, we wouldn't have been asked to put out the food and then clean-up!"

7. Suppose one member of a caterer's staff gets hurt while working at your place of business... are you liable?

8. If the list upon which I found your name is any indication, this is not the first time that you have received a business letter of this type.

9. Back in 1945 Chicago had only 26 licensed caterers. Today there are several hundred!

10. You're one of our best clients. We want you to know that soon only a few people will be able to get their catering from our company. We've decided to begin limiting the total number of events that we take to just three per day.

11. If your present caterer already offers you a 100% money back guarantee, then stop reading this letter right here.

12. Some people have the idea that catering is expensive... and they are absolutely right!

13. Some people have the idea that catering is expensive... but, I'd like you to know that this just isn't so!

14. You owe it to yourself to find out what a catered company picnic would do for your staff's overall morale and productivity!

15. Ask yourself: What will we do if we waited too long to book a caterer for the holiday party!

16. I suppose that it might be a little bit bold of me to ask you for a favor when you are already one of our best clients. However, I do need your help...

17. If my letter has reached the right hands, then finding the better caterers is one of the things on your mind.

18. If my letter has reached the right hands, then finding new and different locations to hold your events is one of your responsibilities.

Examples of Letter Endings

1. Thank you for reading my letter and I hope to hear from you in just a day or two. Please call 555-5555 and ask for extension 33.

2. Go ahead... what have you got to lose... give us a call right now to get the ball rolling! The best time to call us is between 2:00 PM to 4:00 PM.

3. Pick-up the telephone right now and call because you must act now to get our list of "10 Great Recipes" before the supply runs out!

4. Give your company an opportunity to see what we can do. We will arrange a no obligation visit with one of our Event Specialists at your place or ours. I'll be giving you a call later this week to answer your questions.

5. Don't miss this very special opportunity to get better value from your catering dollars. Please call me, or have your assistant call me, and I'll tell you what's new in buffets for 1990.

6. It's easy to give yourself "all of the peace of mind" that goes with working with licensed caterers. Just simply fill in the enclosed card and rush it back to us.

7. We hope that you will accept this invitation. It will mean a great deal to us if you do so, and certainly it will mean a great deal to your company.

8. But right now, all I ask you to do is to let us meet... and that doesn't cost you anything. So, call me right now or even when you get out of bed tomorrow since I'm at work by 7:00 AM each day.

9. This offer is for a limited time only. To take advantage of the savings you need to return the enclosed card by March 25. Or, you may call us at 555-5555.

10. So, why not send for your free recipes today! They're yours to keep even if you don't use ABC Catering.

11. In order to avoid the disappointment of not getting us for your Holiday Party please call us at 555-5555 right away. When you call we will give you a free confirmation number that assures you one of our parties.

12. Please make haste, if you will, since we only have 200 of our booklets "Getting More From Your Catering". We've mailed over 600 of these letters to our best clients. So, call us at 555-555-5555 this week.

Letter for Confirming Appointment

(Date)

Mr. Sallie Sallie
President
Sallie Bowling Ball Company
223 N. Ringo Street
Cleveland, NH 55555

Dear Ms. Sallie,

It was wonderful speaking with you yesterday. This letter will confirm our meeting scheduled for next Thursday, (DATE) at your company. Our meeting will begin at approximately 2:00 PM and will last not more than one hour.

If you wish to speak with me before our scheduled meeting, please call.

Respectfully,

Billy Bill
President

P.S. I've already got our Executive Chef working on some great menu ideas!

cc: Jim James, Executive Chef

CHAPTER 12  QUESTIONS

1. Which of the letters would you use? Why?

2. Which of the letters wouldn't you use? Why?

3. Why are letters important for a caterer to use?

FORMS & LISTS

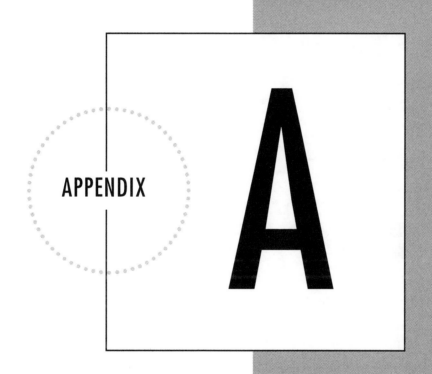

APPENDIX

A

TABLE OF CONTENTS

APPENDIX

A

*"A caterers best advertisement
is, and always be, their
catering!"*

Checklists for Off-Premise Site Inspection

The site inspection is usually done before a proposal is created and prices are offered to the shopper. The reasons are simple. First, if we don't know that a particular site has certain disadvantages, or advantages, we can't determine the right amount it will cost to make it a success.

Here's some suggestions for the creation of your own site inspection checklist:

1. Measure all rooms to determine space planning:
   A. For buffets
   B. For bars
   C. For cooking or reheating
   D. For preparation & plating
   E. For seating
   F. For cleaning & washing
   G. For the band & dancing
   H. For trash
   I. For storage of your boxes
   J. For etc.

2. Determine how much distance there will be between the prep & plating area and the guests.

3. Check for equipment that is already at the location that can be used i.e. chairs, dishes.

4. Check for stairs or multiple floors.

5. Check the kitchen (if available):
   A. For cleanliness
   B. Hoods & exhaust
   C. Number of trash containers
   D. Drains
   E. Hot & Cold Water
   F. Size of doorways
   G. Try all stove burners & ovens
   H. Refrigeration & Freezers
   I. Fire extinguishers
   J. See if your size pans fit into the ovens
   K. Etc!

6. Check electrical outlets to see how many exist and how they are connected to each breaker. Be sure to note where the fuse box is!

7. Determine how the delivery will be made. Through which doors will it come and where it will be placed.

8. Inquire about permission for parking for your staff and your truck.

9. Determine who is in charge of the maintenance at the location.

10. Determine if there is going to be any security staff.

11. Determine how poor weather will effect your performance, especially if using an outside location.

12. Determine where you will place garbage and who is responsible for removing it.

13. Obtain the phone number of the location, especially if there is a pay phone available.

14. If elevators are needed, check to determine the hours that they will be available.

15. Determine which bathrooms, if any, your staff may use.

16. Interview the custodian or maintenance people to see what problems other caterers have had.

Waiver for Leftover Foods

Here's what one caterer does to help limit their liability, when clients ask, or demand, the foods that are leftover at an event. Gaylord Catering Service, Inc. (Madison, WI) requires clients to sign the waiver below, if they wish to keep food used at their event.

Be sure to check this out with your own attorney before using in your area! **REMEMBER:** CaterSource is not giving you legal advice. We're just reporting to our subscribers what others are doing.

Gaylord
CATERING SERVICE, INC.

709 ATLAS AVENUE
MADISON, WI 53714
(608) 222-1267
FAX (608) 222-1487

WAIVER

DATE:

NAME OF EVENT:

LOCATION:

YOU WILL BE BILLED FOR GUARANTEED NUMBER OF MEALS ORDERED.
The customer is entitled to take all meals which are billed for, but not consumed. The customer is not entitled to the 5% amount of food that the caterer prepares over the customer's guaranteed number. Said meals will be made available to the customer, in proper containers, at the conclusion of the event. Upon acceptance of the meals, the customer assumes full responsibility for their transportation and proper storage. The customer agrees that upon customer's acceptance of said meals at the conclusion of the event, Gaylord Catering Service, Inc. is released from all claims, damages, causes of action or liabilities which may arise as a result of the consumption of said meals.

PLEASE SIGN AND RETURN WITH SIGNED CONTRACT.

_____   _____
Customer Signature   Date

Sample Time Line for Events

Set Up Time Line
1:00 PM All morning set up finished - out for security sweep

1:30 Back in to gallery area, continue with gallery set up - food truck arrives

2:00 Back into kitchen area, kitchen & hallway set up
Lead captain arrives to meet with set up captain - check status

2:30 Floor Captains arrive - meet

3:00 Back into Amex Lobby for set up - sanit & bar captains arrive, first sanit crew arrives
Begin Amex lobby set up

4:00 DR set up staff arrives
Reception set up crew arrives
Bar setup crew arrives

4:30 KA's and visiting chefs arrive

5:00 Reception staff #2 and and sanit crew #2 arrives.

5:30 BT #2 crew arrives and dining room crew #2 arrive

6:00 Final Staff arrival

Reception Time Line
5:30 Receptions staff only finish set up - staff meal and meeting

6:15 Ready for guests

6:30 First guests may come - bars open, butler drinks & hors as soon as guests arrive

7:00 Official first guests arrive Receiving line with Mayor

7:45 Guests begin to move to Wintergarden area

Dinner Time Line
6:30 Staff meal and meeting

7:15 Final set up of dining room

7:30 Ready for guests

8:00 Program

8:30 Program finished, first course service

Rest of time line as specified above

Charity Donation Request Form

ow many times a week does your phone ring with a request for a donation of 200 appetizers for a charity auction or a meal for the church? Charity is important to all of us. A business needs to be perceived as a generous one that gives back to the community. Below is a CaterSource template that you would send to those who request a donation... see what you think of it. Just fax this to the person who requests the donation.

(Date)

To: (place the name of the person requesting the donation)

From: (your name)

Subject: Possible Donation

Thank you for your request of a donation from ABC Catering. We would like nothing more than to fulfill all the requests we get for donations of our wonderful food. The problem is that each year we receive dozens of requests.

The simple truth is that we are just unable to provide donations to everyone who calls us. It is our company policy to provide donations to those people, charities, or organizations who have themselves supported our company by purchasing catering over the last twelve months.

If you have ordered catering over the last twelve months, or have members, staff, or volunteers who have done so, please give us their names below and we will respond.

NAMES OF PERSONS ORDERING CATERING FROM ABC CATERING DURING THE LAST TWELVE MONTHS:
(Please give us their names and phone numbers)

1._____

2._____

3._____

PLEASE FAX BACK TO 555-5555.

Thanks for calling ABC Catering.

Marketing for the Host's Eyes

ere's a great template from CaterSource, Inc. In order to get the benefit from this form, you need to realize that it is a marketing and information tool at the same time! To use it properly, you need to place it on top of your delivery boxes that go to the clients office or home.

If it is in clear view, on top of a box, the client will notice it and read what it says. They just won't be able to not read it! As they read, they will be pleased to see that the caterer has provided important information and reminders for the event staff to read.

The client will pay special attention to the "Your Host(s) Request That You:" section of the form. If you've placed some actual client concerns here, you will have a client that is beaming with confidence that the caterer listened well and that the event will be professionally done!

EVENT INFORMATION SHEET FOR STAFF

Host's Name _____ Date: _____

First Reminders:

Please check out your rentals and linens early to make sure all has arrived!

Please check out your food received with the staff copy of the menu!

If there are any questions, Please call the kitchen!

As soon as possible at 555-5555

The Sales Consultant Requests That You:

_____

_____

_____

Your Host & Hostess Selected ABC Catering
Because Of Our Tradition Of Outstanding Service & Food!

Your Host(s) Requests That You:

_____

_____

_____

Each Guest That You Serve Today
Could Be An ABC Catering Customer Tomorrow!

The Kitchen Requests That You:

_____

_____

Seated Dinner Checklist & Guide

There are two types of caterers. Caterers who leave everything up to chance and memory and caterers who put everything in writing. Which is best? What kind of caterer are you? Here's an example of how Eli's Catering (Charlotte, NC) answers the questions. These sheets are given to each server at an event.

Eli's Catering

Seated Dinner
General Decorum

Name : _____   Captain: _____
                                  Partner #1: _____
Tables: ___ ___ ___ ___ ___   Partner #2: _____
                                  Partner #3: _____
         ___ ___ ___ ___ ___   Partner #4: _____
                                  Runner _____
                                  Wine Server _____
                                  Kitchen Mgr _____

Remember these important rules.

1. **Look Sharp!** Aprons not rolled up; sleeves rolled down. You are a professional, let it show.
2. **No** smoking, drinking or chatting on the floor.
3. Respect the privacy of all celebrities, VIP's and dignitaries
4. **Know** the menu and anything you are serving, as well as the room layout and table numbers. Help the guests be seated.
5. Before service, make sure all tables are completely and perfectly set; and chairs out so tablecloths hang free.
6. Serve from left with left hand. Pour and clear from the right with the right hand. Work counter-clockwise around the table.
7. Carry no more than two (2) plates to and from the table.
8. Completely serve one table before going to the next table; clear only when entire table has finished.
9. Keep ashtrays cleaned (wipe out used ones at waiters station) ; keep wine/water/coffee refilled. Wine bottles neatly trimmed and wrapped.
10. Keep the waiter's station organized. Make sure all things you need are there (pitchers of iced water, coffee, setups) . All extra silver, china, glasses, napkins and ashtrays are to be kept neatly stored.
11. Place all plates in front of guests in the same direction.
12. Take only and order only what you need or what is allotted.
13. **Always** work as a team; go to dish-up and breakdown together.
14. Any changes from the above will be covered in the meeting prior to the event.

Table setting: Evenly Space chairs. Place settings "square" with the chair, not the table!
Each table will receive _____ Ashtrays _____ Pairs of Salt & Pepper _____ Set of Cream & Sugar

Scheduling Deliveries & Pick-ups

Caterers keep a hectic pace. Too often the scheduling of how and who will be taking deliveries is overlooked or postponed until it is too late!

EXAMPLE 1 is a CaterSource template form for keeping your show on the road... at the right time!

EXAMPLE 2 gives some idea how caterers might use this form. The right hand column of the form is used to schedule the departure times of your vehicles. In this way the kitchen has a better understanding of deadlines for production of each order.

Pick-ups are a nemesis for many caterers. Keep this sheet with you, or on your desk, to remind yourself of what needs to be picked-up from the previous day, or what needs to be picked-up for today's success.

In essence, a caterer can't ever have enough lists! This particular form has been used by many of CaterSource's clients to bring some order to what is normally a chaotic situation between the kitchen and the sales department.

Owners who do most of their work in the kitchen will find this form a good tool to catch the little things that usually slip by.

Yes, you could have a computer generated listing. However, in the heat of battle, we've found that this oversized form, usually 11 x 14 in size, makes the day go a lot better.

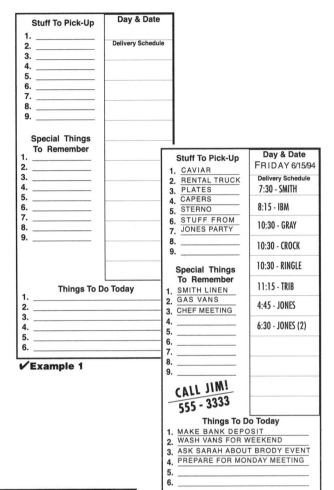

Stuff To Pick-Up
1. _____
2. _____
3. _____
4. _____
5. _____
6. _____
7. _____
8. _____
9. _____

Day & Date

Delivery Schedule

Special Things To Remember
1. _____
2. _____
3. _____
4. _____
5. _____
6. _____
7. _____
8. _____
9. _____

Things To Do Today
1. _____
2. _____
3. _____
4. _____
5. _____
6. _____

✔ **Example 1**

Stuff To Pick-Up
1. CAVIAR
2. RENTAL TRUCK
3. PLATES
4. CAPERS
5. STERNO
6. STUFF FROM
7. JONES PARTY
8. _____
9. _____

Day & Date
FRIDAY 6/15/94

Delivery Schedule
7:30 - SMITH
8:15 - IBM
10:30 - GRAY
10:30 - CROCK
10:30 - RINGLE
11:15 - TRIB
4:45 - JONES
6:30 - JONES (2)

Special Things To Remember
1. SMITH LINEN
2. GAS VANS
3. CHEF MEETING
4. _____
5. _____
6. _____
7. _____
8. _____
9. _____

CALL JIM!
555 - 3333

Things To Do Today
1. MAKE BANK DEPOSIT
2. WASH VANS FOR WEEKEND
3. ASK SARAH ABOUT BRODY EVENT
4. PREPARE FOR MONDAY MEETING
5. _____
6. _____

✔ **Example 2**

TIP: ASK YOUR INSURANCE AGENT HOW MUCH YOUR PREMIUM DROPS IF YOU RAISE YOUR DEDUCTIBLE.

A sight known to all caterers!

Can you see the good and bad in this picture? Future Journals will have an articles on transporting food, equipment and beverages. We'd love to include your ideas and tips. See last page for info on what to do.

Liquor Control Worksheet

Sometimes caterers get into difficult situations with clients who claim that a bartender took some liquor or that some of the liquor was missing the next day when they got around to checking what was left. The form below makes an attempt to limit these, and other problems associated with liquor, before, during and after the event.

As you review this CaterSource template, you will either think that it is great or that it will cause more problems than it solves. That's the wonderful thing about education... we can all use it as we choose.

ABC CATERING LIQUOR CONTROL WORKSHEET

	Total Number of Bottles at Start of Event	Number of Empty Bottles At End of Event	Partially Used, Open and Water-Stained Bottles	Unopened Bottles at End of Event	Total Number of All Bottles At End of Event
SCOTCH					
BOURBON					
GIN					
VODKA					
RUM					
WHITE WINE					
RED WINE					
CHAMPAGNE					

BARTENDERS ARE RESPONSIBLE FOR ACCOUNTING OF ALL BOTTLES. THIS FORM IS TO BE SIGNED BY THE HOST OR HOSTESS AFTER THEY APPROVE OF THE FINAL ACCOUNTING.

COMMENTS _____

_____

_____

_____

_____

I've checked this form and find that the final accounting of the liquor is as it should be. I realize that I am now responsible for the security and liability of the liquor served by ABC Catering at my event.

_____
CUSTOMER'S SIGNATURE

Employee Discipline Notice Template

EMPLOYEE DISCIPLINE NOTICE

Employee's Name_____

Employee's Job Title_____

Employee's Department Supervisor_____

Date of Misconduct_____

_____Verbal Warning   _____Written Warning   _____Day Suspension   _____Immediate Termination

- Unsatisfactory Work Performance_____
- Insubordination/Disobedience_____
- Attendance/Tardiness_____
- Theft_____
- Drug, Alcohol or Food Violations_____
- Failure to Comply with the Equal Opportunity or Sexual Harassment Policies_____
- Disorderly Conduct/Fighting_____
- Grooming/Uniform Violations_____
- Other_____

SUPERVISOR'S STATEMENT / Details of Violation/Comments

_____
_____
_____

Previous Action Taken

_____
_____

By_____ Title_____ Date_____

EMPLOYEE'S STATEMENT

_____
_____
_____

I have received and read this Employee Discipline Notice

Employee's Signature_____ Date_____

**CHECK THIS OUT WITH YOUR ATTORNEY
BEFORE ADOPTING IT FOR USE IN YOUR OWN BUSINESS!**

Function Details Worksheet

Function Details Worksheet

Menu Yr Quoted _____

Date _____   Smoking Reception? _____

Bride: _____ Groom: _____

Group: _____ Contact Person: _____

Address: _____

Daytime Phone: _____ Evening Phone: _____

Daytime Phone: _____ Evening Phone: _____

Day & Date of Event: _____ Location: Pavilion   Other: _____

Type of Event: _____ Time: _____

Expected # of Guests: _____   Minimum Charge _____ Room Charge$ _____

Time of Ceremony _____ Location (Church & Town) _____

Guest Arrival Time _____   Guest of Honor Arrival _____

TABLE ARRANGEMENTS : Registration Table ? _____ Microphone & Podium _____
Head Table ? _____ Shape ? _____ # Guests _____
You will need to provide us with the following assigned seating guest lists:
   1.   A list of all guest in alphabetical order with each guest's table assignment
           and meal choice
   2.   A list of each table and the guests who are assigned to those tables
   3.   Place cards of each guest in alphabetical order with table assignment (OPTIONAL)
   4.   Head table seating arrangement
   5.   A copy of the band or D.J.'s announcement list

LINENS   White Tablecloths   **Napkin Color** _____

CENTERPIECES: Gold   ~   Diamond   ~   Platinum   Other: _____

ENTERTAINMENT: Disc Jockey? (Name & Phone) _____

      Hours will they play? _____   **Will they be eating?** _____

A reputation of delicious food and great service.

P.O. Box 2336, Middletown, CT 06457
Phone: 860-347-7171 Fax: 860-343-1552
www.pavilion-catering.com

INDEX

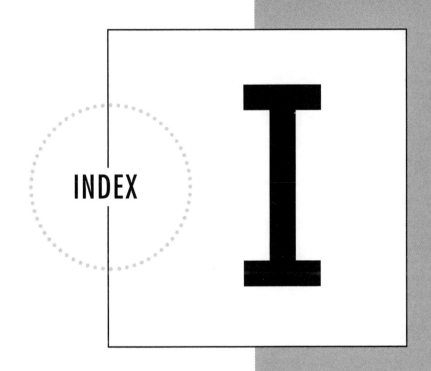

INDEX

I

Index

Index

www.catersource.com